FALCONRY

EMMA FORD

FALCONRY

ART AND PRACTICE

REVISED EDITION

BLANDFORD

First published in the UK in 1992 by Cassell & Co
Wellington House,
125 Strand,
London WC2R 0BB

Reprinted 1993 and 1994
Revised edition 1995

Paperback revised edition 1995

Distributed in the United States
by Sterling Publishing Co., Inc.
387 Park Avenue South, New York, NY 10016–8810

British Library Cataloguing-in-Publication Data.
A catalogue record for this book is available from the
British Library.

ISBN 0–7137–2588–5

Typeset by Columns Design and Production Services Ltd., Reading

Printed and bound in Great Britain by
The Bath Press, Bath

Frontispiece Immature lanner falcon.

I dedicate this book
unreservedly to my husband Steve,
for his unflagging enthusiasm and
support during its completion.

CONTENTS

ACKNOWLEDGEMENTS

I would like to thank my husband Steve for the line drawings and for all his help and encouragement with the text, Stuart Rossell for reading the manuscript and for hours of help with putting the book together, Neil Forbes for the veterinary chapter, Piers Cavendish for his hard work and enthusiasm whilst taking the photographs, Anthony Rhodes for the part-title montages, Carolyn Wilson for typing the manuscript, Penny Spencer for all her secretarial help, Carl Moody for his photograph of the peregrine stooping grouse, Kim Smith for her assistance with the photographs, Derek Cattani for the original rear jacket photograph of the author, and the Hawk Conservancy for supplying the hawks photographed on pages 117, 119, 165, 167, 170 and the colour photographs of the goshawk and the merlin.

PREFACE

Falconers are a fortunate breed. Not only do we have the pleasure of our current hawk, but also, increasingly over the years, the memory of former hawks which were dear to us and individual flights, which are etched in the memory forever.

It is hard to convey this pleasure adequately in words, for it is the little details which are responsible for painting the overall picture – the expression on a hawk's face when she is taken up after a kill, or the spectacle of her enjoying a vigorous bath. Similarly, when writing an instructional manual, it is so very difficult to remember to include all the little details which are intrinsic in the making of a first-class hawk.

I make no apology for using the term 'hawk' throughout the text as, confusingly, even falcons are referred to as hawks in the falconer's language and 'she' is the accepted pronoun. Much of the falconer's language is falling into disuse. The term 'austringer' – one who trains and hunts shortwinged hawks - is one example, but I have tried to use it in specific connection with shortwings and broadwings. For convenience only, I have used 'he' when referring to an austringer or falconer but, obviously, they may be either male of female.

I opened the British School of Falconry in 1982, with my husband Steve. Teaching the sport which occupies one's waking moments virtually continuously, as well as one's dreams, is immensely useful, for it inevitably leads to innovation, as students and instructors endlessly discuss items of furniture and practicalities of housing. It is interesting, however, that there seems to be little new to be discovered in the various forms of hawking. Trained hawk pitted against quarry is an ancient sport and there is a wealth of knowledge which has been passed down from generation to generation. It is in the dissemination of this knowledge that the future of falconry lies. The sport has given me inestimable pleasure and I am grateful for the opportunity to share both this pleasure and what little knowledge I have through these pages.

Emma Ford

PART I
BASIC INFORMATION

1 AN INTRODUCTION TO FALCONRY

Falconry is unlike any other sport in the world. It combines many different elements. Of the falconer it demands a vast array of skills, including fieldcraft, leathercraft, butchery, knowledge of game, manual dexterity and many more less easy-to-classify qualities, such as patience, sensitivity and that indefinable instinctive ability which separates good falconers from bad ones. Within falconry itself there are also many facets, each constituting a different sport – grouse hawking, partridge hawking, lark hawking, rough hawking and hedge hunting to name some of the principal ones. Few falconers will, in a lifetime, be able to become proficient in each – indeed, most settle in their attempt to become master of one.

The principles of training a bird of prey have remained unchanged since the earliest days of the sport, the main one being that of bringing the hawk into the same physical state at which it would hunt in its natural environment. This is achieved by a combination of correct hunting weight and fitness and is known as conditioning. The speed at which this can be achieved depends on the falconer, the hawk and each one's correct assessment of the other. The various species employed in the sport require a vastly differing touch; the delicacy of the sparrowhawk flown in the lush British countryside can in no measure be compared with the inherent hardiness of the saker falcon traditionally hunted under the harshness of the desert sun. Yet the essence of the falconer's art remains the same in both cases and the trials and pleasures of training a

hawk remain unchanging factors in a changing world.

The training comprises various distinct phases. Initially a hawk must be 'manned'. The term literally means becoming used to man and his environment. It is the taming of the hawk, the time when the relationship is formed. During this period, the hawk learns to be carried on the fist, she learns that the falconer will supply food from the fist and she learns to overcome her inherent fear of people in general and of the falconer in particular. This transformation from wildness to comparative steadiness is most easily achieved by regulating food intake. When the hawk is hungry, food can be used to develop and cement the bond between falconer and hawk. Stage one is thereby considered complete when the hawk will feed from the fist and is reasonably relaxed in the falconer's presence. Having obtained food relatively easily, the hawk is then made to work progressively harder for it. She is called over increasing distances whilst tethered to a light training line, called a creance, until such a time as the falconer considers that she can be trusted to fly free. During this time the hawk is introduced to a 'lure' – a device which resembles the intended quarry. Whilst building up the hawk's association with game, the lure also provides the falconer with a means of exercising the hawk and, later, a method of recalling her should she fail to connect with the live game she chases. Through regular daily work, the hawk is rendered fit and is subsequently introduced to live quarry. At this juncture, the training is considered complete and the sport begins.

The over-riding factor for all falconers is the sheer pleasure to be derived from watching a hawk in action. Familiarity cannot taint this pleasure; to see a hawk in flight is to be privileged to watch a master of the air. Your heart soars with the hawk as she pursues her quarry, willing her to connect, blood coursing in your veins. It is a unique hunting partnership – you tame her, tend her, train her and work her to the peak of physical condition, then release her to the elements whilst you become no more than a mere spectator of a totally natural event.

Like all field sportsman, falconers also derive pleasure from the countryside in which they indulge their practices – the wild beauty of moorland on a warm summer evening as the pointers range ahead searching for grouse; the rolling views over open downland as eyes scan the grassland, searching for feeding rooks; and the frosty mornings when duck sit preening on the banks of a flight pond. The

knowledge of the falconer must exceed that necessary to train and maintain his hawk; it must extend to the countryside and to the game he wishes his hawk to catch. Even the rabbit has an entire pattern of social behaviour and habits which must be understood by the falconer if he hopes to furnish his hawk with the best possible chances. The lie of the land, the positioning of the burrows, the nearest cover and the time of sunrise and sunset are factors which cannot be ignored if the falconer is to play his part with distinction. Whilst most falconers will say that the quality of the flight is more important than the kill, neither falconer nor hawk likes to return home empty-handed and recriminations are often clearly apparent on both sides.

When a beginner considers taking up falconry, he must first consider the time required to work a hawk properly, particularly in the shortening days of winter. He must also

Weathering ground at the British School of Falconry.

study the land he will have available to hunt over. This will enable him, after serving his apprenticeship with a beginner's hawk, to choose a species suited to his countryside. The first decision is based on a choice between longwing, shortwing or broadwing – falcon, hawk, buzzard or eagle. Longwings take predominantly flying game, often pursuing their quarry over long distances. If the falconer is to keep his longwing in sight he must be in very open countryside, such as moorland, marshland or downland. Longwings are trained to swing-lures made up from the wings of their intended quarry and, when hunting, are unhooded and put off the fist either to chase the game directly or to get height before stooping when the quarry is flushed. Shortwings and broadwings take quarry on or close to the ground – rabbit, hare, moorhen and game birds – usually when they are on the rise or putting into cover. When the countryside permits, they work from trees, to give them both advantage in spotting game and height to increase the initial speed of their pursuit. At other times they work off the fist. Shortwings can, therefore, be flown in a more enclosed landscape than longwings. They are taught during training to leave the fist instantly in pursuit of a rabbit-lure, which is dragged along the ground. The true eagles and buzzards are classified as 'broadwings'. To work at their best they need to be flown in hill country or rolling downland where they can catch up-draughts and 'slope-soar' whilst looking for prey.

The hawks in each of these three categories are physically adapted to their hunting environments. Longwings have pointed tapering wings which, when closed in a stoop, will assist in streamlining. They have dark eyes and all but the palest species have a 'malar stripe' – a moustachial strip of dark-coloured feathers below the eyes to resist glare. Their tails are relatively short and, in most species, the centre toe is comparatively elongated for binding to their quarry in mid-air. They have a tooth – a projection on the upper mandible – which is used as a pressure point to break the

A common buzzard, the ideal beginner's hawk.

neck of their quarry. Shortwings have rounded ends to their wings and relatively long tails, which assist manoeuvrability when they are pursuing game through woods or along hedgerows. They have a prominent orbital ridge to protect their eyes, which are light in colour – usually yellow, deepening to orange-red with age. Broadwings have broad wing bases to facilitate soaring flight and wide tails which they fan out for buoyancy. Their eyes are mid-brown in colour.

14

For a beginner, the choice of longwing, shortwing or broadwing should be one faced only when choosing their second hawk, for all novices are advised to start with a common or European buzzard. Until recent times, most beginners were advised to start with a kestrel. Kestrels, however, hold little appeal for the serious beginner, for what falconer wishes to fly a hawk in partnership with which the pinnacle of his hunting achievement might be a beetle or a mouse?

Birds of prey used for falconry throughout the world fall into three main categories in the falconer's language – eyasses, passagers and haggards. Eyasses are young birds taken from the nest in their wild state or bred in captivity. Passagers are birds trapped during their immature year. Haggards are birds trapped in their adult plumage. These three types behave and respond differently when trained for falconry. Eyasses have never flown and hunted in their natural state and, consequently, are totally lacking in experience. Thus they require a high level of skill and patience on behalf of the falconer. Eyasses will also 'imprint' very readily if they are hand-reared or taken from the nest too young. Imprinting can result in anti-social tendencies, such as mantling over food, aggression and screaming, stemming from social reaction towards the falconer. Passagers have many advantages over eyasses, including fitness, experience in taking game and a total absence of imprinted traits. Haggards are not as highly regarded as passagers because they are much harder to train and more easily lost, having matured in the wild and learned during that time to be wary of man.

In the UK, with very few exceptions, falconers now fly captive-bred eyasses. All native birds of prey are protected and cannot therefore be trapped from the wild as passagers or haggards. Until 1987, few licences to take eyasses from wild nests were granted each year by the Department of the Environment to falconers in the UK. Now, due mainly to the escalating success falconers have enjoyed in breeding birds of prey in captivity, licences to take hawks for falconry have ceased to be granted, as hawks no longer need to be acquired in this way. British falconers must possess the necessary degrees of skill and patience previously mentioned if they are to bring their captive-bred eyasses to the peak of physical perfection prerequisite for them to take wild quarry in fine style. Without the benefit of a parent bird to teach the eyass to hunt, this is by no means an easy task. Any person who can train an eyass to take wild quarry in its natural habitat, by definition and by merit, deserves the title of falconer. Similarly, anyone who keeps a hawk merely to sit on a block or to fly to the fist or lure does not.

A beginner can therefore look forward to an eyass buzzard as his hunting partner in the early days, whilst he masters the basics of his craft and seeks the knowledge and ability which will enable his advance in a sport rich in variety and pleasure.

2 GENERAL HUSBANDRY

HOUSING

Accommodation for a hawk should provide adequate shelter, be free from draughts and be easily cleaned. It should also provide protection against vermin and other birds or animals, domestic or non-domestic, which might harm the hawk or, in turn, be harmed by her.

Falconers used to keep their hawks indoors in a mews, putting them out on the lawn in the daytime. The more modern approach to housing a hawk is the weathering. In this three-sided, roofed structure, a hawk can enjoy the elements whilst being adequately protected from the heat of the sun and from showers of rain. When the falconer is in the vicinity he can still put his charge onto the lawn to offer her a bath, but at other times, with his hawk under the cover of a weathering but in the open air, he need feel no guilt if his work takes him away until flying time.

The system, adopted by a small and uncaring minority, of leaving their hawks out on the weathering lawn day and night, regardless of weather conditions, is despicable. It is natural for any animal or bird to seek shelter in times of bad weather. A falconer has no right to deprive his hawk of this privilege.

A weathering is most easily constructed from larchlap fencing panels. Three 6 ft × 6 ft panels will create the basis of a weathering, suitable in size for all but eagles. To this, a solid sloping roof, a netting floor covered in gravel, a netting front and a protective blind are added to complete the ensemble. As the anti-vermin netting on the floor will sub-

TABLE 1 MATERIALS REQUIRED FOR WEATHERING CONSTRUCTION

	Quantity	Size	Material
	3	6 ft × 6 ft	larchlap fence panels
	4	3 in × 3 in × 8 ft	fence posts
	2	8 ft × 8 ft	felt board
	1	7 ft × 7 ft	1-in mesh chicken wire
	4	2 in × 2 in × 7 ft	lengths of sawn timber
	¼ ton	—	uncrushed pea gravel
	1	6 ft × 6 ft	PVC blind
	—	—	nails
	—	—	roofing clouts
	—	—	roofing felt and adhesive
	—	—	catapult elastic
	—	—	flashing strip
	6	2 in × 2 in × 6 ft	lengths of sawn timber
Front 1	1	6 ft × 6 ft	section of plastic-coated 1-in mesh
	2	3 in	door hinges
	—	—	staples
	—	—	hasp
	—	—	padlock
	1	8 ft × 6 ft	piece of Cintoflex
Front 2	3	2 in × 1 in × 6 ft	length of sawn timber
	2	2 m × 15 mm	electrical cable ties
	—	—	staples
	—	—	hasp
	—	—	padlock

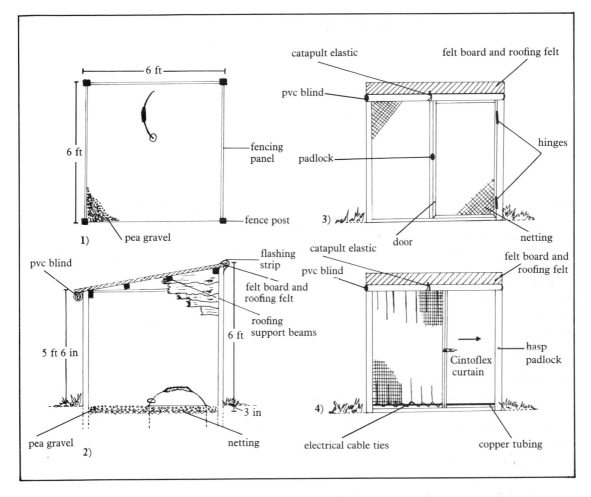

Weathering construction: 1) aerial view, 2) side view, 3) front 1, 4) front 2.

sequently be covered by gravel, it need only be chicken wire, but the mesh at the front should always be plastic-coated. The gravel must consist of small, rounded stones, often referred to as uncrushed pea gravel, or pea beach, as a hawk will sometimes pick up and swallow stones to aid the digestion. The stones, known in the falconer's language as 'rangle', are later regurgitated.

Sand should not be used to floor weatherings as it is highly abrasive and can cause damage to a hawk's feet, should it get under her scales. It can stick to food and impact in the crop if the hawk is fed whilst in the weathering. It is also difficult to keep clean and inclined to stick to the leash if at all damp. Generally speaking, it is most unwise to experiment with alternative ground cover-

ings – straw and wood bark, for example, can cause the fungal respiratory disease called aspergillosis.

The blind at the front of the weathering is designed to give extra protection when driving rain or snow prevails. It is also useful to drop the blind if the grass immediately in front of a nervous hawk's weathering needs cutting. Some species of hawk native to warmer climes, notably the Harris hawk, suffer from frostbite in their toes and wing tips if the temperature falls below freezing point. To obviate this risk with hawks sensitive to cold, a ceramic heat bulb of the type used for pigs should be suspended at a height of approximately 2½ ft above the hawk's head. When a cold night is anticipated, the bulb can be switched on and the blind dropped to keep in the small amount of heat necessary to maintain the weathering above freezing point. A maximum/minimum thermometer, placed at ground level in the weathering, will enable the falconer to ensure that these precautions are working.

The siting of the weathering is important. Ideally a hawk should be situated so that she can see some sort of activity, which will keep her entertained and will assist with her manning in the early stages. At the very least, she should have a view of the garden. Prevailing winds should also be taken into account.

To clean a weathering, a hose-pipe and scrubbing brush, or preferably a power-hose should be used. Once or twice a week, the hawk can be blocked out on the lawn to bath, in the accustomed manner, whilst the falconer thoroughly cleans the gravel, the perch and, if necessary, the walls of the weathering. A light spray of a solution of Virkon S (Vet Drug) disinfectant, after completion of the operation, will help to inhibit the growth of bacteria.

When a broadwing is fully trained, she can be kept loose in a chamber (see illustrations on page 25). This system has several advantages over and above maintaining her in a weathering. Firstly, if the chamber is fairly high and of substantial dimensions, she will keep reasonably fit. This can be encouraged in the design of the chamber, by incorporating high perches, level with high viewing windows. If the remainder of the chamber is solid-walled, the hawk will naturally gravitate towards the high perches, from which she can enjoy the view they afford. An area of 12 ft × 12 ft and a height of 9 ft, sloping to 8 ft in the front, is ideal for most hawks. It is important that the sides of the chamber are not constructed wholly or partially from netting of any sort, as a keen hawk will damage her feathers, and possibly also her feet, by hanging on the netting. The roof must be covered to the extent of 50 per cent to provide her with adequate shelter. The perch under the roof should be as high as possible to give the hawk shelter.

By keeping her loose, boredom is alleviated, together with the risk of frostbite (see Chapter 9, Harris hawks). She can be fitted permanently with field jesses and called to the fist for food when it is time to fly her. She will not, therefore, get twisted-up as she may do when tied down, and she is less likely to pick at her equipment through boredom or to suffer from jess rubs and scale displacement. Altogether, it is a far better way to keep a trained hawk, because of the comparative freedom and variety which she is afforded and, when she is put down to moult, she can be left in there (see Chapter 2, Moult).

Unfortunately, it is not possible completely to replace the weathering with a chamber. Before a hawk is fully trained, she will become wayward if she is turned loose. Some *Accipiters* become unruly if turned loose at any stage during the flying season. Longwings need to be assessed individually by the experienced falconer to see if this style of accommodation would suit the hawk in question. However, there is a great deal to be said for including a chamber as well as a weathering in the design of a facility, as the potential uses for it – including times when the falconer is away for intervals – are numerous. In addition, such a structure is easy to convert to a breeding aviary, should the need arise, simply by adding a nest site under cover of the roof.

FEEDING

The diet for a hawk should consist solely of raw meat. The meat must be lean and fresh. Roughage, in the form of fur or feather, must also be included in the hawk's regular feeding pattern. Hawks use roughage to clean out their crop, regurgitating pellets 12–24 hours after eating. These pellets or 'castings' as they are correctly termed, are small pellets of fur or feather. They are covered in gleam to enable the hawk to cast more easily. Roughage should be fed at least twice a week – most falconers feed it every day.

When feeding whole food to a hawk – the game that it has caught or an item from the deep-freeze – it is a wise precaution to remove the internal organs, lest there be any risk of the game being infected. Unfortunately, this does deprive the hawk of the trace elements which it would ingest from eating the vital organs of its kill in the wild. These, however, can be introduced in the form of supplements – for example, SA 37 is a multi-vitamin supplement commonly used and Collo-Cal D replaces calcium. Both are obtainable from veterinary surgeons or pet shops.

Beware of anything that has been killed with a shotgun and may contain lead pellets. Hawks will get lead poisoning if they ingest lead, and sharp slivers of pellet can slice the gut. Only rifle-shot game is safe. Even game which the hawk has caught may contain shot from a previous encounter with a gun and should be checked carefully before being fed.

Road casualties should only be fed if the falconer himself has knocked over the victims.

Basic hygiene techniques should always be observed when feeding a hawk. Clean food trays, clean hands, well-scrubbed hawking bags or waistcoats and, above all, fresh meat are essential. Never feed food which has been frozen more than once and protect defrosting food from flies. Fat hawks in aviaries should not be overfed and all the food given should be eaten on the same day. A very fat hawk is not a healthy hawk and an excess of internal fat may result in a heart attack.

DIET
DAY-OLD CHICKS
Cockerel chicks, culled by hatcheries at a day-old, form the staple diet of many hawks in captivity. They have the advantage of being abundantly available, relatively inexpensive, and constituting a whole food diet – one that is fed in its entirety, including roughage. Some falconers feed them exclusively, but on the negative side, they cannot be described as a diet of high quality. It is better, therefore, if the diet is varied periodically to include something both richer in meat quality and more substantial in terms of roughage. The

yellow down covering of day-old chicks is sufficient to enable a hawk to produce a casting, but rabbit fur or gamebird feathers are a superior roughage material and should be fed if the hawk produces a slushy casting on chicks.

Day-old chicks still contain their yolk sac. This yolk sac contains carotene which will eventually colour the cere and feet of a hawk bright yellow. There have been some fears regarding the cholesterol content of yolk when fed excessively, but to date, no conclusive facts along these lines have led to the feeding of chicks becoming less popular. The yolks do make them messy to feed, however.

The best chicks are those obtained blast-frozen rather than fresh. Much care has to be taken with the freezing down of fresh chicks, which give off a lot of heat and thus are at risk of growing *Salmonella*. Fresh chicks must therefore be obtained by the falconer immediately after killing and must be allowed to cool completely before being frozen down in layers, rather than in a big mass. Blast-frozen chicks, by the nature of the process, are properly frozen down from their fresh state. They can be held for long periods in a domestic deep-freeze, one can be broken from another easily in the frozen state and they defrost much better than chicks initially frozen down in a normal deep-freeze.

QUAIL
Quail are an excellent food source for hawks. They are high in protein and contain good quality roughage. Unfortunately, they are also comparatively expensive. One way round this problem is for falconers to breed their own, provided that they have the time and facilities.

In the field they are useful as most hawks enjoy the taste of quail. In an emergency they can also be used as a lure.

BEEF
Being so readily obtainable, beef is an easy and clean foodstuff for hawks. It lacks calcium and roughage, but both can be supplemented. The cut must be lean, with all fat scrupulously removed. Shin of beef is an

ideal buy as it is an inexpensive cut and will not be ripped up too quickly by a hawk. This is important, particularly when putting beef on a lure for a longwing. It is useful that both beef and chicks have a similar effect on a hawk in terms of weight control, so the one may be easily substituted for the other in portions of similar size.

RABBIT

Rabbit has a low nutritional value – a fact easily recognizable from its pale flesh. Generally speaking, therefore, to achieve the same weight, a larger quantity of rabbit has to be fed to a hawk normally maintained on chicks, quail or beef.

Fed exclusively, rabbit is a somewhat anaemic diet. It is not a diet on which to maintain an active longwing or a sparrowhawk.

HARE

The flesh of hare is quite rich and therefore the amount fed must be carefully regulated. It is not a meat often fed by falconers as it tends to end up in the pot. However, those who do feed up their hawks on hare will find it to be an energizing diet, quite unlike rabbit.

RATS AND MICE

Rodents contain a high proportion of protein. They are obtainable in large quantities from specialist food suppliers and so can be acquired more cheaply than from pet shops.

Small longwings, particularly merlins, which need a high energy source, do well on mice. Some hawks, especially those accustomed to chicks, unfortunately do not appear to find them palatable and cannot be persuaded to eat them. They do not need gutting before being fed, so rats and mice contain many trace elements and therefore constitute a diet which does not need supplements. It is worth avoiding the feeding of white rats if one is using an albino ferret.

GAMEBIRDS

Comparable to quail, these are excellent fodder for hawks. Like hare, they tend to end up in the cooking pot, unless a hawk of prowess accounts for a regular number, whereupon she may find herself occasionally rewarded with more than the head.

PIGEON

Pigeon carry trichomoniasis, which causes the cankerous disease of the mouth termed 'frounce' by falconers. It should never therefore be fed fresh to hawks and, if fed at all, should only be given after being frozen for at least a month, with head and guts carefully removed. The flesh is very rich.

ROOK

Similar in food value to beef, a crop of rook will not upset a rook hawk's flying weight. Some longwings appear to dislike the taste of rook, preferring to wait for the falconer's well-garnished fist.

SQUIRREL

A squirrel is a tough prospect for a hawk to break into. As such it is good exercise and will keep a hawk gainfully occupied, As a meat, it is of middling nutritious value.

MOORHEN

Although too rich to be fed safely to a hawk in flying condition, it is worth having a few moorhen in the deep-freeze for a hawk in low condition. As usual, the guts and head should be removed, as should the skin which is greasy. A sick hawk requires only breast meat.

OFFAL

Liver is useful to feed to sick hawks as it is high in iron and other minerals. It can be fed in small, easily digestible slivers.

Heart has a low food value and is consequently of little use except as a slightly more nutritious washed-meat substitute.

Kidneys and other vital organs should never be fed to hawks.

WASHED MEAT

The feeding of washed meat is uncommon but it can be used during a period of weight reduction for eagles, which tend to become anorexic when deprived of food for several

A peregrine falcon enjoying her daily bath.

days.

Strips of beef are soaked in water in a refrigerator overnight. They are then squeezed out in warm water and dried. Nearly all the colour and goodness will be washed out during this process. The object is not to hold weight on a hawk but to keep its digestive system functioning.

No hawk should be kept on this regime for more than 2 days without being given a little proper food. This is important as otherwise the blood-sugar level may fall too steeply, causing the hawk to go 'low'.

The process of losing internal fat is called 'enseaming'.

TIRINGS

Tirings are tough pieces of meat on the bone – mainly sinew. Wings and necks are the best forms. They are given to hawks to build up muscle, which is acquired when the hawk pulls at the tirings to take off the small amount of meat. Care must be taken to ensure that a hawk cannot swallow the tirings whole.

It is particularly useful to give tirings to a partially manned hawk to keep her occupied on the fist.

DAILY MANAGEMENT

Every morning, a hawk on jesses should be picked up and checked. A good falconer will know immediately if anything is awry, his eye promptly noting the signs indicative of a sick hawk or a broken item of furniture. Only daily observation will teach a beginner this; one must first be familiar with a happy, healthy hawk with neat, correct equipment, and assessing its condition at a glance.

21

Opposite Whilst in training, hawks are weighed every day.

On fine days, the hawk can be blocked on the lawn and offered a bath. If business then takes the falconer away until flying time, someone else must take the bath away, leaving the hawk time to dry out. Longwings, especially peregrines, will usually bath quite quickly, but shortwings are notorious for taking all day to think about it, often taking the plunge just as the falconer appears to fly them in the afternoon.

Some individuals seldom or never bath. Others, particularly those originating from hot countries, prefer a dust bath. This can be accommodated by offering a tray of sand. If a hawk has gone a while without taking a bath, the hose-pipe can be employed on fine days to sprinkle her liberally and thus to encourage preening.

Hawks should be weighed immediately before being flown. If roughage was fed the previous day, a fresh casting must be produced before weighing, lest her weight is falsely boosted by the presence of a casting in her crop. In sticking to a regular daily flying time, there should be little risk of a hawk failing to cast before flying. After flying, the hawk should be returned to her perch to put over her crop in peace.

Usually the novice will keep a weight chart to monitor his hawk's early progress, but once his hawk is taking quarry, a diary or game book is more appropriate. The flying weight will, by this time, be established and the falconer will want only to record their adventures in the field, for his bedtime reading during the long summer months when hawks are moulting and his sport is in abeyance.

Extract from a game book.

Month September Week 3 Year 1990						
Braco Castle Moor						
Hawk Chanel – intermewed eyass falcon	(with Anthony Rhodes')		(on Arrow Flats)			
Date Sunday 16th	Monday 17th	Tuesday 18th	Wednesday 19th	Thursday 20th	Friday 21st	Saturday 22nd
Weight 1·14	1·13½	1·13¾	1·14	1·14	1·14¼	1·13¾
Comments Not flown – Sunday	Perfect stoop 250 ft approx. first flight – knocked down, took on reflush	Saw one late – stooped but failed to connect. Feathered and put in another	Storming flight on Grey Hen-three consecutive flushes from one covey-third put in too far for reflush	Bound awkwardly to one wing, but brought down safely	Lost when raked away towards beaters on Drummond; v. high - 1000 ft. Tracked and recovered	One false point. Put one in but dog re-flushed too soon. Bound to another but dropped it
Weather	Wet and windy	Abysmal -very stormy	Bright after rain - grouse very jumpy	Windy, overcast	Still and bright	Low cloud -difficult conditions
Food ½ breast quail	head of grouse + ½ quail	½ quail	breast meat of quail	head of grouse + ½ quail	one side of quail breast	breast meat of quail
Quarry	Adult cock grouse (over Nell)		(Unlucky - put in all three in quick succession)	Grouse - adult cock (over Duke)		

Whilst striving to keep his hawk in perfect condition, the falconer must even pay attention to her droppings, which give many indications of the state of his charge's health. Longwings 'mute' around the base of their perch, whilst shortwings and broadwings 'slice', firing their excrement like a ribbon towards the walls of their weatherings or mews. A healthy mute should be black and white. Brown mutes indicate richness of diet – maybe several yolks from day-old chicks. Greenish mutes indicate that the hawk has no food passing through the gut and will therefore be passed in the few hours immediately prior to flying time, when all the food from the previous day will have completed its passage. Yellow mutes will occur if the hawk is on antibiotics or, occasionally, if chick fluff is passed through the gut, rather than being regurgitated as a casting. Blood-stained mutes are usually indicative of a heavy worm infestation and the falconer should lose no time in taking a fresh mute sample to his veterinary surgeon for examination. Blood-stained mutes can also occur through trauma, whereupon the problem will generally resolve spontaneously. A hawk should be wormed every 3 months with a general-purpose wormer such as fenbendazole (Panacur, Hoechst UK) which will cover most but not every type of infestation which she is liable to pick up. Abnormal weight loss is also a symptom of a worm infestation and requires prompt action.

Hawks should also be periodically sprayed for mites with Johnson's Anti-Mite or another insecticide, which must be pyrethrum-based. Other insecticidal bases can be highly toxic to raptors.

Once a week, jesses should be greased with a suitable leather grease, such as Kocholine, to keep them supple. Dirty leashes should be exchanged for clean ones.

THE MOULT

Most species of hawks moult annually, the exception being eagles, which can take up to 2 years to complete a moult. The moult generally starts in early April and continues for 5 to 6

fret marks and hunger traces

pinched feather

Feather defects.

months. Whilst a hawk is moulting, she needs extra rations to facilitate the growth of new feathers. For this reason, it is not usual for a falconer to fly his hawk during the moulting period – the extra rations would obviously render the hawk over flying weight. If insufficient food is given at this time, the moult will be severely slowed down, which will be to the detriment of the next flying season. The hawk may also grow damaged feathers, showing 'hunger traces'. It is not entirely disadvantageous that hawks moult during the summer months. It is often too hot for them to perform well and all the game is out of season. In addition, with the trees in full leaf and an abundance of ground cover, it is difficult both to keep trace of shortwings in trees and to spot ground game, such as rabbits, which are one of the few quarry species which can still legally be hunted in the UK at this time of year.

The onset of the moult is stimulated by two main factors – the photoperiod, or day length, and the food intake. The former is dependent on daylight hours – when the winter days lengthen into spring, a hawk's internal clock will tell her that it is time to start moulting. The latter is dependent on the falconer – if a hawk is held at a tight flying weight she is unlikely to start the moult. As there is no merit in delaying proceedings, the best course of action is to feed her up in mid-March, in the hope that she will start throwing her old feathers soon and be finished in time for the next season.

Although it is possible to moult most hawks on jesses, it is advisable to moult them loose, preferably in a seclusion aviary or a chamber. Even the weathering, suitably adapted, will suffice as a small loose chamber. In this way a hawk can exercise a little and keep herself in better trim, whilst enjoying freedom of movement. Her aylmeri anklets (see Chapter 4) can be left on, but the mews jesses should be removed.

A moulting shed or 'loose mews' should be light and airy, with a bath and a suitable ground covering requiring minimum attention. In a chamber, natural ground will suffice,

Chamber: perspective view with cutaway sections.

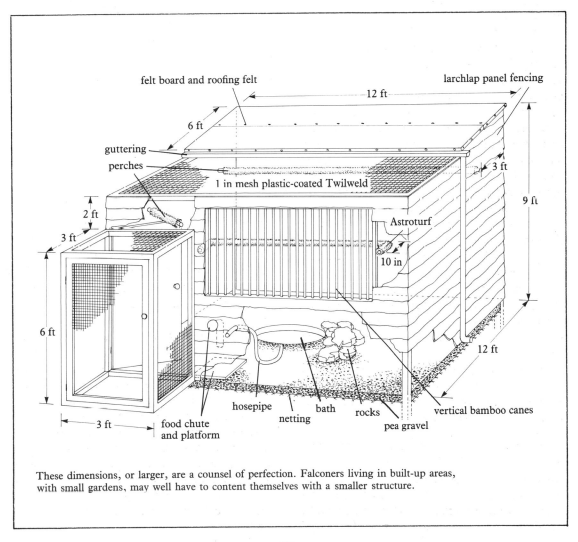

felt board and roofing felt

larchlap panel fencing

12 ft

6 ft

guttering

perches

3 ft

1 in mesh plastic-coated Twilweld

9 ft

2 ft

Astroturf

3 ft

10 in

6 ft

12 ft

hosepipe

bath

rocks

vertical bamboo canes

netting

pea gravel

3 ft

food chute and platform

These dimensions, or larger, are a counsel of perfection. Falconers living in built-up areas, with small gardens, may well have to content themselves with a smaller structure.

provided that vegetation is cropped short. In weatherings, the gravel will require more frequent attention as the smaller space will become soiled more quickly. Only steady hawks, therefore, which can be removed weekly without upset while the weathering is cleaned, can be moulted in this way.

A hawk should be disturbed as little as possible whilst moulting, or she will grow feathers with fret marks – a fault bar caused by a fright whilst the feather is growing. At worst she will throw out pinched feathers. This is a trait to which *Accipiter*s, which turn very wild during the moult, are particularly prone. It occurs if they are severely upset. The feathers will re-grow eventually but this will prolong the moult. Sparrowhawks and

goshawks are also prone to throwing fits, particularly towards the end of the moult when they are at top weight. It seems as if their bodies have stored so much food that they feel the need to burn it off in a violent and most distressing manner. These fits often become more frequent, eventually proving fatal. For this reason, *Accipiter*s should never be moulted on the bow perch. Equally, they must never be moulted loose in the weathering, where they would have insufficient space to exercise and in which the weekly process of cleaning out, involving the picking up of a fat hawk, would undoubtedly cause fret marks and possibly pinched feathers.

Before a hawk is turned loose to moult, her beak and talons should be thoroughly coped. She should also be sprayed with Johnson's Anti-Mite and wormed. Her food intake can be increased so that she has as much food daily as she wants.

Normal secondary moult sequence of a longwing, shortwing and broadwing. The secondaries are moulted from the innermost (1st) outwards.

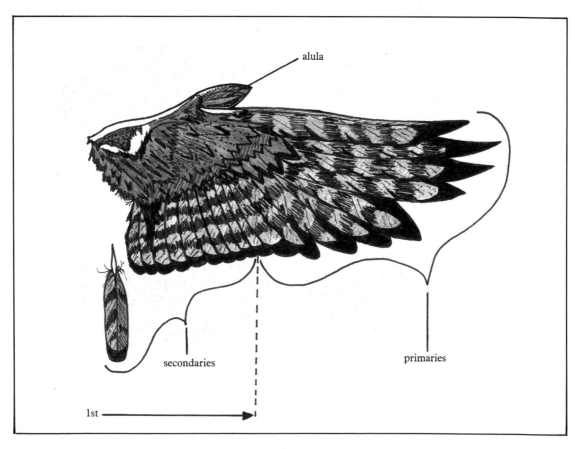

alula

secondaries

primaries

1st

26

The falconer is only interested in the perfect moulting of his hawk's flight feathers – primaries, secondaries and tail. Often some body feathers will not be dropped during the first moult.

All the perfect moulted flight feathers should be collected and saved carefully, lest there is cause to imp (p. 31) the hawk at a later date.

All feathers are generally dropped in matched pairs and although the secondaries, primaries

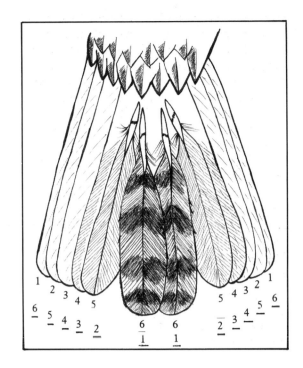

Right Normal tail moult sequence of a shortwing and broadwing. The outside numbers correspond to the sequence of moult.

Below Normal primary moult sequence of a shortwing and broadwing.

Bottom Normal primary moult sequence of a longwing.

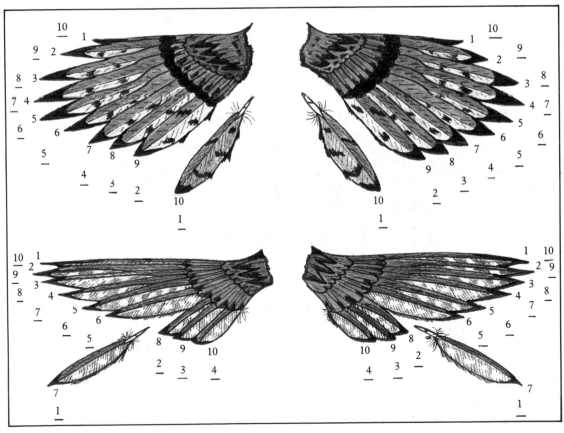

and tail are moulted in that order, these banks of feathers will overlap, so the first tail feathers will be dropped when the hawk is mid-way through her primaries. Once a feather is moulted, it will re-grow to approximately one-third of its eventual length, before the adjacent feather is dropped. This growth will take approximately 7 to 10 days and this is why the moult takes so long.

Whilst a new feather is growing, the shaft is encased in a sheath filled with blood. As the feather grows, the blood recedes and the webbing appears, to be preened into place by the hawk. When feathers are 'in blood', they are very delicate and the slightest knock can cause them to bleed. This is also the time when hunger traces and fret marks occur - hence the importance of leaving a hawk undisturbed and well fed.

Through careful observation, the falconer will know when his hawk has completed her moult, with the outer train feathers 'hard down'. Ideally the hawk's weight should then be partially dropped whilst she is still in her moulting chamber, before she is taken up again. She will then be known as 'intermewed'.

Hawks completing their first moult remember a great proportion of their training from their immature season. They will only need to be reduced in weight and given a brief retraining session before being back to normal, although totally unfit. Often they will fly at a slightly heavier weight than in their immature year.

COPING

In her natural state, a hawk keeps her beak and talons short by constant wear against rocks and the bones of her prey. In captivity, both beak and talons will grow too long and it is the responsibility of the falconer, therefore, to cut them back, filing them into shape.

It is difficult for the novice to assess when coping is necessary. As a basic guideline, the beak of an immature should not need coping until just before her first moult, unless she should bite hard on a bone and cause a crack to appear. Her talons, however, should be clipped as soon as she is taken up for training.

This will save her from grabbing herself in the foot and making a puncture hole, which can result in the dreaded 'bumblefoot' (p. 39). After her first moult, it is advisable to cope her at the start and end of the flying season, although it may be necessary to cope her more frequently. A novice may find it useful to take a close photograph of his hawk with perfect beak soon after he obtains her as a young immature. Thus, he will have something with which to compare her beak later in the season.

The instruments necessary for coping are a pair of dog's toenail clippers – the sort that cut in a circular motion – and various files. Chainsaw files are the most useful to do the bulk of the work, complemented by a set of needle files of various shapes, including a flat one and a round one. A silver-nitrate stick, obtainable from a veterinary surgeon or chemist, is also useful, to stem the flow of blood if the beak or a talon should be accidentally clipped too short, reaching the quick.

Before being coped, a hawk must first be cast – held firmly in the hands of a assistant. A towel or cloth should be used to wrap the hawk, to protect the waterproofing 'bloom' on her back. This matter is simple enough in the case of a hooded longwing, which cannot see the towel used to wrap her. With a shortwing or broadwing, which does not take a hood, it is an entirely different matter. If one is very quick, it is sometimes possible to drop the towel over her whilst she is on the fist of the assistant, lifting her bodily off the glove with both hands clasped around her wings, thumbs on her back and fingers on her chest. If this approach fails, it will be necessary to cause her to bate off the glove. Her legs can then be held firmly, whilst she is lowered onto her back into the towel, which is then wrapped around her. Once in the towel the hawk can be positioned with a cushion under her chest whilst the coping takes place.

COPING SHORTWINGS AND BROADWINGS

Shortwings and broadwings have a curve in their upper mandible, called a 'festoon'. If this grows too long, it will become thin and

can crack easily. The severity of the crack will increase if it becomes impacted with meat. Attention has to be paid to both the upper and lower mandibles of the beak. Like a dentist, the falconer must check that the bite, or relationship between the two mandibles, is correct once he has finished.

1) Clip the tip off the beak, taking it back to the right length.
2) File the underside of the tip flat with the flat file to prevent cracks.
3) File the sides of the beak down towards the tip to put back the point.
4) File down the front of the tip and up over the curve and sides of the upper mandible

Coping is one of the skills which has to be mastered.

to remove excess growth and any grey flaky granulation which may have accumulated.
5) Open the beak carefully by getting the hawk to bite on a gloved finger.
6) File inside the upper mandible in the curve inside the point and reshape the festoon.
7) Run a flat file across the lower mandible to remove any inward growing curve.
8) File back the tip of the lower mandible.
9) Check that the two mandibles meet correctly and finish with a gentle polishing with moistened fingertips. This will show up any remaining defects.

29

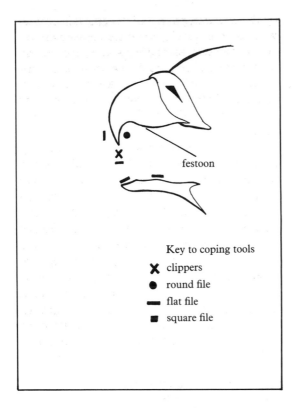

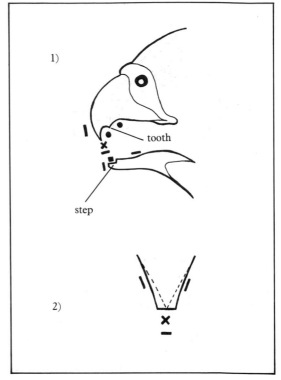

Key to coping tools

X clippers
● round file
▬ flat file
■ square file

Coping of upper and lower mandibles for shortwings and broadwings.

Coping of upper and lower mandibles for longwings: 1) side view, 2) end-on view of point of beak.

COPING LONGWINGS

Longwings have a tooth on their upper mandible. They use this as a pressure point to break the necks of their quarry by slotting it into the vertebrae. This tooth fits into a step in the lower mandible.

1) File back the tooth to the correct position.
2) Clip the end off the tip of the beak – the amount you need to remove will be apparent once the tooth has been taken back.
3) File with the flat file under the tip.
4) File the sides of the tip downwards and the entire outside of the upper mandible.
5) Open the beak and shape the tip and the tooth from the outside, using the round file to shape the tooth.
6) File flat across the lower mandible and reshape the step which accommodates the tooth.
7) File back the tip of the lower mandible.
8) Check the bite and polish with moistened fingertips.

If a crack appears in a beak, the correct approach is to file it out, filing quite deeply into the crack itself from the outside surface of the upper mandible. It may take several sessions to remove a crack, leaving time for the beak to re-grow in between to prevent excessive thinning.

Coping the beak is a good opportunity to clean the crines – the little hair-like feathers around the lower mandible – if necessary. Partially obscured nares can be cleaned out, with extreme care, with the blunt end of a needle.

Coping of talons.

Talons can be clipped to remove the sharp points. The curve in the underside can then be filed to bring back the point and to remove excess scale which will accumulate in this area. Large hawks have a well-defined groove under their talons which needs cleaning with the point of a file, as rotten meat can build up here. As a guideline to talon length, a hawk should be able to stand flat-footed, without the curve on the talon causing the toes to lift away from the perching surface.

IMPING AND FEATHER CARE

Imping is a traditional skill which must be numbered amongst the falconer's accomplishments. The repairing of a broken feather is unfortunately a service which few falconers will escape during the course of a season, if they are flying their hawks vigorously at game.

The quality of feather varies from species to species. Hawks from hot climates tend to have softer feathers, whereas those from cooler parts will have harder feathers, better able to cut through the wind and to shrug off rain. Adult feathers are usually harder than immature feathers.

The falconer is only concerned with the repairing of broken flight feathers – tail, primaries and secondaries. When choosing a feather with which to repair a broken one, it is obviously best to use the corresponding feather from the same bird, thrown out in a previous moult. The exception will be with tail feathers from the first moult, for these shorten noticeably in length in adult plumage. A replacement feather should preferably be from the same species and obviously from the same sex, as female feathers will be larger than those of the male; it should also be from the same side of the body.

Often, the falconer may be able to pick up the piece of broken-off feather, enabling him to imp it straight back into place. If a feather is 'hanging by a thread' it can be secured by bridging with super-glue, or splicing underneath with a short length of spare feather shaft, cut longitudinally and superglued onto the shaft below the webbing, to bridge the weakened point. With a complete break, however, the imp must be secured by means of plugging the hollow shaft with an imping needle – a peg or pin which runs between the end in the hawk and the replacement feather.

MATERIALS FOR IMPING
PEGS AND SPLINTS

These must be made from flexible material to match the flexibility of feathers and include:

Bamboo: preferably green, houseplant canes
Carbon fibre: obtainable from anglers and fishing shops in the form of broken carbon fibre rod tips
    Note: handle with care as slivers under the skin will not dissolve
Sewing needles: a range of sizes, including gloving needles

OTHER EQUIPMENT

The following items will also be required:

'Super-glue': not the type that sets immediately on contact
Sharp knife: scalpel, or modelling knife
Chopping board
File: for filing carbon-fibre imping needles
Card

BASAL IMPING

Prepare by casting the hawk, leaving the wing

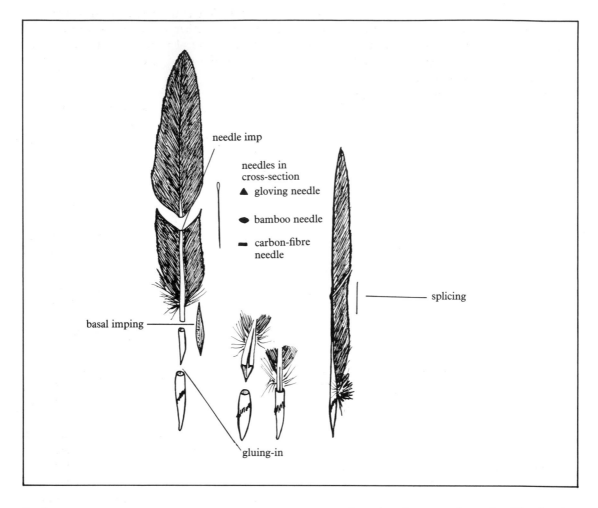

needle imp

needles in
cross-section
▲ gloving needle
◕ bamboo needle
▬ carbon-fibre
needle

splicing

basal imping

gluing-in

Imping.

or tail to be imped uncovered. Isolate the broken feather by running a piece of card under the stub and over surrounding feathers.

1) Cut the broken feather at the point where the webbing starts, leaving a good stub in the hawk, well below the flesh line.
2) Offer up a matching feather and cut carefully to length, lining up with the feathers on each side.
3) Form an imping needle, either by whittling a bamboo peg or filing down a length of carbon fibre. Depending on the size of the hawk, the imping needle should be between ½ in (merlin) and 2 in (golden eagle) long

and pointed at each end. No imping needles should ever be round, as they would rotate in the feather.
4) Gently try half of the imping needle for a friction-tight fit in the broken stub. If the peg is too large and you push it in too firmly, you can split the shaft, rendering a bad situation worse and yourself heavily reliant on the powers of super-glue to hold the broken stub together. Above all else, never push the imping needle so far that it exceeds the point at which the hawk's flesh line starts.
5) Check the needle for fit in the prepared cut feather.
6) Once the two halves of feather have been married up for length, with the needle fitting completely inside them, remove the

needle and glue each half of it in turn. Insert it first into the new feather and then, pushing it carefully home, into the cut stub. When the two halves meet, the peg should be totally obscured.

7) Twist the feather into the right plane, so that it lies correctly between the neighbouring feathers. Wipe off any surplus glue and wait for the adhesive to set.

8) Bridge above and below the join with super-glue.

NEEDLE IMPING

This form of imping is carried out with sewing needles. If the break is low down on the feather – a broken tip – the falconer has the choice of cutting out the feather high up and performing a basal imp or of putting back the tip, or a corresponding one, by means of a needle imp.

From base to tip, the shaft of a feather becomes thinner, with solid tissue inside, rather than being hollow. Sewing needles have the strength to hold firm when imped in low down in the shaft, at a point where the falconer could not carve a peg fine enough without it breaking. Just how fine an imp a falconer will attempt depends on his level of skill and the availability of suitable needles.

Gloving needles are preferable, as they have triangular points which will help to prevent rotation. Unfortunately, however, they are fatter than normal sewing needles and are therefore unsuitable for very fine imps. The imp is performed in exactly the same manner as the method described above for basal imping, with the obvious exception that the sewing needle is not filed to shape, although the eye may have to be cropped off.

GLUING IN

Instead of the similar, outdated method called 'sewing-in' it is possible these days, with the excellent range of adhesives on offer to secure a feather solely with glue.

The principle is to fix the actual shaft of the replacement feather inside the hollow shaft of the stub, instead of running an imping needle in between the two. The glue then secures it in place.

1) The broken feather is cut as for basal imping.

2) A complete corresponding feather is offered up for length and cut so that it will extend into the stub, but not go beyond the flesh line.

3) The shaft of the replacement feather is split longitudinally to a length of an inch or so, depending on the size of the feather. The cut end is pointed with a knife or scissors, to form a quill.

4) The split shaft is then crimped with the fingers, dipped in glue and pushed home into the shaft of the stub.

5) The plane of the feather is corrected before the glue sets.

STEAMING, DIPPING AND WASHING

Sometimes a hawk may bend a flight feather, but not actually sever or damage the shaft. This commonly happens with primaries when a hawk is transported in a travelling box. Bent feathers can be straightened by being steamed over the spout of a boiling kettle, taking care to keep the hawk out of the jet of hot steam.

An untidy tail can be vastly improved by being dipped into warm water, but this must not be done too frequently or the feathers will become brittle.

Dirty feathers can be wiped, or gently scrubbed in the direction of the webbing with a nailbrush or toothbrush. If a hawk's body feathers ever need to be washed in a major fashion due to some disaster or misadventure, much of her waterproofing will be removed as the natural oils are washed out. These can be replaced by lightly wiping a cotton wool pad, moistened with a minute amount of baby oil, over the feathers after they have dried.

3 IN SICKNESS AND IN HEALTH

by Neil Forbes, MRCVS, B.Vet.Med.

Under UK law there are certain procedures which the falconer is permitted to perform on his hawk, whilst others must be carried out by veterinary surgeons. The falconer is permitted to render first-aid care, give tablets or pills, and administer food or drugs by crop tube (see p. 36). Under a veterinary surgeon's direction the falconer may give injections and apply dressings. However, no layman is permitted to perform invasive techniques – opening of the skin for any reason. Obviously the falconer should find a good, willing veterinary surgeon, before he acquires his hawk.

THE SICK HAWK

RECOGNITION

A sick hawk will be first recognized by a change in its demeanour, behaviour or bodily function. The following are some of the commonest signs which might indicate an illness or injury:

1) Loss of weight.
2) Loss of appetite.
3) Change in the appearance of mutes or castings.
4) Vomiting food.
5) Huddled appearance, with feathers fluffed up.
6) Difficulty in keeping eyes open.
7) Increase or decrease in wariness towards human beings.
8) Reluctance to stand on one or other leg.
9) Reluctance to move.
10) One or both wings dropped.
11) Abnormal appearance or sound of breathing.
12) Breathing with the mouth open.
13) Change in voice.
14) Tremors, twitching, fits or convulsions.

TREATMENT AND NURSING

A sick hawk should be handled as little as possible, for this will increase the level of stress. If the cause of the problem is not obvious and there is no simple remedy, then expert assistance should be summoned.

In the treatment of sick hawks, skilful and diligent nursing is as important as medication.

The hawk should be placed in a quiet, warm and dark place, such as a well-ventilated enclosed cardboard box, positioned next to a radiator. Most sick hawks will benefit from the administration of oral fluid therapy. This is a simple technique which will help to save many hawks. To give fluids by mouth, a crop tube should be used. This is a length (4–6 in) of plastic or rubber tubing attached to a syringe. One person holds the hawk's shoulders from behind, whilst the other takes the head in one hand, stretching the neck by placing a finger between the hawk's mandibles. The tube is then inserted using the other hand, so that the tube passes to the side of the opening to the windpipe (seen at the back of the tongue as a slit) and into the crop.

Fluids may be given by mouth or by injection under the loose skin between the

Opposite The parts of a hawk.

34

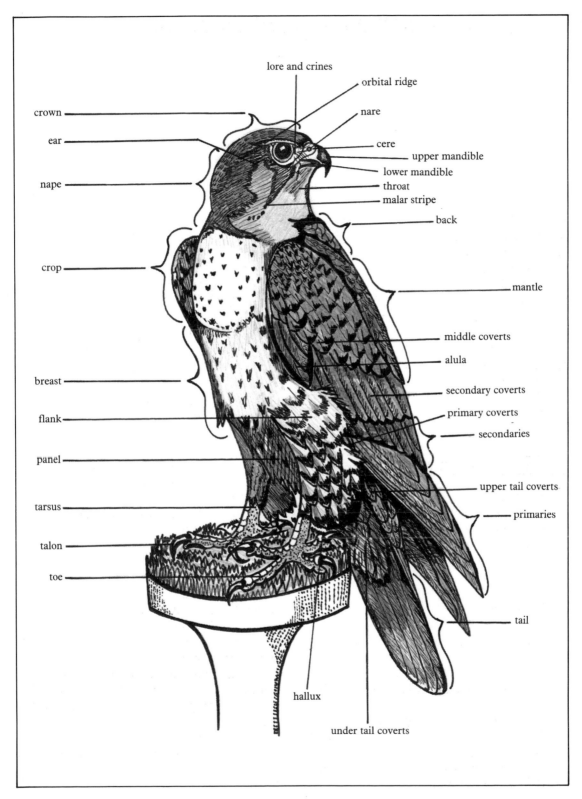

crown

ear

nape

crop

breast

flank

panel

tarsus

talon

toe

lore and crines

orbital ridge

nare

cere

upper mandible

lower mandible

throat

malar stripe

back

mantle

middle coverts

alula

secondary coverts

primary coverts

secondaries

upper tail coverts

primaries

tail

hallux

under tail coverts

TABLE 2 RECOMMENDED DRUG DOSAGES

Drug	Form	Dosage per kg	Length of treatment (days)
ampicillin	soluble powder	100 mg po tid	3–5
ampicillin	long-acting injection	150 mg im sid	3–5
amoxycillin	tablets	100 mg po tid	3–5
amoxycillin	long-acting injection	250 mg im sid	3–5
aureomycin	wound powder	ad lib topically bid	as req'd
bromhexidine	powder	3 mg po bid	3–5
carbenicillin	injection	100–200 mg im bid	3–5
calcium EDTA	injection	35 mg im bid	as req'd
cephlexin	tablets	50 mg po qid	3–5
chloramphenicol	injection	30 mg im tid	3–5
ciprofloxin	tablets	40 mg po bid	5–7
collo-Cal D	liquid	0.5 ml po sid	as req'd
clauvenate-potentiated amoxycillin	tablets	125 mg po bid	3–5
doxycycline	syrup	25 mg po bid	3–5
fenbendazole	liquid	50 mg po once	
frusemide	injection	10 mg im once	
ivermectin	injection	200 μg sc once	
itraconazole	syrup	10 mg po sid	7–10
ketoconazole	syrup	5 mg po bid	5
lincomycin	tablets	175 mg po bid	5
lincomycin	injection	20 mg im tid	5
metoclopramide	injection	2 mg im bid	1–2
metronidazole	tablets	50 mg po bid	5
miconazole	injection	10 mg im sid	5–7
oxytetracycline	long-acting injection	40 mg im sid	3–5
prednisolone	injection	30 mg im sid	as req'd
spectinomycin	injection	50 mg im bid	3–5
tobramycin	injection	10 mg im bid	5–7
trimethoprim	injection	50 mg im bid	3
trimethoprim	syrup	80 mg po bid	3
tylosin	injection	20 mg im bid	3

Key
sid	*Once daily.*	po	*By mouth.*
bid	*Twice daily.*	sc	*Subcutaneously.*
tid	*Three times daily.*	im	*Intramuscularly.*
qid	*Four times daily.*	ad lib	*At will.*

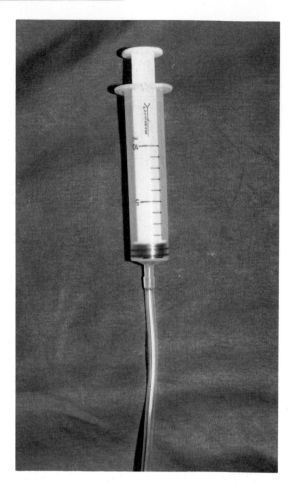

A 10-mm syringe with plastic tube attached to form a crop tube.

inside of the thigh and the body wall or directly into the vein or bone (the latter two techniques should only be used by veterinary surgeons). Generally speaking, oral fluid therapy is usually most suitable. It is quickly and easily carried out and hence less stressful to the patient. For oral therapy, the fluid used does not need to be sterile and it is available from all chemists and veterinary surgeons. It is sold as 'electrolyte' in a dry powder form, which is reconstituted with water. In an emergency, mix together a heaped dessertspoonful of glucose and half a level teaspoonful of salt in 1 pint of warm water. The fluid should be given at a rate of 1–2 per cent of the

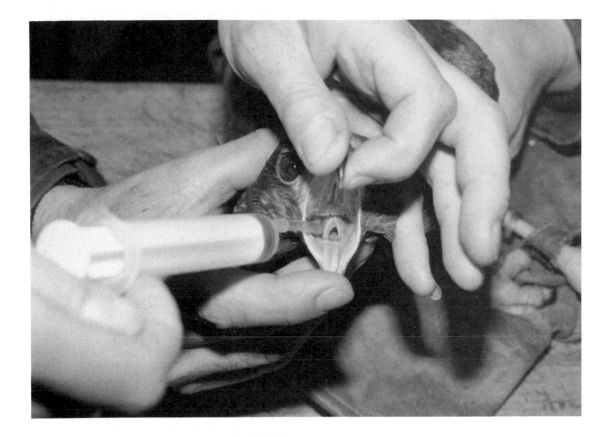

hawk's body weight hourly (i.e. a 1-kg hawk would receive 10–20 ml hourly) until recovery or demise.

Once the hawk has received fluids, it should be confined in a box or similar receptacle either next to a radiator, over a heated pad or under a heated lamp. If the hawk is in low condition, then, after one dose of glucose saline, a more nutritious oral therapy may be used. Suitable compounds are: Ovigest (Coopers Pitman-Moore), Milupa and Complan (Farley Health Foods Ltd), Build Up (Carnation Foods Ltd). These should all be given by crop tube at the same dosage as described for the electrolyte. If the crop empties, then small pieces of finely chopped meat can be added to the gruel. It is important at this stage to ensure that the crop empties fully before further food is given. Any hawk which has been vomiting is always treated according to this regime. In cases of vomiting, meto-clopramide chloride (Emequell, SmithKline

Tubing a sick hawk. The tube is coated with K-Y Jelly and passed down the hawk's throat to the side of the tongue. Care must be taken to avoid the windpipe, which is clearly visible at the back of the tongue.

Beecham) may be given by injection (see Table 2 for suggested dosage).

If food is not emptying from the crop into the stomach after several hours, then this needs to be removed as a matter of urgency. If this is not done then the condition known as 'sour crop' ensues rapidly, leading to death. In this condition, the food in the crop goes off and poisons produced during this process soon reach the bloodstream, leading to death. If the food in the crop is dry, this can be readily milked up from the crop using a retrograde massaging action of the finger and thumb. If, however, the crop contains any amount of fluid, this may be inhaled. This can only be avoided by a veterinary surgeon anaesthetizing the hawk and placing an inflated tube down the windpipe to prevent fluid passing down.

Any hawk which is this low in condition (unless it is known to be simply due to starvation) will certainly require antibiotics. No one antibiotic can control all possible infections, but, an experienced veterinary surgeon will have a good idea what is likely to be effective. In this situation amoxycillin is one of the most suitable drugs. In the UK, such antibiotics are termed 'prescription-only medicines' and are available only from veterinary surgeons, who are legally obliged to see the patient before prescribing any prescription-only medicine.

DISEASES

PARASITIC CONDITIONS
INTERNAL PARASITES

These are numerous, the main groups being:

1) Round worms (including intestinal and gapeworms)
2) Tapeworms
3) Fluke
4) Protozoa (including Coccidia, Giardia and Amoeba)

Diagnosis is made by faecal examination and should be done twice yearly by a veterinary surgeon experienced in this field. Most internal parasites are treated using fenbendazole (Panacur, Hoechst UK) or ivermectin (Ivermec, MSD Ag. Vet.). (See Table 2.)

EXTERNAL PARASITES

These are also numerous and are usually indicated by a hawk showing signs of pulling feathers out or excessive preening. Most, but not all, ectoparasites are visible to the naked eye. Check the hawk carefully both during the day and also after dark, because some parasites, in particular the red poultry mite *Dermanyssus gallinae*, only feed on hawks at night. Most ectoparasites are efficiently controlled using Johnson's Anti-Mite.

Some feather parasites actually live within the shaft of the feather and diagnosis by a veterinary surgeon with access to a laboratory and a microscope is necessary.

FEATHER DISORDERS

The majority of feather disorders are caused by parasitic infestation, but, there are other causes. If a feather is knocked out then the best immediate action (presuming that the feather is clean and only recently shed) is to push the feather firmly back from whence it came. Often a replaced feather will settle back down, but if not the feather follicle will be kept open thereby allowing a new feather to grow down in the near future. 'Pinched feathers' may arise where there is a nutritional deficiency, a viral infection or severe shock. Zinc or biotin may be deficient so it might be prudent to give a moderate supplement of both of these.

NERVOUS DISORDERS
HYPOGLYCAEMIA

These low-sugar fits, most often seen in smaller species, in particular muskets, are caused by an unnaturally low blood-glucose level and will occur when levels fall as low as 60–80 mg/dl. A drop of blood from a shortened talon is enough to confirm diagnosis. Treatment is by immediate supplementation with glucose. The quickest and easiest method is for the falconer to mix a concentrated glucose solution and administer this orally or by crop tube. A veterinary surgeon may then give further glucose subcutaneously or intravenously (a 10 per cent solution is used at a rate of up to 4 per cent of the hawk's body weight, i.e. 40 ml/kg of body weight in 24 hours).

HYPOCALCAEMIA

Fits due to a shortage of calcium are seen in three distinct situations:

1) They may be seen in young hawks on a severely calcium-deficient diet. In this case, the long bones (femur, tibia, fibula, humerus, ulna and radius) are likely to be severely affected. This can be verified by

taking an X-ray which is likely to reveal considerable bowing of these bones. If the bones are severely affected then euthanasia may well be advisable. If the bones are not badly affected, initial treatment with calcium borogluconate, given intravenously or subcutaneously and accompanied by dietary correction, will alleviate the problem.

2) Hypocalcaemia may be seen in the female during egg laying.

3) Hypocalcaemia will occur when a hawk is under stress, and is frequently seen when *Accipiters* are being initially manned. In all the above cases, diagnosis can be confirmed by blood sampling (normal levels are 8–10 mg/dl). Treatment is with 5–10 per cent calcium borogluconate, given slowly intravenously, at a rate of 3–6 ml/kg body weight depending on the concentration used. Dietary supplementation with Collo-Cal D may also be useful.

THIAMINE DEFICIENCY

This has often been blamed for causing many fits in hawks. Thiamine is one of the B group of vitamins. Characteristically the hawk tips her head upside down (bent right over backwards), whilst demonstrating a variety of other tremors or fits. Sadly, few of these hawks respond to thiamine treatment alone, although it should always be administered. More recently, Harris hawks have been found to suffer from repeated fits, which could be prevented by maintaining the hawk on a large daily dose of thiamine.

LEAD POISONING

This can cause all manner of bizarre nervous signs. In the early stages of the disease, the hawk is usually slightly weak with dropped wings. However, the hawk soon takes up a characteristic position – sitting back on her hocks, with her feet turned inwards, clasping. Any hawk exhibiting nervous signs should undergo whole-body radiography to check for the presence of lead. Calcium edetate (Sodium Calciumedetate, Vet Drug) should be injected, prior to surgical removal of the lead.

STRYCHNINE POISONING

There is sadly no direct antagonist for this horrifically powerful poison. If the hawk is believed to have ingested some poisoned meat (usually evidenced by a pile of other poisoned birds and animals near the bait), then this must be milked up from the crop immediately, by massage between finger and thumb. The hawk should be wrapped up warmly and taken straight to a veterinary surgeon, who may give sedatives or anaesthetics to control the spasm, as well as fluid therapy in an attempt to flush the poison out of the system.

TRAUMATIC INJURIES

Glucocorticosteroids such as prednisolone as well as diuretics such as frusemide (see Table 2) should be administered if a hawk has suffered concussion. Complete recovery after injury to nervous tissue can be a lengthy process; it may take up to 6 weeks or sometimes longer.

GOSHAWK CRAMPS

This is a serious disease which affects a small number of goshawks each year. Characteristically the hawk's toes and feet become flaccid and non-functional whilst, in herself, the hawk appears totally normal, eating, flying, vocalizing, etc. This flaccid paralysis moves up to include the legs and then the toes become tightly clenched and immovable. Degeneration of the sciatic nerve which supplies the feet and legs is responsible; the cause is unknown and few hawks recover. Immediate treatment is required if the hawk is to have any chance of survival. Treatment involves the use of antibiotics, steroids, vitamins and good nursing.

INFECTIONS
BUMBLEFOOT

Bumblefoot is probably the single largest cause of referral of birds of prey to veterinary surgeons. The condition is an inflammatory and usually infected reaction on the plantar aspect of the foot. The disease can be divided into three broad types:

Type 1 A small reddened area or even just a smooth shiny area, evident on the foot, caused by inappropriate perching or badly fitted furniture (e.g. jesses, bewits etc.). Simple rectification of the husbandry defect will lead to the regression of the lesion. In all cases, reducing the hawk's weight to flying weight, flying the hawk regularly, and applying a haemorrhoid cream (e.g. Preparation H, Whitehall Labs) to the feet twice daily will aid recovery.

Type 2 Where some penetration of the skin has occurred or where severe and often repeated trauma has occurred to the foot or ankles. Supportive treatment, as listed above, will also be useful for these cases. However, they will almost certainly require immediate antibiotic treatment as well.

Type 3 Severe distortion of the contours of the foot and/or toes, resulting from the infection causing considerable damage in the foot.

The duration of the infection is not the only factor which determines whether or not type 2 progresses to type 3. The pathogen (i.e. the type of infection) has an important effect on the course of the disease. The most commonly encountered infections are: *Staphylococcus*, *Streptococcus* and *Escherichia coli*. These pathogens are relatively easy to control, whilst others, i.e. *Pseudomonas*, *Proteus*, *Candida*, *Aspergillus*, are considerably more difficult, and, on occasions, impossible. There are a number of ways in which the pathogen may enter the foot initially, including puncture wounds, bites, jess rubs, poorly designed perches, etc.

Veterinary assistance is required when dealing with type 3 bumblefoot. No one antibiotic controls all infections. In the author's experience the two best first-choice antibiotics are amoxycillin and lincomycin (see Table 2).

Before administering antibiotics, swabs should be taken from the wounds and the organisms cultured and tested for antibiotic sensitivity. Following a 5–7-day course of

appropriate treatment, the case should be re-evaluated. If the improvement is dramatic, further drug therapy may be indicated. Conversely, if there is still considerable swelling, surgery by a veterinary surgeon is required. All the infected material must be removed from the foot, after which the incision may be closed. If there is considerable sepsis, it may be prudent to leave the wound open to granulate naturally.

Bumblefoot treatment can be a long and frustrating undertaking. However, recovery rates in the region of 90 per cent are achieved by most veterinary surgeons experienced in this field.

TRAUMA
BITE WOUNDS

These should be treated on the spot with wound powder and be washed immediately on return with a general-purpose disinfectant such as Hibiscrub or Pevidine Iodine. A light dressing should then be applied. A severe bite should be treated by giving antibiotic cover. This will certainly be necessary if the foot is becoming more swollen after the first 8 hours.

BROKEN TOES

It is not uncommon for hawks to break toes when binding to quarry. It is important with any fracture that the two broken bone ends are immobilized completely.

INJURIES CAUSED BY EXCESSIVE BATING

As well as contributing to bumblefoot, this may give rise to scale displacement and fractured legs. In the latter case, the injury caused is invariably a fracture of the top third of the tibia. This fracture is almost always seen in young hawks soon after they are first jessed because bating puts pressure on weak bones. It is best treated by placing an intramedullary pin down the length of the bone.

FRACTURE REPAIR

In any situation where a bone has been broken, the two broken ends of the bone must be immobilized. This may be accomplished by

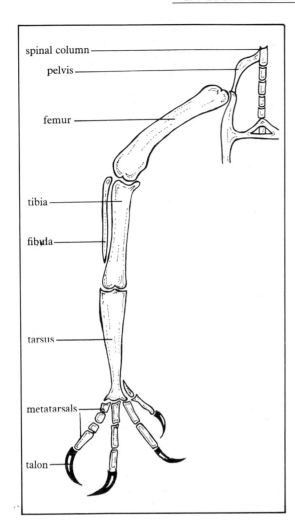

a number of means. Joints above and below the fracture must be fixed if the limb is to be plastered. Only some bones lend themselves well to this technique. If the fracture cannot be restrained by this method then some form of intra- or extra-medullary device is necessary to serve the same function.

For fractures of the tibia, femur (thigh bone) or humerus (bone of the upper wing), a good intra-medullary repair may be effected by inserting a sterile stainless steel pin of correct diameter and length down the shaft of the bone.

If the radius or ulna (bones of the lower wing) are fractured, then a splint may be applied to the outside of the wing. Sutures are passed through a mesh-like splinting material (cut or made to size) and around the shaft of each secondary feather. As the secondary feathers insert onto the ulna bone itself, if these feathers are maintained in a straight line then the fracture will also heal in correct apposition.

It is important that the bone ends are as close together and as straight as possible. It is equally important that the hawk is able to resume using her joints as soon as possible.

Left Bones of the leg.

Below Bones of the wing, showing a midshaft fracture of the humerus reduced by internal fixation.

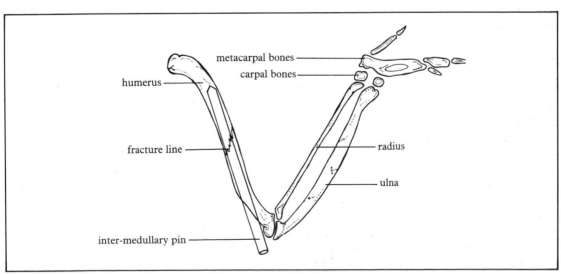

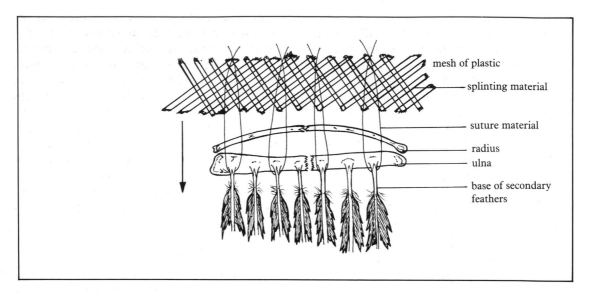

mesh of plastic
splinting material
suture material
radius
ulna
base of secondary feathers

A fracture of radius and ulna, stabilized by external fixation.

Lengthy immobilization can cause long-term problems – principally arthritis. If the fracture is in the wing, the affected wing should be restrained in a natural position for up to 6 weeks, depending which bone is affected. This may be accomplished by the use of a body stocking or with bandages around the wing or whole body.

Signs of a fracture are varied. If a leg is damaged, the hawk will be standing quite happily on the remaining good leg, with the affected leg held up. Fractures in the wing can be recognized by a dropped wing and usually occur whilst flying. Any hawk who hangs a wing should have an X-ray taken. Fractures in either the ulna or radius, but not both, are often missed. However, the intact bone acts as a splint for the fractured one.

DISEASES AFFECTING THE WINGS
BLAIN

This is the common name applied to carpal bursitis. Initially, a soft fluid-filled swelling is recognized over either the elbow or the wrist joint, usually preceded by some form of trauma to the area. Unfortunately, the swelling often becomes infected, frequently leading to an arthritic reaction in the joint concerned, ending the hawk's flying career. The fluid must be drained, using very strict aseptic techniques, and systemic and topical antibiotics and steroids must be given.

FROSTBITE

Sadly this has been an increasing problem. The condition has been recognized most frequently in lanners, luggers, Harris hawks, and certain eagles. It is usually seen from October to April in the UK and affects hawks which are restrained near ground level, on nights when the temperature has fallen to below freezing. The condition is most frequently seen at times of year when the owner does not expect frosts, i.e. early autumn and late spring.

An affected hawk will be seen with both wings slightly dropped. The ends of the wings, where the primaries emerge, will be significantly swollen, with characteristic cold fluid–filled blisters. The further up the wing the swelling extends, the worse the prognosis. A haemorrhoid preparation (such as Preparation H, Whitehall Labs) should be applied to the affected areas and the hawk should be given frequent short flights. The aim is to encourage the return of the normal blood supply to the wing tips. The hawk should also receive a course of broad-spectrum antibiotics, as the chilling will often have affected the normal gut flora of bacteria, giving rise to a severe enteritis or even septicaemia. The final outcome may not be known for several weeks. It may appear to be improving, when suddenly, up to 6 weeks later, the distal tip of the wing dries up and literally falls off, with the permanent loss of several or all primaries on that side. This is a tragic ailment, but one which can be avoided.

PARATYPHOID INFECTION

This is an infection by *Salmonella* organisms which affects a number of different sites in the body. The liver is one of the primary sites, becoming swollen and bronze in colour. The elbow and wrist joints of both wings may also be affected, demonstrating marked painful swellings. Treatment is rarely effective.

COLDS AND CHILLS

Any hawk which shows symptoms such as loss of weight, loss of appetite, laboured breathing or unexpected exhaustion should have an immediate mute test carried out and be put on a course of antibiotics (e.g. amoxycillin, see Table 2).

RHINITIS

This is commonly known as 'cold' or 'snurt' and hawks are said to be 'sniting' (shaking their heads and sneezing). It is caused by a number of different infections or results from trauma.

STOMATITIS

Also known as frounce, this is most frequently caused by *Trichomonas gallinae*. The hawk usually has reduced appetite, and may flick food. On examination of the mouth, a white plaque-like lesion is most commonly seen. Treatment is simple and effective. Metronidazole (Flagyl, RMB Animal Health) is the drug of choice.

If an abscess occurs in or above the roof of the mouth, this may cause respiratory problems. External swelling of the face may be evident, but, more frequently, one sees a depression in the roof of the mouth. In the author's opinion, this commonly arises as a result of food or other foreign material entering the slit in the roof of the mouth (choanal slit). This caseous pus needs to be surgically removed and the area cleaned up. This is a delicate procedure, due to the proximity of several major blood vessels, and needs to be carried out under anaesthetic.

Stomatitis may also occur due to parasitic infestation with *Capillaria* worms, yeast infection due to *Candida*, alkali or acid burns, foreign bodies wedged in or around the mouth and other traumatic injuries.

RESPIRATORY DISEASES

Respiratory diseases are the single greatest cause of death amongst raptors. There are numerous different causative agents and it is essential that a proper diagnosis is made before treatment is commenced. The different conditions affecting the respiratory tract are discussed below.

SINUSITIS

More accurately described as the 'sinusitis, rhinitis and conjunctivitis complex', this condition may be seen as a nasal discharge, a swelling below and slightly in front of the eye around the orbit, or by a weeping eye. *Mycoplasma* infections have been demonstrated to be present in some such lesions, although the pathogenesis is not proven at present. In most cases, these infections respond rapidly to therapy with lincomycin (Lincocin, Upjohn). tylosin (Tylan, Elanco) or spectinomycin (Spectam, Ceva). If, after a 5-day course with such drugs, the problem is still evident, then microbiological testing should be carried out. On occasions, it may be necessary to inject directly into the sinus with one of the above drugs, sometimes repeatedly for several days.

If mycoplasmas are not responsible for the disease, one will often find that *Pseudomonas* organisms are present. In this case carbenicillin (Pyopen, SmithKline Beecham) or ticarcillin (Ticar, SmithKline Beecham) are usually effective.

Abscesses in the mouth and persistent oronasal infections can be associated with vitamin A deficiency; thus, supplementation with this may be useful. When giving any vitamin supplement, dosages must be in line with the manufacturer's recommendations or those of a veterinary surgeon. Simply speaking, vitamins B and C are not harmful when given to excess, as any surplus is excreted via the kidneys. Conversely vitamins A, D and E, if given to excess, may cause severe problems.

Conditions which affect the upper respiratory system render diagnosis and treatment relatively simple. Moving down to the trachea and lung, diagnosis and treatment is more complicated.

INFECTIONS OF THE TRACHEA AND DISTAL RESPIRATORY SYSTEM

Hawks affected usually have severe respiratory distress and find it difficult to breath. They are very easily stressed and over-zealous handling alone can lead to a rapid demise.

To make an accurate diagnosis, the veterinary surgeon will need to carry out a number of tests. Firstly, a mute sample should be tested for the presence of parasitic infestation. The common pathogen in this case is *Syngamus trachea*, the gapeworm. It is essential that this test is carried out, rather than simply using a worming preparation 'just in case', for a wormer will kill off any worms that are present. Whilst this may be the correct first stage of any treatment regime, it will not stop the respiratory distress until after a period of 6 to 7 weeks. Hence, if one was not sure if the worms were there in the first place, it will not be known why the signs are persisting. The continued signs are caused by the presence of dead worm material still in the windpipe. During this period, broad-spectrum antibiotics, such as amoxycillin, and mucolytics, such as bromhexidine (Bisolvon Powder, Boehringer Ingelheim), should be used. The worm infestation, if present, would be treated with fenbendazole (Panacur, Hoechst UK). (See Table 2.)

If the mute test is clear, a swab should be taken from the trachea and tested for bacterial and fungal pathogens. A blood sample may also be taken for *Aspergillus* serology. Unfortunately, using the tests that are available at present, only 10–12 per cent of infected hawks will show as positives.

If bacterial infection is present, the most effective antibiotic should be used. If the hawk does not respond to antibiotic therapy, or if fungal infections are actually isolated, drugs such as itraconazole (Sporonox, Janssen), miconazole (Daktarin Inj., Janssen) or amphotericin (Fungizone, Squibb) should be used. The fungus *Aspergillus* is prevalent everywhere, but particularly in mouldy environments, rotting or decaying vegetable matter and wood or bark chips. Some species of hawk are more susceptible to *Aspergillus* infection than others. This is due to a less well-developed immune reaction against the organism. Such species include gyrfalcons, golden eagles, and black sparrowhawks. Infection will be most commonly seen in young hawks and recently stressed hawks (e.g. following importation). Species that are particularly sensitive should be given a precautionary course of treatment, for once there are clinical signs of the disease, prognosis is poor. Success rates for the treatment of aspergillosis will depend on how quickly treatment is instigated, as well as how high the level of infection is in the lungs and air sacs. Taking X-rays of the lungs and air sacs in an attempt to make a diagnosis in respiratory cases is relatively unrewarding.

AVIAN TUBERCULOSIS

This is the commonest cause of death of wild raptors in many countries. Infection most frequently arises by ingestion of infected wild birds. The disease is characterized by chronic weight loss, although the hawk continues to eat well. Thirst may be excessive. In some cases, lameness is the first sign of disease. In view of this, any case of unexplained lameness, swollen bones or joints should be checked for tuberculosis. If an open wound or swollen lesion is present, a sample from this may reveal the causative bacteria. Frequently no such lesions are found and tuberculosis can only be suspected as a result of the weight loss. In this situation, a blood sample may give further supportive evidence. A characteristic blood sample will reveal a dramatically increased white blood cell count, a severe increase in monocytes, sometimes an increase in heterophils and usually an increase in fibrinogen. Final diagnosis can only be made by endoscopic examination of the surface of the liver for the characteristic white lesions and a liver biopsy can be taken.

Having made the diagnosis, the decision has to be made as to whether treatment should be attempted. Drugs must be administered by crop tube daily for a period of 2 months and the person who administers them must have no contact with other avians. The bacteria is very resistant and, for as long as an affected hawk is alive, it may be excreting further infection. Thus it may contaminate its environment still further, risking a spread of the infection. Affected hawks in a collection should be destroyed. If one positive is found, all the other hawks on the premises should be sampled. Those suspected on the blood test should be isolated, awaiting the results of serial blood samples. It is also important to try and ascertain the origin of the infection. The two main sources are wild birds given as food and faecal contamination of the aviaries by an indigenous population of feral birds. If the latter is the case, either these birds need to be 'controlled' or the tops of the aviaries need to be closed in order to prevent further contamination. Whichever the cause, it is important that the aviary is well disinfected before it is used again with a suitable disinfectant such as Virkon S (Vet Drug).

INTESTINAL DISORDERS

Conditions affecting the oesophagus, crop and proventriculus are most commonly found in a hawk with a decreased appetite, who is flicking food or vomiting. It is important to identify the causative organism. It may be trichomoniasis (frounce) or *Capillaria*, whereupon the same white lesions may be found, but the characteristic bipolar plugged worm eggs will be found in the mutes. Treatment is carried out with fenbendazole (Panacur, Hoechst UK) or ivermectin (Ivermec, MSD Ag. Vet.).

The same signs may also be seen in the case of yeast (*Candida*) infections. In this case itraconazole (Sporonox, Janssen) or nystan (Nystan Oral Susp., Squibb) should be used (see Table 2). The diagnosis of candidiasis is made after smears from the crop are examined under a microscope.

Alternatively, vomiting and foul-smelling mutes may be caused by a bacterial imbalance of the gut. All animals, human beings and hawks have a balance of micro-organisms in their gut. Severe shock, stress, change of diet, chilling, or a course of antibiotics can cause an imbalance of these organisms. The result may be vomiting, loss of appetite or diarrhoea. In any case of a gut upset, even if the cause is *Capillaria* or *Candida*, antibiotics should be given in order to control secondary bacterial infections. Antibiotics which are useful in this situation are amoxycillin (soluble powder) or doxycycline (Vibramycin Syrup, Pfizer). If the vomiting is not controlled, an intramuscular dose may be given. If proper treatment is not quickly given, the hawk commences a rapid and often intractable decline, which involves repeated vomiting and loss of strength. Treatment should be specific and symptomatic, i.e. therapy for the vomiting, dehydration, and loss of energy as well as against the infection. Vomiting is best controlled in a warm environment using metoclopramide chloride (Emequell, SmithKline Beecham), together with fluid therapy by crop tube or subcutaneously. Impacted proventriculus can occur.

MISCELLANEOUS

IDENTICHIP

This is a relatively new technique in which a 'passive transponder' micro-chip 8 mm long by 1.5 mm wide is inserted under the hawk's skin. The ownership of a hawk thus implanted can be proven at any time in the future, even if the DoE ring is lost or removed. The chip is implanted in a conscious hawk by a veterinary surgeon. It has 3 particular uses:

1) A deterrent to would-be thieves.
2) Ownership can be proved, with or without a ring.

3) Permanent identification for pedigree records, in an effort to prevent inbreeding.

PROBLEMS ARISING FROM INBREEDING

As there is a relatively small genetic pool for some species bred in captivity, there is a severe risk of excessive inbreeding.

However, the problem does not arise simply due to lack of different blood lines in the country, for it is often for reasons of convenience and greed that father–daughter and brother–sister pairs are put together. Examples of congenital and probably inherited abnormalities have already arisen, such as congenital cataract, micropthalmas, curvature of the spine, spina bifida, deviations of the long bones, inactive preen glands and thiamine-responsive fits.

It is essential that all breeders keep good records and make a conscious effort not to breed from closely related stock. In the author's opinion it is now time that breeding pedigrees were made compulsory for all raptors bred in captivity in this country.

THERAPEUTICS

Drugs may be given by a number of different routes.

1) *By inhalation* This is used for treating respiratory infections. The drug is placed in a nebulizer, which then distributes the drug into the air as a fine mist. The hawk is confined in a sealed box to inhale the mist.

2) *Orally* This is the most commonly used route and is convenient for treating gut conditions or systemic ailments, using drugs which are readily absorbed from the gut. The drug may be hidden in a piece of food or alternatively given by tube into the crop.

3) *Subcutaneously* This route may be used for fluid therapy and certain other drug treatments, such as Ivermec worming.

4) *Intramuscularly* This is the most widely used injectable route and is frequently used for the administration of antibiotics. Strict aseptic (sterile) technique must be used. The back of the thigh or the pectoral muscles are the sites used. The pectoral is most accessible – the needle is inserted ½–¾ in to the side of the keel bone, into the muscle. If repeated injections are to be given, the exact site should be varied.

5) *Intravenously* Via a vein, only to be used by veterinary surgeons.

The drugs commonly used in raptor therapeutics are listed in Table 2, together with recommended dosages and routes of administration. All these drugs can only be used under direct veterinary supervision and veterinary surgeons inexperienced in the treatment of hawks may find this list useful.

4 FURNITURE

BLOCKS AND PERCHES

In their natural state, longwings perch flat-footed and shortwings and broadwings perch in trees; therefore falconers give their longwings flat-topped block perches and their shortwings and broadwings bow perches, to resemble branches. All perches must be covered with Astroturf. Astroturf keeps the feet clean and its use prevents pressure points forming, which can swell and be punctured by a talon, causing bumblefoot.

Most equipment suppliers sell good perches, but Astroturf must be requested specifically.

THE BLOCK PERCH

The best style of block perch is the Arabic type, with the correct size of top for the species. The flat top sits on a supporting pole, around which the tethering ring can rotate freely. These poles can be attached to heavy metal bases for indoor use or to spikes, which can be pushed into the ground in weatherings or on the weathering lawn.

The principal advantage of these Arabic-type blocks, over and above the traditional European shape, is that the sides of the perch do not get soiled by mutes.

The size of block top and height, must be in proportion to the species as shown in the table. If the top of the block is too small, or the jesses too long, the longwing can straddle the block, with jesses slipping over opposite sides of the top, leaving her pinned against the support pole at the point where the jesses join the swivel. This can result in severe feather damage or even internal rupture.

TABLE 3 SIZE AND HEIGHT OF BLOCK TOP IN RELATION TO SPECIES

Species	Diameter of top (in)	Height (in)
Jack	3½	10
Kestrel, merlin	4	10
Lanneret, male lugger	5½	11
Lanner, lugger, tiercel, male prairie	6	11
Falcon, sakret, female Prairie	6½	12
Saker	7	13
Jerkin	7½	13
Gyr	8	15

THE BOW PERCH
OUTDOOR BOWS

Made from metal piping on spiked legs, these perches must be well padded with Astroturf. The Astroturf can be secured with electrical cable ties, with the ends wrapped in insulating tape (equipment suppliers often sell them unpadded). The metal ring must be of a diameter wide enough to pass over the Astroturf. The height must be sufficient to accommodate the length of the hawk's tail.

INDOOR BOWS

The outdoor-bow design is modified for indoor use by substituting the spikes with two heavy metal feet – usually scaffold piping filled with cement.

LOOP PERCHES

This is a relatively new design of perch which has proved to be ideal for shortwings. It is

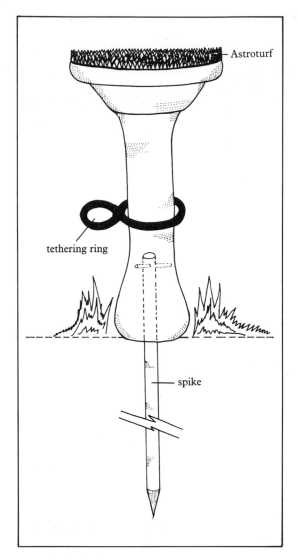

Arabic-style block perch.

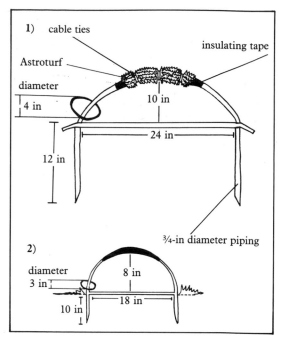

Bow perch suitable for: 1) broadwings and shortwings, 2) sparrowhawks – a fine grade of Astroturf must be used.

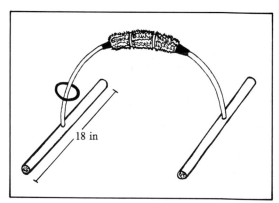

Indoor bow perch.

constructed from a solid length of timber, running across the entire width of the weathering, at a height of approximately 12 in. The top is padded with Astroturf and a metal loop, holding the tethering ring, is positioned centrally and sunk into the ground each side of the perch.

The particular merit of this type of perch for *Accipiter*s, over and above the bow perch, is that *Accipiter*s tend to bate more than broadwings and will often get the ring of the bow perch stuck in the bristles of the Astroturf. The leash then pulls through their train, with the concurrent risk of tail feathers being broken. On a loop perch, this cannot happen, as the tethering ring passes freely up and over the metal loop, thereby leaving the leash flat against the ground.

Many other types have been used in the

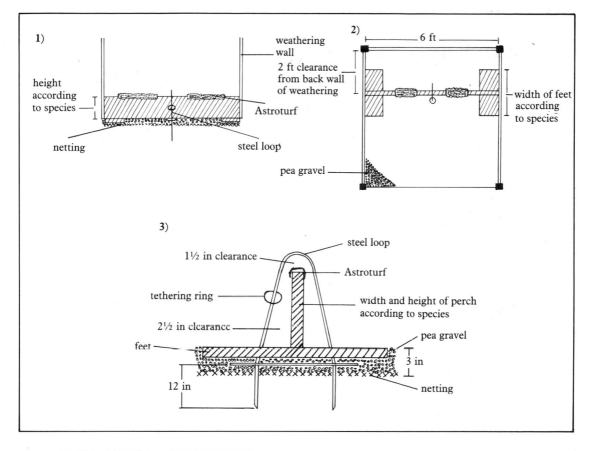

Loop perch: 1) front view, 2) aerial view, 3) cross-section.

TABLE 4 DIMENSIONS OF THE LOOP PERCH

	Height (in)	Width of feet (in)	Length (ft)	Width (in)
Spar	7	18	6	¾
Male goshawk Black sparrowhawk	9	24	6	1
Female goshawk Red-tailed buzzard Harris hawk Common buzzard	12	24	6	1½

history of the sport, including the notorious screen perch, but most of these are now considered outdated, unsuitable or unsafe.

SCALES

As daily weighing is such a critical part of training a hawk, the scales are an important item of equipment. The old-fashioned balance-type, suitably adapted with a perch at a height to accommodate the train, are reliable. Any spring-balance scales will flicker when the hawk moves and the calibration may alter, because the spring stretches over a period. Balance-type scales are consistent – provided that the one side balances with the other, they will give an accurate weight. Top-quality electronic scales, suitably adapted, can also be used.

It is important to have weights descending to ¼ oz. Falconers flying jacks and muskets

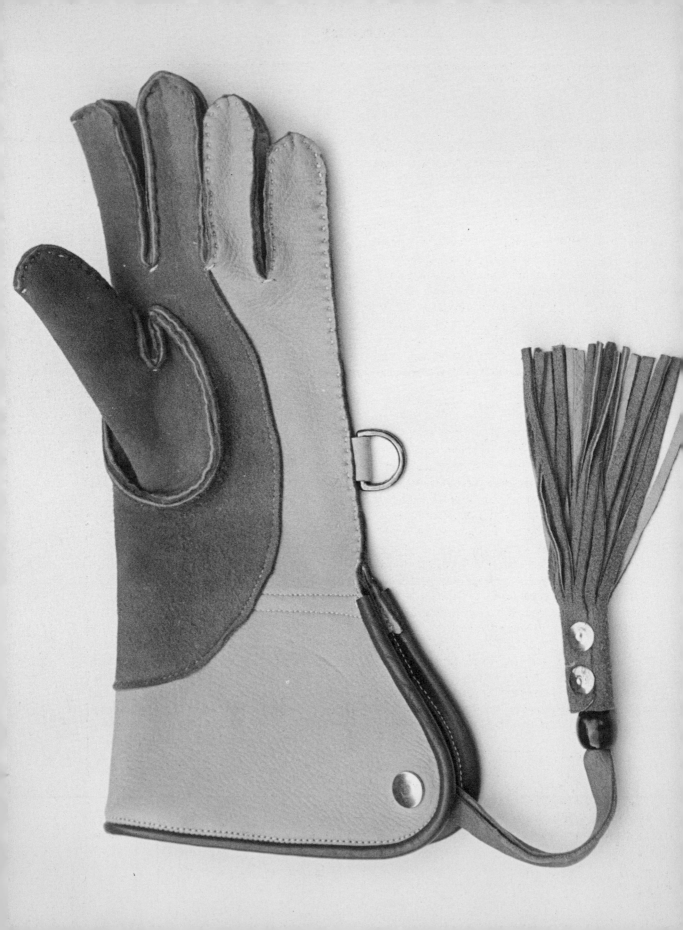

Opposite Falconer's glove. This glove is double thickness and is suitable for most species of hawk.

should have weights accurate to ⅛ oz. Most equipment suppliers now sell scales suitable for hawks.

BATHS

Hawk baths should be of a good size and deep enough for the water level to reach up to the top of a hawk's legs when she is standing normally; this depth will be sufficient for her to get her shoulders under when she dips her wings. Some equipment suppliers sell baths, but mailing them is extremely awkward as they are so large and difficult to wrap up. For this reason, the falconer may have to collect the bath or go to the expense of a door-to-door carrier.

GLOVES

To make a falconry glove is quite an undertaking. If the leather is to be tough enough to withstand the hawk's talons, it will be difficult to stitch. The pattern is all important to get a good, comfortable fit and acquiring the right leather, which must be supple as well as strong, is extremely difficult. Bearing in mind that one's hand is going to spend a great deal of time in this glove, it is a better option to buy one ready made from a reputable equipment supplier. He will have ideal leather and the necessary expertise to produce a glove which is really comfortable. If the species for which it is needed is specified, the glove will be of suitable thickness and length. Sending a tracing of the hand ensures a good fit. Falconers carry their hawks on the left hand.

JESSES AND AYLMERIS

Traditional jesses, made from one piece of leather and attached around the hawk's legs by folding through a series of splits, have been outdated by aylmeris. Aylmeris take the form

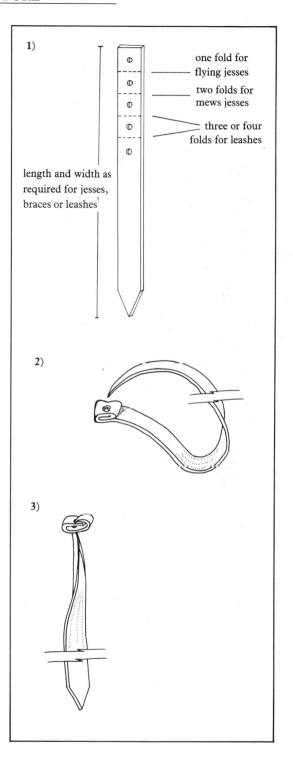

1)

one fold for flying jesses

two folds for mews jesses

three or four folds for leashes

length and width as required for jesses, braces or leashes

2)

3)

The making of a button: 1) folding, 2) passing the pointed end through the punched hole, 3) pulling it tight.

TABLE 5 LENGTH OF JESSES FOR VARIOUS SPECIES

Species	Length of mews jesses (in)	Length of flying jesses (in)
Merlin Kestrel Sparrowhawk	5	6
Lanner Lugger Tiercel Black musket Male prairie	7	8
Common buzzard Red-tailed buzzard Ferruginous buzzard Black sparrowhawk Goshawk female Goshawk male Saker falcon Sakret Gyrfalcon Jerkin Peregrine falcon Female prairie	8	9

The above measurements are approximate according to the size of perch. The measurement is taken from the point of the jess to the underside of the button.

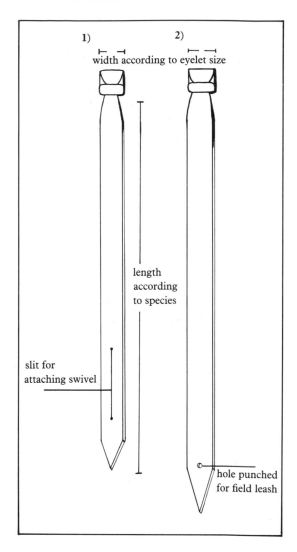

Jesses: 1) mews jess, 2) field jess.

of a separate anklet, fastened around the tarsus and secured by a metal eyelet. Through this, a separate jess is threaded, with a button on one end, large enough to hold it in the eyelet. Mews jesses are inserted when the hawk is at home in the weathering, with a slit in the end to accommodate the swivel. Field jesses, with no slit in the end, which could get caught up in trees or on the barb of a fence, must be inserted when the hawk is flying free.

The leather from which aylmeris are made must be extremely strong, but also supple. The exact weight of the leather will depend on the size of the hawk, but it must be tested against tearing.

Falconers must always make their own aylmeris, as the anklets have to be fitted exactly around the hawk's leg and secured with eyelet closers *in situ*. To order jesses ready made from an equipment supplier really is the height of laziness and inefficiency. What will arrive will usually be a false aylmeri, to thread like a traditional jess, with the eyelet beyond the threading slits, or a set of anklets to pop-rivet around the leg. The former is inclined to trap the back talon of the hawk through the eyelet, whilst she moves around on her perch; the latter are unsafe as they have been known to open. Above all other considerations, however, jesses should always be hand-made by the falconer to fit his hawk,

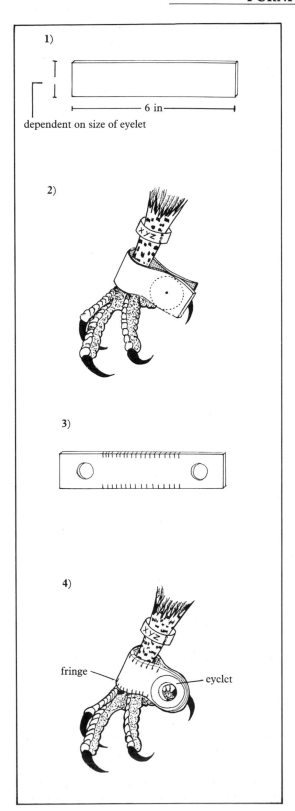

1)

dependent on size of eyelet

├── 6 in ──┤

2)

XYZ

3)

4)

fringe ——— ——— eyelet

Left Making and fitting of aylmeri anklets for longwings and broadwings.
1) Cut a 12-in length of leather. The width is dependent on the size of eyelets required for the species of hawk. Cut this in half width-wise, leaving two 6-in lengths.
2) Fold a length of leather around the hawk's leg and place the eyelet on one side so that the anklet will rotate comfortably without being too loose. Mark the middle of the eyelet with a leather awl.
3) Open the leather strip and punch out the eyelet holes. Make small nicks along the top and bottom edges in between the eyelet holes to create a soft fringe against the hawk's leg. Repeat on the second length of leather.
4) Replace the anklet around the leg and secure with the eyelet. Cut off excess leather and repeat on other leg.
Always make sure that the anklet is below any rings or other equipment.

Below Fitting of wide alymeri anklets for shortwings to reduce scale damage.

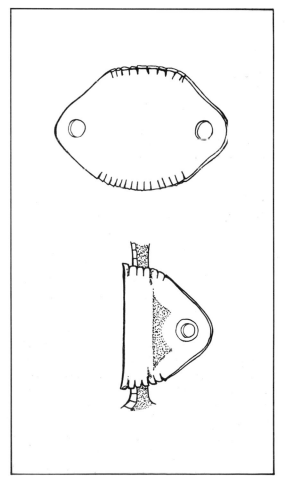

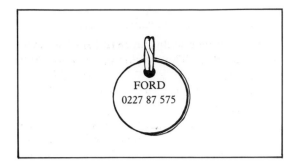

Identity tag, showing name and telephone number of owner.

Below Making and fitting a bewit.

1) Cut a strip of leather 6–8 in long and the width of the keeper on the bell. Fold in half to find the middle. Punch hole 1 just to one side of the centre. Punch hole 2 at a distance corresponding to approximately half the diameter of the hawk's tarsus. Just beyond hole 2, two nicks can be cut, angled like an arrow head.

2) Thread the bewit through the keeper on the bell until the bell lies in the centre of the bewit.

3) and 4) Pass point A through hole 1 and pull tight. This must be done so that there is a smooth soft surface around the hawk's leg at all times.

5) Place the bewit around the hawk's leg and pass point A through hole 2. Punch hole 3 in the end without nicks, as close as possible to the point where the bewit passes through hole 2. (This cannot be punched earlier as its position depends on the thickness of the hawk's tarsus.)

6) Pass point B through hole 3 until the nicks are through and secured. Cut off the surplus leather.

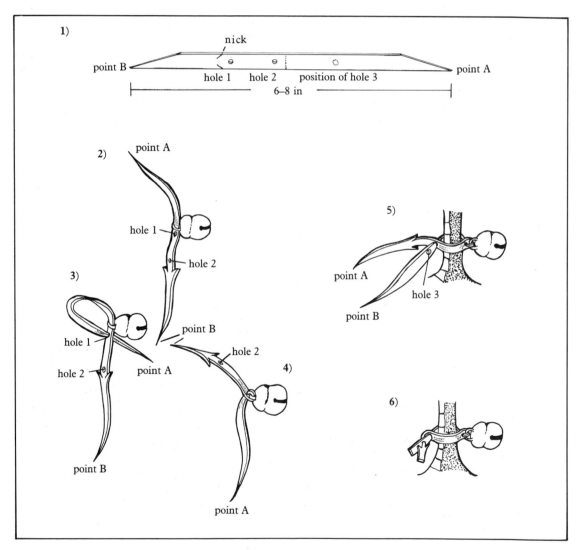

and this last criteria cancels the justification for ordering ready-cut anklets of any sort.

To make aylmeris the following equipment will be required:

Leather: available from some equipment suppliers or a local tannery or leather shop

Eyelets: from equipment suppliers in small, medium or large sizes

Eyelet applicators: from equipment suppliers, in sizes to match eyelets

Hole punch

Steel ruler

Scalpel or leather knife

Awl

Leather grease: saddler's or equipment suppliers

The latter items are available from any shop selling leather tools, or an ironmongers.

The making of aylmeris is most easily explained when depicted. Always remember to cut the leather across the grain to avoid stretch and grease the strips well before use.

A telephone number can be written on a field jess with a waterproof marker, lest the hawk be lost. Alternatively an identity tag can be attached to the bell/bewit.

BEWITS

Used to hold bells on the hawk's legs, there are various different designs of bewit – traditional, button and a recent innovation, the cable-tie bewit. Only the former should be used. Button bewits are too loose, resulting in the bells hanging too low and impeding the hawk. Cable-tie bewits are dangerous as the tubing covering the cable-tie will often sever, leaving the sharp edges of the cable-tie free to cut into the hawk's tarsi, aided by the weight of the bell.

Like aylmeris, traditional bewits should also be made by the falconer to fit his hawk. Bewits must always be put above the aylmeri anklets, but below the DoE ring. If there is no space on the tarsus for all three, the leg which does not bear the DoE ring should have a bewit fitted.

BELLS

There is quite a wide choice of bells for hawks available now. The traditional 'Lahore' bells come from Pakistan. These are the least expensive and, if selected with care from a number, have a good tone. Unfortunately, they do not last as long as some of the more expensive bells, often cracking after a season.

Asborno bells from the USA are probably the best bells available, but this is reflected in the price. They last virtually indefinitely, being much more strongly made and their pitch is generally excellent. Other bells have been produced in an attempt to emulate the Asborno or 'Acorn' bells and some of these are quite good. The best are Steve Little bells, again from the USA, but extremely expensive.

The choice of a pair of bells depends largely on the ear of the individual. Ideally, a falconer should have the facility to choose from a big carton of bells at an equipment suppliers. The more discordant the ring, the further it carries.

Hawk bells.

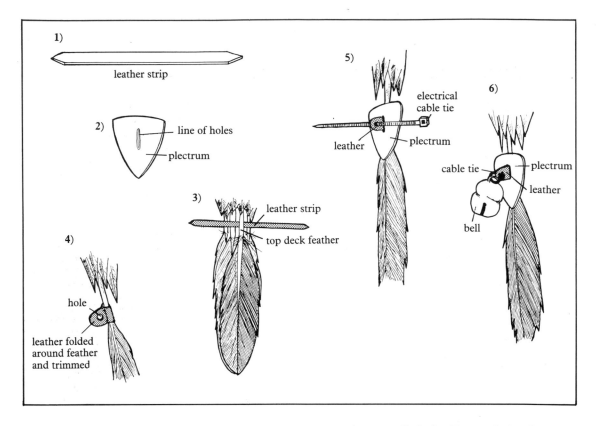

Attaching the tail bell. First method.
1) Cut a strip of leather 6 in long and ¼ in wide.
2) Punch a line of holes in the centre of the plectrum to a length of ¼ in.
3) Pass the strip of leather under the shaft of the top deck feather at the base near the upper tail coverts.
4) Folding the strip of leather around the shaft, apply super-glue and pinch together with a pair of pliers. Punch a hole and cut off the surplus leather.
5) and 6) Push the plectrum onto the leather tab. Pass an electrical cable tie through the hole and attach the bell. Cut off any excess cable tie.

TAIL BELLS

Tail bells are essential for shortwings, which wag their tails when in trees, but can also be used on broadwings and longwings, for with the DoE ring on one leg, taking up space, the tail is the obvious alternative site for mounting the second bell of the pair. The mounting for a tail bell can also be used for attaching a transmitter. The smallest size of bell should always be used.

There are several different methods of mounting a tail bell. Two of the best are shown in the illustrations above and opposite.

LEASHES

Leashes can be purchased ready made from equipment suppliers or they can be made from a suitable material by the falconer. The material used to make a leash is woven or braided terylene, which will not rot and is relatively easy to tie and untie. This material can be divided into two types – flat and round. The round leash material is yachting cord, which can be purchased off the roll in a variety of colours from ship's chandlers. A knot is tied in the end of a 4½-ft length to form the leash. Both ends are then sealed with a flame to prevent them from unravelling.

Flat leash material comes in various weights and thicknesses. A hawk with a propensity to pick at her leash should be tested on both types to see which she makes least headway with, for if she should free herself from the

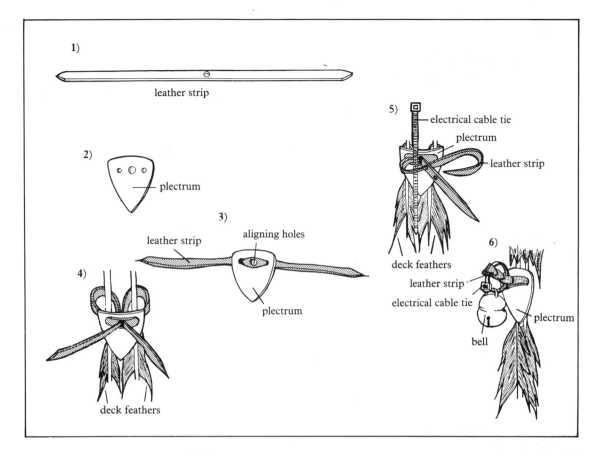

1) leather strip

2) plectrum

3) leather strip / aligning holes / plectrum

4) deck feathers

5) electrical cable tie / plectrum / leather strip / deck feathers

6) leather strip / electrical cable tie / bell / plectrum

weathering lawn with jesses and swivel attached, she will easily become tangled in a tree and may hang upside down and die. Never use leather leashes which are prone to snap without warning.

BUMPER LEASHES

These have been designed for *Accipiter*s which generally bate a great deal when first jessed. The tarsi of *Accipiter*s are very slender and a great deal of strain is therefore put on them when the hawk bates. They are also prone to scale displacement.

To alleviate the problem, a piece of knicker elastic can be threaded down part of the length of a flat leash, giving the leash some degree of elasticity. Such leashes are made by punching a series of holes in a normal flat leash, for a total of 7 in. The elastic is then threaded through the holes and secured at each end by stitching into place.

Attaching the tail bell. Second method.
1) Cut a 10-in strip of leather, pointed at both ends and narrow enough to pass through the holes to be punched in the plectrum. Punch a large hole in the centre of the strip.
2) Punch three holes in the plectrum, the centre one slightly larger than the outer two.
3) Scratch the back of the plectrum with a scalpel to roughen it. (This will help to stick the plectrum to the shafts of the feathers when glue is applied.) Pass the pointed ends of the strip of leather downwards through the two outside holes in the plectrum, so that the hole in the leather lies directly above the central hole in the plecturm.
4) Fold the two pointed ends of the leather strip inwards and pass them around the deck feathers. Together, bring them upwards through the central hole in the plectrum. Apply glue to the deck feathers and pull tight on the pointed ends of the leather to secure.
5) and 6) Punch a hole near to the plectrum in one of the leather strips. Feed the opposite pointed end out through the hole and, before pulling tight, place an electrical cable tie in position. Pull tight and punch another hole and pass the pointed end through once more, applying a small spot of super-glue to secure. Cut off excess leather, then pass the cable tie through the keeper on the bell, so that the bell hangs close to the plectrum but loose. Cut off surplus cable tie.

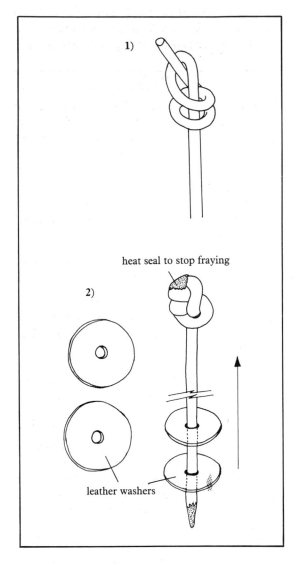

Tying a figure-of-eight knot on the end of a leash:
1) method, 2) addition of leather washers to enlarge the knot.

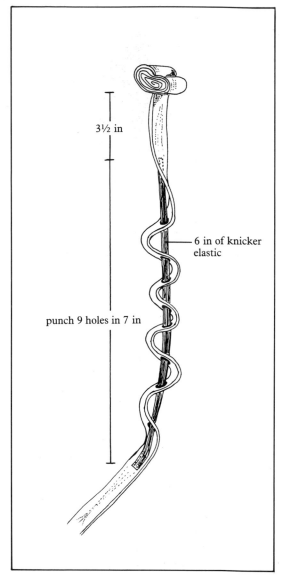

Making a bumper leash. Two strips of elastic should be used for a male goshawk or a black musket and three strips for a female goshawk or a black sparrowhawk.

Neither of the above types of leash should be longer than 4 ft. If a leash is too long, the hawk will get up too much speed when bating before she reaches the end of the leash. When pulled up short at speed, she can damage her legs.

Avoid any leash colours that look like food – red, for example, which may encourage picking.

FIELD LEASHES

The field leash has been developed for use when the hawk is fitted with field jesses. It is a short piece of creance material, approximately 2 ft in length, with a loop tied in one end. The loop is passed through the tassel or thong of the glove, with the end threaded through to

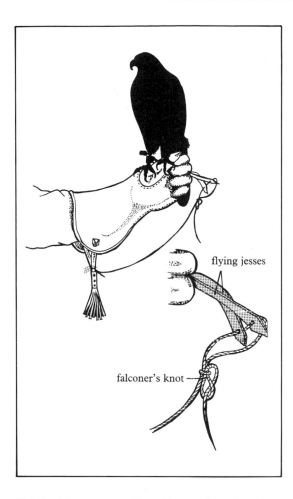

Field leash in use, secured by a falconer's knot through the holes in the flying jesses.

secure it. The end is then passed through tiny holes punched at the ends of both field jesses and secured with a falconer's knot.

The field leash provides a security measure when the hawk is on the fist. It saves the hand from becoming too tired whilst hanging on grimly to the field jesses and it can be untied quickly and easily with the right hand.

SWIVELS

The best swivels are the stainless steel D type. These are available from most good equipment suppliers. They are unlikely to wear and they are easy to use. A selection of sizes is available, according to species. As with all items of the hawk's furniture, swivels should be checked regularly for signs of fracturing.

CREANCE

The creance is used when a hawk is in training, until she can be trusted to fly free. It should consist of 50 yd of lightweight braided terylene, attached at one end to a stick, around which it is wound in a figure-of-eight manner. The ability to wind both creances and lure lines thus is one of the skills which a falconer should possess, and can be mastered with practice.

LURES

Swing-lures

Longwings, shortwings and broadwings are flown to swing-lures, which are supposed to resemble a bird in flight. The *only* type of swing-lure which is acceptable is a pair of wings, tied back to back. Some falconers insist on using lure-pads, on which wings (sometimes) and meat are tied. The weight and size of these pads vary enormously, but all are dangerous. If a hawk collides heavily with such a lure, either thrown in the air or through bad lure-swinging on the part of the falconer, it can do her damage. Pads can also bruise the feet of a longwing taking it at speed.

Proper lures are made from the wings of the intended quarry species, or one of similar colouration. The wings are dried in an open position, then tied together firmly with a cable tie and by passing thin nylon cord around the bone. The ends of the nylon are left extended to tie on meat (beef, never chicks). The longer of the two ends is then passed through a tiny swivel on the end of a lure line and tied in a reef knot. A chunk of beef, tied on fresh daily, will give the lure all the weight it needs.

Lure lines should be made from about 4 yd of braided cotton, which will not burn the fingers when swung vigorously. Unfortunately braided cotton will rot in time if it gets wet, which it inevitably will. It should be checked

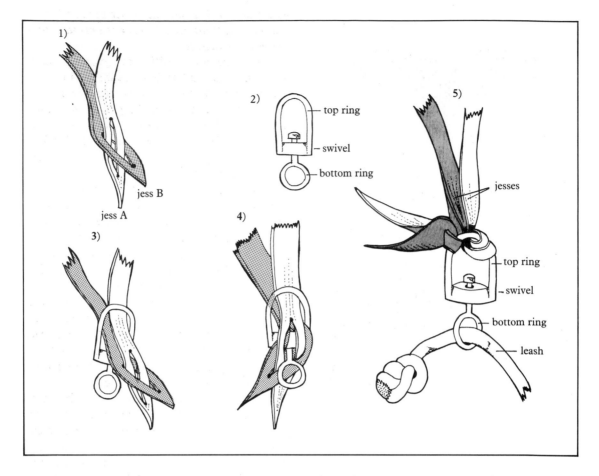

Attaching a swivel.
1) Pass the end of the jess A through the slit of jess B to make one slit.
2) and 3) Pass jesses through the top ring of the swivel together so that the slit is lower than the bottom ring on the swivel.
4) Open slit and pass it over the bottom ring of the swivel.
5) Push both sides of the slit of the jess all the way to the top of the upper ring on the swivel until in position. Pass leash through bottom ring. This method alleviates the problem of the second jess slipping down the swivel.

periodically because it is most unfortunate to have a lure line snap and it can result in a long walk, particularly with a fit longwing in a good breeze. Most equipment suppliers sell lure lines in small, medium and large sizes, related to species.

RABBIT-LURES

Rabbit-lures are used for broadwings and shortwings. They are made from the well-cured skin of a rabbit, which must include the tail. Rabbit-lures must be well padded lest the hawk should hurt its feet on impact. Turner-Richards training dummies for retrievers form excellent bases on which the skin can be mounted. The tail is important, as this flash of white is generally what appears to catch the hawk's eye. Strings for meat are attached by stitching close to the 'head end', together with a swivel and line. The line, which should be approximately 15 ft in length, has a loop for the fingers at the far end.

HOODS

Fundamentally, a hood is a more sophisticated version of a simple blindfold. Hoods are used for a variety of purposes in falconry. The most common and probably the most important

Swing-lure.

which are too big and allow her to see through the beak opening merely do not perform their intended function.

There are many different types of hood. Some are more difficult to make than others, particularly 'blocked' hoods – those which are soaked during their making and stretched over a hood block, then dried to take the shape of the block, remaining rigid when drying is complete and the block is removed. Blocked hoods, such as the Dutch hood, have the advantage of keeping their shape, unless completely crushed. Softer hoods are much easier to make, particularly the Anglo-Indian which is made from one piece of leather.

When confronted with acquiring a hood for a hawk, the falconer faces something of a dilemma. Many falconers take pride in the fact that they make a large proportion of their equipment themselves, in particular, items which can be hand-made to fit the hawk. However, whilst one is likely to be able to make a respectable job of a pair of aylmeris, hood-making is a more demanding art. With the aforementioned risks inherent with badly-made hoods, many falconers prefer to buy their hoods from equipment suppliers, most of whom possess the prerequisite level of skill, not to mention the correct materials for the job. If a hood supplied by an equipment supplier does not fit, he will change it for one a touch smaller or larger, as required. It is worth seeking out a really good hood-maker – this is not an area in which to economize.

If one really feels confident about attempting to make a hood, it is best to stick to the Anglo-Indian design, where it is possible. through a tried and tested pattern, to make a hood which fits from a single measurement of the hawk's head. When completed, if the hood looks less than perfect, it should be thrown in the bin, not put on the poor hawk in a vain attempt to justify the hours spent in making it. Typical sins in the first attempts include: hoods which have been pulled too tight on one side when stitched and therefore are not symmetrical; hoods which let in light through the stitch holes; badly-cut beak openings and hoods with knots from the

usage is on longwings, where the hooding is an essential part of the training. Hoods are used also for shortwings and broadwings – usually eagles rather than *Buteo*s. Essentially, hoods are used to make hawks sit quietly during manning, during travelling and whilst being carried, particularly if another hawk is being flown at the time. Hoods are 'struck' (opened) and 'drawn' (closed) by two leather braces mounted at the back of the hood, operated by the right hand and the teeth when the hawk is on the fist. A top knot enables the falconer to put the hood on and lift it off without crushing the sides.

Hoods must be comfortable. If a hawk is once left wearing an ill-fitting or badly-made hood, she can be rendered permanently hood-shy. Obviously hoods which are too small are those most likely to upset a hawk – those

Dutch hood

stitching high inside the seams, where they can damage the hawk's eyes.

The following are the three principal patterns used nowadays.

DUTCH HOOD

Made from three pieces of leather – a central body piece and two side panels – these blocked hoods are generally used for longwings as they suit the shape of their heads. The side panels are usually a different colour from the body of the hood.

Dutch hoods usually have a feather plume. The art of making a Dutch hood has advanced so far in recent years that they are no longer the rather heavy hoods that they used to be.

BAHREINI HOODS

The hood most favoured by Arabs for their saker falcons and shaheens (peregrines), these hoods have become increasingly popular with

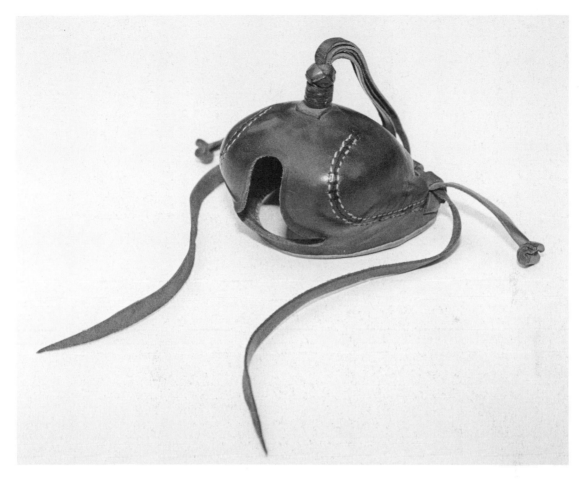

Bahreini hood

British falconers in the last decade. The pattern is particularly good for *Accipiter*s, but is also widely used on longwings, particularly now the technique of blocking Bahreinis has been mastered.

The true Bahreini is made from one piece of leather, although there are some most attractive hybrid versions being marketed, with coloured side panels, like the Dutch hood. The braces are interwoven through a series of slits at the back of the hood, causing the leather to concertina like a purse when the hood is struck and drawn. The top knot is usually a straight forward leather tab, or a Turk's head knot.

ANGLO-INDIAN HOOD

Anglo-Indians are widely used and ideal for making a hawk to the hood initially. Like the Bahreini, an Anglo-Indian has a leather tab or Turk's head knot as a top knot and the best of them are now blocked. This innovation, whilst taking the hood away somewhat from its original concept, helps the shape enormously.

MAKING AN ANGLO-INDIAN HOOD

The hawk must first be measured. To do this accurately, she should be cast and the widest point across the top of her head, directly behind the eyes, measured with pin-point precision, to the nearest millimetre. The measurement thus attained is used to construct the geometrical pattern, which will result in a perfect fit, provided that the pattern is drawn accurately.

Anglo-Indian hood.

The paper pattern is transferred onto leather, which should be lightweight but not stretchable. When cutting the pattern with a sharp leather knife or scalpel, it is safer to make the beak opening slightly smaller than on the paper pattern – it can always be opened up later, after fitting. The opening should also be chamfered or shaved with the scalpel at a slight angle on the inside edge, so that it will sit more evenly against the hawk's cere and gape. Slits must be cut for the top knot and braces and holes punched for the throat lash, as shown on the pattern. It is advisable to use a stitch-marker on the inside of the seam. The hood is now ready for stitching.

Although it is considerably more difficult, it is worth going to the effort of stitching through the seams, rather than stitching in an over-and-over manner. The end result will be much more light-tight, as well as being neater in appearance. Waxed linen thread or dental floss knotted at one end, is used to start the stitching on one side at point P. The needle is pushed into the leather, approximately $\frac{1}{10}$ in from the edge to be stitched, then out again through the edge of the leather and in through the corresponding edge to be joined, emerging $\frac{1}{10}$ in in on the opposite side. The stitch must be pulled tight extremely gently to avoid the

The author and her husband.

Student at the British
School of Falconry with
a common buzzard.

Adult female Harris hawk.

Blue hare hawking.

Peregrine in flight.

Stephen Ford with falcon and
pointer.

Peregrine on red grouse.

Merlin.

Hooded immature peregrine falcon.

Adult female goshawk.

Peregrine and grouse.

Adult female peregrine.

The Gleneagles Hotel, 1990.

A point on Braco Castle Moor.

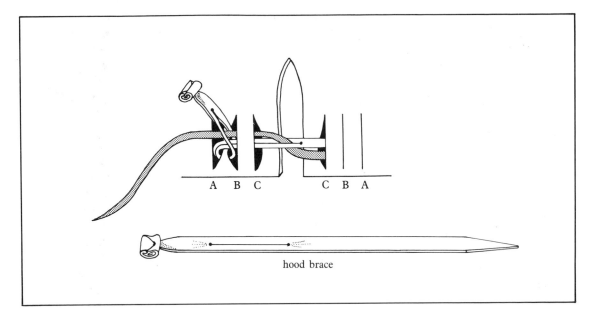

hood brace

thread snapping or the leather tearing. Obviously the smaller the stitches the better, within reason. The end result should be a perfect edge-on-edge join, finished with a small knot, hammered flat into the bottom of the seam. The process is then repeated on the other side and at the back.

After completing the stitching, the hood should be domed by placing a broom handle, or similar object, inside against the top of the seam and hammering with a small wooden mallet. This defines the curve and closes up the seams by flattening the leather against itself. Check the seams by holding the hood up to the light – if daylight is still visible, nail varnish can be painted along the seams.

Now the hood is ready to have the braces fitted. Cut two lightweight strips of leather narrow enough to lie inside the brace slits. Cut them to equal length and make a long point on one end. Make buttons at the other end. Punch a hole in each brace at a point about ¾ in away from the button and thread the hood. Open the hood fully, then cut off the long ends, leaving pointed ends about 1½ in longer than the buttons.

Cut a strip of leather for the throat lash, thin enough to thread through the holes already punched. This strip is usually of a

Braces. 1) Threading braces in a hood. Pass the brace: *a.* down B, *b,* up A, *c.* through slit in brace, *d.* down B, *e.* up C, *f.* repeat on other side, *g.* pass right-hand brace through slit in left-hand brace, *h.* down C, *i.* up B, *j.* pass through slit in other brace, *k.* repeat last three instructions on other side. To finish, tie knot in pointed end of brace. 2) A hood brace.

different colour leather to match the leather used for the top knot. Leave a small flap inside at each end, to be stuck flat against the sides of the hood. The purpose of the throat lash is to support the lower edge of the hood, so that it keeps its shape. An alternative is to put a rolled edge around the base of the hood.

To make the top knot, cut a strip of leather, pointed at both ends and fractionally narrower than the slits cut for the top knot. Feed the strip down one side and up the other. Punch a hole and pass the opposite end through it, then repeat. The Turk's head knot is unfortunately too complicated either to depict or to describe in words and must therefore be learned from another falconer or leather craftsman who is familiar with it.

Finally, the hood must be fitted on the hawk. The following guidelines will enable the beginner to tell if the fit is correct and will

PATTERN FOR ANGLO-INDIAN HOOD

MODIFIED FROM AN ORIGINAL DESIGN BY H.J. SLIJPER.

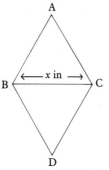

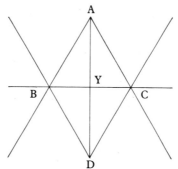

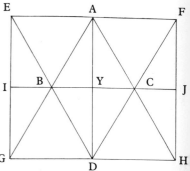

1) Measure across the top of hawk's head at widest part directly behind the eyes. Using BC as this measured width of *x* in, draw equilateral triangles ABC and BDC, with BC as common side.

2) Join AD to cross BC at Y and extend all lines from B and C.

3) Draw EG and FH parallel to and the same length as AD and join EF and G Extend BC to I and J.

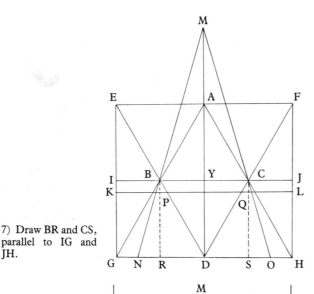

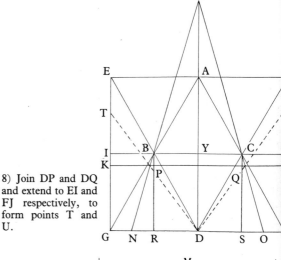

7) Draw BR and CS, parallel to IG and JH.

8) Join DP and DQ and extend to EI and FJ respectively, to form points T and U.

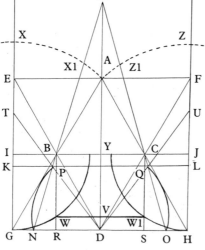

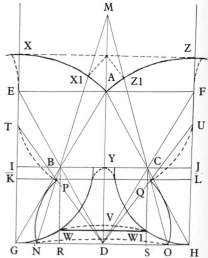

11) Extend lines GE and HF. With compass point on K and radius KA, draw arcs cutting GE extended at X and MN at X1. Extend slightly beyond X. With compass point on L and same radius, draw arc cutting HF at Z and MO at Z. Extend on slightly beyond Z.

12) *a*. Draw curves TP, UQ, NO and WW1 by hand.
b. Join E to the extended arc AX and F to the extended arc AZ by hand.
c. Join X and Z, to meet MA at the same level as XZ.
d. Where arc from G and arc from H join IJ, draw curves to point Y for top of beak opening.

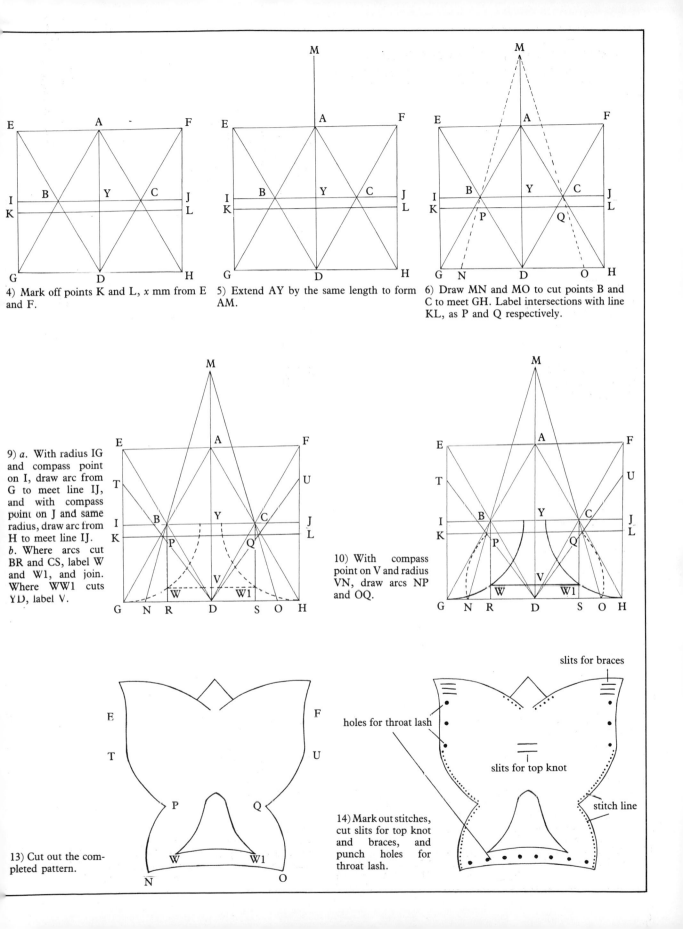

4) Mark off points K and L, *x* mm from E and F.

5) Extend AY by the same length to form AM.

6) Draw MN and MO to cut points B and C to meet GH. Label intersections with line KL, as P and Q respectively.

9) *a*. With radius IG and compass point on I, draw arc from G to meet line IJ, and with compass point on J and same radius, draw arc from H to meet line IJ.
b. Where arcs cut BR and CS, label W and W1, and join. Where WW1 cuts YD, label V.

10) With compass point on V and radius VN, draw arcs NP and OQ.

13) Cut out the completed pattern.

14) Mark out stitches, cut slits for top knot and braces, and punch holes for throat lash.

slits for braces

holes for throat lash

slits for top knot

stitch line

Opposite Waistcoats are a more practical option than hawking bags.

apply equally to hoods purchased from equipment suppliers:

1) The hood should pop easily over the hawk's head.
2) The braces should draw without choking the hawk.
3) She should not be able to see out of the beak opening.
4) The whole of her gape should be visible through the beak opening.
5) When the top knot is rocked back and forth, there should be little movement on the head.
6) When the hood is removed, there should be no moist patches indicating that her eyes were touching the inside of the hood, or that it was cutting against her gape.
7) The hawk should appear comfortable.

The latter point cannot necessarily be a hard and fast rule with a hawk that is being hooded at the very start of her training, when she is unfamiliar with wearing a hood. Some hawks will take a hood without fuss right from the outset, whilst others, although taking the hood well, will fuss when the braces are drawn, even in a hood that fits them properly.

WHISTLES

To recall a hawk on the wing, it is common practice to blow a whistle or to whistle with the mouth. If one is unable to whistle oneself with gusto, the artificial version will be essential. However, every falconer is well advised to carry a whistle as, if he finds himself in hot pursuit of a flight, he is equally likely to find himself completely out of breath and unable to achieve a noise of any volume from his lips. The best type of whistle is the Acme Thunderer – available from sports shops, where they are sold for referees. The plastic ones are better than the metal variety, which feel very cold to the lips on a freezing winter's day.

FLYING WAISTCOATS

To carry meat and the quarry that his hawk has accounted for, traditionally the falconer wears a bag, suspended from a belt or shoulder strap on his right-hand side. These bags have been largely abandoned in favour of a lightweight or waxed waistcoat, of the sort used by fishermen and photographers. The chief advantage that the waistcoat holds over the bag is that it is less cumbersome and will not snag when the falconer climbs over a barbed-wire fence.

A great many useful features can be incorporated into the design of the waistcoat, which can either be purchased from an equipment supplier or bought as the aforementioned fisherman's waistcoat from a field-sports shop and adapted. Waistcoats should have a large back pocket as this is essential for holding lures and game. The right-hand side pocket, used for meat, should be lined with washable waterproof material. A field-jess holder should be incorporated, as should a whistle on a lanyard. Spare pockets can be used for a lock knife, an extra set of equipment (but not bells) lest an item be lost in the field, a basic emergency medical kit – wound powder and sticking plaster – and the game licence, for which there is usually a convenient inside zipped pocket.

TELEMETRY

There is no disputing that telemetry is a great asset to the modern falconer. It is not merely useful for locating hawks which have been lost through unfortunate circumstances whilst flying, but also for finding hawks on kills. There are several systems currently marketed. The first point to bear in mind is that units, even from the same supplier, seem to vary enormously. Each supplier, therefore, will have the blessing of some of his clientele and the damnation of others. The strengths and weaknesses of a receiver unit lie in the following areas:

1) *Range* This will vary according to the

Telemetry units should be as portable as possible.

area in which the hawk is being flown. Obviously the more open the area, the greater the range of a particular unit. Trees, built-up areas, hills and electrical pylons, will all cause a reduction of the range over which the system will effectively operate. Generally speaking, a greater range is required for longwings than for shortwings.

2) *Directional finding* Some receivers fall down in their ability to find a hawk at close range. They will give a strong signal to let you know that the hawk is close by, but will not allow you to pin-point her exact location. Contrary to what the novice may expect, the gain or volume knob should be repeatedly turned down as low as possible, for if it is on too high a setting, the signal will be received over such a wide arc that the operator will not know in which direction to search. Some units will enable the operator to disconnect the antenna lead when at really close quarters and to use

the end of the lead to track down the precise location of the hawk, which may be necessary if she has killed in dense cover.

3) *Portability* If a unit is to be of any real use, it should be able to be carried easily by the falconer when in the field. Many units fall down in this respect. Valuable time and distance can be lost if the falconer has to return to his car, or, still worse, home, in order to pick up his unit.

4) *Easy assembly* The antenna is collapsed when not in use. Some units have a system of rods to be slotted into place. All this takes time – the antennae that open out from fixed points are infinitely quicker and less irritating. Better still are the units which have the antenna actually mounted on the receiver itself and which can be pointed, like a gun, in the direction in which the hawk disappeared.

5) *Channel selection* Telemetry units have a number of channels which enable the user to operate several transmitters at the same time.

It is therefore important that the channels are not too close together on the waveband, lest there is overlap. A fine-tuning knob enables the operator to tune into each transmitter so that the best signal is received. The easiest receivers to operate are those with numbered push-button channel selection. In practice, if a hawk is lost at a time when a number of other hawks are fitted with transmitters, it is best to collapse the other transmitters before seeking the lost hawk. This prevents any possible confusion – one does not want to spend several hours attempting to locate the hawk sitting on the fist of one's companion.

6) *Needle meter* When the wind is howling, as is so often the case when one is in pursuit of a lost hawk, it is most depressing if one is unable to hear the beep because it is drowned out by a gale. In such circumstances, a meter indicating the strength of the signal by means of a moving needle will come into its own.

7) *Additional features* A unit should have a socket for earphones, which will help enormously in gale conditions. It is also helpful to have a unit which can be powered by a socket inserted into the cigar lighter of a car. A magnetically mounted car-roof aerial (mag-mount) can then be utilized to help the falconer search over long distances, for when no signal is received it is the unhappy task of the falconer to travel with grim determination in the direction in which the hawk was last seen disappearing, until she comes into range. If this approach fails, he must then broaden his search in a wide arc in an attempt to pick up the signal.

Batteries should be removed from a unit at the end of the season, for they may corrode and damage it. The size of the transmitters is in direct proportion to the size of the batteries. Depending on the size of the hawk and how much weight one feels it can carry, the choice of transmitter varies from single stage (one battery) to three stage (two batteries and two aerials). It is worth being extravagant with batteries, for the life left in them dictates how long one has to find a lost hawk. Lithium batteries last much longer and are suitable for larger transmitters.

Transmitters are attached daily before flying

Tail-mounted transmitter.

and removed immediately afterwards so that the batteries can be taken out. Consequently, an easy and safe way of attaching the transmitter has to be adopted. The falconer has the choice of attaching it either to the tail or leg. There are pros and cons with each option. On the leg, the hawk may well remove the aerial. In the field, this will reduce the range to the point where the transmitter is, to all intents and purposes, useless. It may also impede footing. If the transmitter is tail-mounted, it is not unheard of for the falconer to track his absent charge, only to pin down the deck feather(s) to which it had been attached, swinging, complete with transmitter, on the barb of a fence. However, better the loss of the deck feathers than a wrenched leg. Tail-mounting therefore seems the preferable option. There are two principal methods of attaching a transmitter, dependent on the design. If the transmitter has a metal keeper at the top, an electrical cable tie can be passed through this and slipped through the tail bell mount or the aylmeri. Cable ties are the only safe ties to use for attaching transmitters in this fashion. Unfortunately, a cable tie is used and cut off every time the transmitter is attached, but the very small type of cable tie suitable for this operation is relatively inexpensive.

The alternative method of mounting can be employed if the transmitter is fitted with a spring-clip system. These are designed exclusively for use on the tail. They are supplied with a small metal tube which is glued around a deck feather. The clip is then squeezed with the fingers and pushed into the tube, opening up when released to hold it in place. In theory, this sounds like an excellent idea, as it saves wasting a cable tie each time the transmitter is used. In practice, however, its ease of use depends largely upon the hawk – some, when keen, simply will not hold still long enough to enable the little prongs of the spring clip to be lined up with the tube on the tail.

There are two principal types of transmitter – the type where the batteries are pushed into a brass holding slot and the cap-and-barrel variety. The first type, where the batteries are pushed into place and secured with a surrounding rubber loop, are better. The cap-and-barrel variety, where the batteries are dropped into the barrel the right way up before the cap is screwed into place, have a tendency to loosen a fraction while the hawk is on the wing, breaking the contact point between the base of the barrel and the positive terminal of the battery.

The exact frequency of the transmitter is determined by the crystal. Different frequencies require different lengths of aerial. From the falconer's point of view, the shorter the aerial the better, lest it should impede the hawk's progress. In the UK, of the two frequencies usually marketed by telemetry firms, 216 MHz is illegal, but requires shorter antennae, both on the receiver unit and on the transmitter, than the other legal frequency usually encountered – 173 MHz. It is important that all transmitter antennae are coated in plastic so that they cannot blow up if they should trail down against an electrical wire.

Telemetry does not guarantee the safe return of a hawk. The use of telemetry, however expensive and effective the system, is no substitute for sound training and proper practices. It is essential to practise with a unit before entrusting the hawk to the façade of security it represents.

TRANSPORTATION

TRAVELLING BOXES

It is normal procedure to transport longwings, and shortwings when possible, hooded on a cadge. Broadwings, however, generally need to be transported in a box, as indeed do all hawks when first collected from the breeder. The best boxes available are plastic crates, used for domestic pets and supplied by most pet shops. Vari-kennel is one of the suitable makes. They bolt together in two halves, with a frame door opening from one side. This door must be covered to black it off and thus prevent hawks bouncing against it. Carpet should be cut to fit the base. Newspaper or other coverings which will slide about should never be used. Whatever type of box is used, it should always be substantial, well-ventilated, large enough for the hawk to be able to turn around in comfortably and easily carried in such a way that the hawk will not be unbalanced. Perches in travelling boxes are unnecessary for broadwings.

'MODIFIED HOODS'

There is a trend towards using a box with a perch in it not just for transporting a trained hawk, but even to carry it out into the hunting field. This is an American idea, rather fatuously named the 'modified hood'. Devised mainly for imprints which do not take a hood, such a box is so-called as it performs the same function as a hood without the hawk actually having to wear one. This seems a rather cumbersome alternative, but such boxes are useful for travelling *Accipiter*s because, being

perched, they are less likely to damage their tails. The box must be completely blacked out for this purpose. Air holes, therefore, such as the sort around the top of the aforementioned plastic crates, which provide good ventilation but also let in light, are not a viable prospect. An ingenious way around the problem is to use a hollow perch made from plastic piping, but covered with Astroturf, with the hollow ends flush with the outside sides of the box. The perch then has sections cut out on its underside, allowing air from the outside to enter the box. A similar ventilation pipe can be incorporated at the top of the box.

CADGES

There are two types of cadge – the box cadge for travelling and the field cadge for carrying

'Modified hood'.

Combined field and box cadge.

Field cadge ready for use.

several hawks in the field. At the British
School of Falconry, a combination of the two
has been devised, whereby the field cadge fits
inside the box cadge. This works extremely
well. Box cadges have solid sides which are
necessary for the hawks to brace their tails
against when travelling. The field cadge has to
be of a lighter weight and of a size whereby
the cadger can fit inside it and walk, with the
cadge well balanced, suspended from his
shoulders by means of straps and supported
by his hands holding the frame on each side.

The top edge of the cadge, where the hawks
sit, should be of a width to comfortably
accommodate their feet and padded with
something which they can grip into – hessian
backed carpet with the hessian on the outside,
works well.

The ideal dimensions for a combined box/
field cadge are 3 ft × 2 ft × 1 ft high. This is
a suitable size for six large longwings. The
base of the box cadge should have a small
piece of rubber matting glued at each corner,
to prevent it from slipping and sliding in the
back of a vehicle.

Hawks should not be left unattended on a
cadge. To tie a hawk on a cadge, the leash
should be split in half, knotted at the swivel
and passed around the top of the cadge,
through the tethering slot. A knot is tied, so

that the hawk has only the freedom of movement afforded by the length of her jesses.

When a number of hawks are to be flown,
one after the other, it is useful if they can be
secured on the cadge by their field jesses.
With a small hole punched in the end of the
field jess, in the same manner as for a field
leash, swivel-mounted spring clips in a small
size can be permanently attached to the cadge,
enabling the falconer to clip on his hawk
between flights, having equipped her in
readiness before leaving home.

TAIL SHEATHS

It is common practice, when transporting a
newly acquired and untrained hawk in a
travelling box, to tape her tail to protect her
feathers. When arriving home, the tail tape is
then removed and the hawk equipped and put
into the weathering. Here she will inevitably
bounce around as she becomes accustomed to
her new circumstances in general and to being
tethered in particular. At this time, the tail of
a shortwing will be particularly vulnerable –
more so than that of a longwing or broadwing,
both of which have shorter trains. To alleviate
the risk of serious damage to the tail in these
early stages, a tail sheath can be fitted to a
shortwing until such time as she is considered
steady.

74

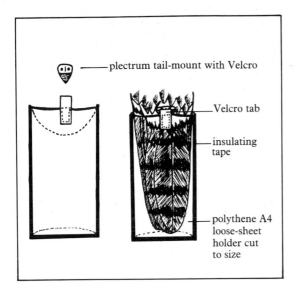

plectrum tail-mount with Velcro

Velcro tab

insulating tape

polythene A4 loose-sheet holder cut to size

Tail sheath.

A tail sheath is most easily made from a polythene A4 loose-sheet holder. It should be secured on the cut edge and strengthened around the edges with insulating tape, leaving the top and bottom open so that it can be slid over the tail. A shallow semi-circle is cut out of one half at the top of the sheath to accommodate the under tail coverts and the vent. The hawk must be tail-mounted, as though for a tail bell, but around two feathers and incorporating a Velcro tab on a plectrum. The corresponding piece of Velcro is attached as a tab on the top of the tail sheath, facilitating easy attachment and subsequent removal from the tail. The length of the sheath can only be correctly assessed when an allowance has been made for the length of the Velcro tab and the positioning of the tail mount. Ideally, the tail sheath should give only fractional clearance for the extent of the tail tips. As soon as the hawk is well manned, the sheath can be removed.

EQUIPPING

To equip a hawk without an enormous degree of difficulty, an assistant is required. It is the assistant's responsibility to hold the hawk in the cast position, wrapped in a towel, with her chest supported comfortably by a cushion. It is also his or her responsibility to prevent the recumbent hawk from either footing or biting the equipper.

The prelude to most occasions when a hawk is to be equipped is the act of catching her in a travelling crate. Given the small amount of space involved, the novice would be forgiven for assuming that this would not represent much of a challenge. His misconception will be swiftly corrected for the gymnastic ability of the untrained hawk in a box no larger than the size of a tea chest is indeed remarkable. Attempts to grab both legs in the gloved hand will be accompanied by the sickening sound of primaries flailing against the sides of the box. Even after securing the offending feet, the catcher cannot risk merely pulling her unceremoniously from the crate, for, if she leaves her wings open, she may easily wrench one or both against the box opening as she exits. Instead, the catcher must guide her wings out in the closed position with his right hand.

Once she is out, the towel is employed, to protect both the waterproofing bloom on her feathers and the assistant and the equipper from her attempts to bite them. This is most easily accomplished by suspending her by the ankles from the gloved fingers and lowering her onto her back into the protective folds of the towel; this is then wrapped loosely but firmly around her, covering her head completely. Once she is propped on her breast on the cushion, the assistant should spread his hands over her back, pushing her gently downwards into the cushion, rather than gripping tightly around her wings. He must also maintain a good grip on both legs, with two lower fingers, enabling him to pass each leg in turn over to the equipper to fit the aylmeri anklets. The leather for these should have been pre-cut and greased in a strip of suitable width. When both anklets have been fitted, the ready-prepared mews jesses are inserted and swivel and leash attached. The bells are also put on at the same time and any other services which are required – such as steaming bent feathers, imping, coping, etc. –

A hawk cast in preparation for equipping.

are carried out. If the hawk in question is a longwing being equipped for the first time, a hood can be fitted whilst she is in the cast position.

However arduous and stressful a novice's initial attempts at equipping a hawk may be, he can be comforted by the thought that this, like all skills, is one which improves with practice.

In conclusion, it has to be said that a feather-perfect hawk, sitting on a clean perch, with well-greased jesses and a clean leash, in proper accommodation, is a pleasure to behold. Hawks wearing poor and ill-kept furniture, sitting on filthy blocks and perches and in no proper accommodation are a disgrace to the falconer and, indeed, to the sport.

5 THE LAW

Despite being the most heavily legislated field sport in the UK, including shooting, falconry lacks one major item of protective legislation – that of limiting the keeping of birds of prey to those who are proven to have the necessary degrees of knowledge and expertise. In the USA, the novice is not allowed to acquire a hawk before he has sat a formal examination and acquired suitable accommodation and equipment. He is further required to be apprenticed to an experienced falconer for a period of 2 years. In the UK, no such safeguards exist. However, the unwieldy *Wildlife and Countryside Act (1981)* does exist and it is under this act that falconry is legislated.

The act is implemented by the Bristol-based headquarters of the Department of the Environment (DoE). Here, the Chief Wildlife Inspector, his assistant and a team of civil servants in the registration department orchestrate the system of registration of captive hawks as outlined under the act. Up until 1993, the law required all diurnal raptors held in captivity to be registered with the Department. Since 24 May 1994, only species listed on Schedule 4 of the *Wildlife and Countryside Act (1981)* are now registrable. At the time of writing these species include golden eagle, goshawk, peregrine falcon, gyr falcon, Barbary falcon, and their hybrids, together with rarer species of birds of prey not generally used for falconry purposes. Common or European buzzards, kestrels, sparrowhawks and the majority of non-indigenous birds of prey used for falconry, such as Harris hawks and red-tailed buzzards no longer need to be registered. A comprehensive list of registrable species can be obtained from the DoE.

Each hawk which is registrable has its own uniquely numbered ring and registration document, similar to the log book of a motor vehicle. If a registered hawk is sold or passed on to a new keeper, the registration document must be returned to the DoE and amended, and a fee is payable.

The hawks held legally in captivity originate from various sources. It is to the credit of falconers that by far the largest group are hawks which have been bred in captivity in the UK – a branch of falconry largely instigated by falconers in the late 1960s. This group can be bought and sold freely under the Act, subject to certain provisos. The second group are injured hawks which are unable to be rehabilitated back to the wild due to the severity of their injuries. These hawks cannot be sold. The third major category are hawks taken from the wild or imported under licence. It is no longer possible to take a wild eyass from the nest in the UK under licence for the purpose of falconry, as it is considered that there are sufficient captive breeding stocks in the UK to supply the needs of falconers. A route to take further native hawks from the wild will only be opened if the captive gene pool is assessed in the future as being detrimentally small. Hawks may be imported under licence but, generally, for falconry purposes, only applications to import hawks which have been captive bred will be granted.

Certain well-established falconry clubs enjoy 'recognized club status'. Their members benefit from reduced registration fees due to the fact that the clubs undertake to inspect a proportion of their membership annually, thereby saving the DoE the financial burden of carrying out inspections. At the time of writing, the principle of recognized club status is due to be reviewed. The recognized clubs also pay a levy to fund the Hawk Board, the government advisory panel on captive hawks. The Hawk Board liaises with the DoE and the Nature Conservancy Council, who provide scientific input for the DoE when requests are received for the granting of specific licences and exemptions.

Thus, in broad terms, it can be seen that falconers are not licensed, nor do they necessarily require a licence in order to acquire a hawk because the vast majority of captive-bred hawks can be sold freely under specific sales exemptions issued by the DoE. The following notes are designed to act as a guide only. Detailed information sheets can be obtained from the DoE.

REGISTRABLE SPECIES

Under the *Wildlife and Countryside Act (1981)* all birds of prey in captivity were ringed and registered with the DoE. On 24 May 1994 many species were removed from Schedule 4 and ceased to be registered. In most cases, these hawks still wear their DoE rings, but the Department no longer keeps a record of them. The remaining registrable species are either ringed with a uniquely numbered cable tie – if they were bred in captivity prior to the 1983 breeding season – or with a DoE close ring if they were bred from 1983 onwards. The keeper is obliged to pay registration fees in respect of these birds and to provide the Department with a record of their movements, by using the registration document to notify the transfer of one of these hawks to a new keeper.

If a registrable species wearing a cable tie persistently bites the cable tie off its leg, the keeper may eventually be issued with a registration document bearing a number prefixed by UR, and a licence allowing the bird to remain unringed. If a cable tie becomes illegible, it must be cut off and returned to the DoE with the registration document and a note of explanation. A replacement cable tie will then be issued.

When a young hawk of a registrable species is bred initially, it is registered in the name of the keeper and an initial registration fee is payable. Once the registration document has been received by the breeder, provided that the hawk is close ringed and all is in order, he can then sell that eyass on, if he so wishes. The new keeper and former keeper fill in the relevant section of the registration document and return them to the DoE, together with a transfer fee. Hawks are re-registered triennially on the anniversary of their first registration. At the time of writing, the fee scale, which should be checked with the DoE, varies if the falconer is a member of one of the recognized clubs.

Periodic inspections of registrable species may be carried out by the Department's Wildlife Inspectorate. There are two purposed to these inspections: they may be to witness ringing of a registrable eyass, or they may be to check that the DoE's records match the hawks held at the premises and their respective ring numbers. Notification of the latter type of inspections is not always given.

If a falconer takes a registrable hawk away with him for more than 3 weeks – for the grouse hawking season, for example – he must notify the Department in writing of his temporary address, the ring number(s) of the hawk(s) he has taken with him and the dates during which he will be resident at the new location. If a registrable hawk spends more than 3 weeks at a new location with a new keeper, a transfer of registration must take place. If a registrable hawk remains at its registered address, but is looked after by someone other than the registered keeper, a transfer of registration must take place after 6 weeks.

NON-REGISTRABLE SPECIES

Although there is no legal requirement that a non-registrable hawk is fitted with an appropriately sized close ring, the DoE strongly recommends that keepers continue to fit them as, without a ring, the hawks cannot be sold. Captive-bred non-registrable hawks fitted with the correctly-sized ring can be bought, sold or displayed provided that they conform to the terms of a specific exemption licence issued by the DoE, without the need to apply for an individual licence. Sale or transfer should also be accompanied by documentary evidence of captive breeding.

Now that close rings can no longer be obtained from the DoE for non-registrable species, rings should be obtained from specialist manufacturers or suppliers – many of whom advertise in the specialist press. These suppliers should provide a list of the appropriate size of ring for the species in question. Ring sizes are denoted by a letter of the alphabet. The rings are generally fitted when the hawk is between 1 and 2 weeks old. A correctly-sized ring will not be able to be taken off the leg when the hawk is fully grown.

LOST HAWKS

If a registrable species is lost, the registration document must be returned to the DoE, but the falconer is advised to keep a photocopy. The loss will be logged on the DoE's computer and the Department will contact the keeper if the hawk is found and reported to them. The registration document will then be re-issued free of charge.

Hawks which are no longer registrable cannot be traced by the DoE, unless they were reported as lost before 24 May 1994. It is therefore essential that falconers flying non-registrable species ensure that such hawks carry some aid to identification. Close rings and identichips (see Chapter 16) may help the police or another falconer to trace the keeper of a lost hawk, but if the hawk is picked up by a member of the public, the attachment of a small identification tag, engraved with the falconer's telephone number, is much more likely to lead to the hawk's safe recovery. There are also many independent registration schemes which have been set up for keepers of non-registrable species, but these can only operate effectively if members of the general public who find a lost hawk know to telephone these schemes.

Licences to operate a manually-operated bow trap to recover a lost hawk can be issued by the Department. If the hawk in question is a registrable species which is cable tied or unringed (issued with a UR number on its registration document), a licence to recover the hawk by any means will be required. A licence to trap can be incorporated within this licence. These may be requested by telephone and can be faxed.

BUYING AND SELLING

Apart from the previously mentioned transfer procedures relating to registrable species, a falconer must also be aware of the exemptions related to buying and selling hawks. There are 9 specific exemptions/licences which can be used by any person, provided that all the conditions attached to the exemption can be met. These licences are applicable both to registrable species and non-registrable species. Documentary evidence of captive breeding must accompany all sales made under these specific exemptions. This evidence must state that the hawk in question was 'bred by _____ on _____ from parent birds, ring numbers _____ and _____' which were legally held in captivity at the time the egg was laid. If the sale is not covered by one of these specific exemption licences, details of which can be obtained from the DoE, a person can apply for an individual licence, either to the DoE in Bristol or to the Scottish Office, if they live in Scotland.

Certain guidelines can be considered standard. No injured wild birds of prey can be sold, nor can hawks taken from the wild under licence, either native or imported. Captive-bred imported hawks can only be sold if an individual sale licence is granted. All individual sale licences only hold good for one transaction – the subsequent owner will have to apply again.

DISPLAYING

Specific exemptions authorize the 'display to the public for commercial purposes' as well as sale, keeping for sale, offering for sale or transporting for sale. A hawk not covered under the terms of one of these specific exemptions may not be displayed for commercial purposes unless an individual licence authorizing its display has first been obtained form the DoE or the Scottish Office, as appropriate.

IMPORTING AND EXPORTING

IMPORTING

To import a hawk for falconry purposes, a CITES application form will have to be filled in. The success of the application is dependent on several factors. Firstly, the hawk should be captive bred. Secondly, the application is likely to progress most smoothly if the country of exportation subscribes to CITES and provides a CITES export document. This may not always be applicable, however, as some CITES countries do not have every species of raptor under Schedule 1 protection. In such cases a general government export permit should suffice. Thirdly, documentary evidence of captive breeding should be supplied by the breeder. Finally, importations from some countries, or of some species, are occasionally restricted on a temporary basis due to certain problems with legality. This is worth checking in advance with the DoE. Assuming that the above criteria are satisfactorily met, the import licence should be granted in 3 to 6 weeks and will be valid for 6 months.

When import and export licences have been granted, an application for a further import licence must be sent to the Ministry of Agriculture, Fisheries and Food. This licence concerns quarantine and health regulations and a quarantine premises must be cited. Details of how to establish quarantine quarters can be obtained from the Ministry at their London headquarters. A Divisional Veterinary Officer will be sent to inspect the quarantine premises. The importer should name a Local Veterinary Inspector (LVI) whom he would like to supervise the quarantine, or one will be appointed. Britain will allow birds of prey to be imported from some countries within the European Community without quarantine. At the time of writing, these countries include Germany, France and Belgium, with Denmark soon to follow. However, import licence applications must still be submitted to MAFF for these countries. Up-to-date information should be obtained from MAFF. For countries within the EEC for which there is still a quarantine requirement and for countries outside the EEC, a licence should be issued provided that quarantine premises are passed. Part of this licence must be sent to the exporter for the attached veterinary certificate to be completed, declaring that the hawk to be imported is in good health and has not been inoculated.

The exporter must ship the hawk in a crate which conforms to International Air Transport Association (IATA) standards. Details of these can usually be acquired from the airline. When the hawk arrives in the UK, the importer is liable for freight charges, if these have not already been paid, and also for value added tax (VAT). It is cheaper if the hawk travels with someone as excess baggage, but some airlines will not accept livestock as excess baggage. VAT is payable on the 'open market value' of the hawk in the country of origin, plus the freight cost and is unavoidable, even if the hawk was a gift. Customs will request copies of invoices and if these are not made available, they can ascribe an arbitrary figure. It is therefore essential to have some financial paperwork, endorsed by the exporter, to show them.

Ports through which the hawk can arrive are specified. If a different port of entry is required, written permission has to be granted by the DoE. Heathrow is usually the best option as the Animal Quarantine Station (AQS) there will take the hawk off the plane and release it when the formalities of paperwork have been completed. If the hawk arrives at Gatwick, for example, there is a risk that it may be transferred to Heathrow to pass through AQS, although for small, non-commercial consignments this should not happen. AQS charge a small handling fee. It is essential that paperwork is in good order, lest the waiting hawk is ensnared in red tape. Plenty of cash must be taken to pay the freight, for if it cannot be paid in full, the hawk will not be released. Airline estimates concerning freight and handling charges are notoriously unreliable.

EXPORTING

Exporting is less complicated. A CITES export permit should be granted by the DoE, provided that a copy of the declaration of captive breeding is produced and that the hawk is correctly registered and ringed if appropriate. MAFF regulations now require that premises from which birds are to be exported to the EEC become registered holdings. Forms for this are available from MAFF and the application is a simple, self-certifying procedure. For most countries within the EEC, an owner's declaration, written on the day of export, stating that the hawk if free from disease, will then be sufficient, but some EEC countries still require a veterinary certificate. Outside the EEC, some countries will send their own veterinary surgeon's certificate to be filled in, others will accept a local veterinary surgeon's declaration of good health. In the former instance, the certificate has to be stamped by an LVI. The importer has to provide a copy of the import licence from his country and some airlines will request written confirmation from him that he will be at the airport at the correct time to receive the hawk. IATA boxes are again necessary. Usually the hawk has to be at the airport up to 4 hours before the flight, unless it is travelling as excess baggage, when it can be checked in with the passenger. Some Middle Eastern countries require a certificate of origin. This should be ascertained by telephoning the relevant embassy before attempting to ship the hawk. If it is required, it is easiest to engage a consular agent to acquire the certificate. He will need an invoice, on letterheaded writing paper, and other details, to authenticate at the Chamber of Commerce.

GAME LAWS

The falconer must have knowledge of, and comply with, the legislation concerning quarry. In simple terms, the species which a hawk is liable to be flown at can be divided into three groups – game, vermin, and other species with some degree of protection under law.

TABLE 6 OPEN SEASONS FOR GAME SPECIES IN THE UK

Type of game	Start of season	End of season
Pheasant	1 October	1 February
Partridge	1 September	1 February
Grouse	12 August	10 December
Blackgame	20 August	10 December
Ptarmigan	12 August	10 December
Moorhen	1 September	31 January
Coot	1 September	31 January
Snipe	12 August	31 January
Woodcock	1 October	31 January
Woodcock (Scotland)	1 September	31 January
Wildfowl (above high water mark)	1 September	31 January
Wildfowl (below high water mark)	1 September	20 February

Hare are protected on moorland and unfenced arable land between 1 April and 31 August.

GAME

Game species are protected in their breeding season, but there is an open season when they can be hunted. These seasons are shown in Table 6.

It is unlawful to hunt any of the above on Sundays or Christmas Day. A game licence, obtainable annually from the Post Office, must be acquired for hunting all of the above, except moorhen. The Home Office has announced that game licences will be abolished, but details or the effective date have not been announced at the time of writing. Up-to-date details concerning game licences can be obtained from the British Field Sports Society.

VERMIN (UNPROTECTED)

The following are unprotected by game seasons and may be hunted at any time:

Rabbit	Sparrow
Crow	Starling
Pigeon	Squirrel
(wood and feral)	(grey)
Jackdaw	Collared dove
Magpie	Gulls,
Jay	herring
Rook	greater black-backed and lesser black-backed

PROTECTED SPECIES OTHER THAN GAME

A quarry licence must be obtained from the DoE to take any species which enjoys year-round protection under law. This applies to the taking of such species with both registrable and non-registrable hawks. From the falconer's point of view, this would include, most notably, skylarks and blackbirds. A quarry licence stipulates dates, the number that can be taken and the ring number of the hawk which can flown at the species in question.

Quarry licences for use in Scotland should be acquired from the Scottish Office.

All field sports have enough problems without the exponents bringing their sport into disrepute by taking game out of season, hunting protected species without a licence, or taking game without a game licence. A game licence costs only a few pounds and it is an offence to take game without one.

Poaching is equally as serious an offence for a falconer as it is for a man with a gun. Falconers are largely reliant on the goodwill of land-owners for their sport, so it is essential to acquire their permission before hunting on their ground.

LICENSED REHABILITATION KEEPER STATUS

On occasion, falconers will be brought an injured or sick wild hawk by a member of the public who has picked it up or, occasionally, been responsible for its injuries. When the *Wildlife and Countryside Act* was drawn up, it was recognized that those who are frequently called upon to look after wild hawks in this manner would be under a considerable financial burden if special provision was not made to accommodate this type of work within the Act. 'Approved Keeper' status was therefore introduced, later to be called Licensed Rehabilitation Keeper (LRK) status. Anyone who receives a regular flow of wild disabled hawks can apply for LRK status. The main criteria for being granted the status are the possession of suitable aviaries and quarters to house injured hawks, the possession of a well-stocked and well-labelled medicine chest and the knowledge necessary to hack back wild hawks, assuming that they recover fully. An LRK must also name a local veterinary surgeon to whom he will be prepared to take hawks which are handed in for treatment. LRKs have to document each hawk that is handed in to them. They pay a blanket fee every 3 years for their licence. The DoE will provide the name of the nearest LRK to whom an injured hawk can be handed.

The advantage of having LRK status used to be that LRKs, like vets, had 6 weeks before they had to register a wild disabled hawk. This was often long enough to get the hawk fit for release. However, now that so few species need to be registered, the Department is proposing to abolish LRK status. It may or may not be replaced by a similar scheme. Up-to-date information should be requested from the DoE.

6 PREPARING TO RECEIVE A HAWK

Before finding a source for his first hawk, the complete beginner has much to do. As well as being in possession of the necessary equipment and facilities, he must also personally possess the necessary skills which will be in daily use in the maintenance of his hawk.

PERSONAL SKILLS

Whilst a book may be a useful store of information and an invaluable reference, it is no substitute for practical example. No beginner should ever attempt to train his first hawk purely on the basis of information read in a book. No written manual can really describe in words how to make a hawk comfortable on the fist, how to help her to regain the glove if she both bates and bites at the same time, or how to feel from the sharpness of her breast bone when she has reached flying weight. In these and in many other respects, the only way to learn is with the help of an experienced falconer.

Such help can be found in one of two ways – either from a local falconer who is willing to give of his time and to allow his own hawk(s) to be handled by his pupil, or at a school which runs reputable and recognized courses, such as the British School of Falconry. Here, in one week of intensive training under experienced instructors, the beginner can be taught the practical skills and techniques necessary to equip him for the task ahead.

One of the practical skills which must be mastered before acquiring a hawk is the tying of the falconer's knot. The knot has been de-vised so that it may be tied and untied quickly by the falconer with one hand, whilst his hawk is perched on the other. The beginner would be further well advised to practise putting on and taking off a swivel, using the right hand only, and tying the falconer's knot through the swivel with creance line which, being considerably finer than leash material, often presents a new difficulty to the novice.

CHECKLIST OF EQUIPMENT

The following must be acquired before the hawk is received.

Bow perch. as a list for a beginner, it is assumed that the first hawk will be a buzzard
Portable bow perch: can be used on the weathering lawn, or inside in an emergency
3 × leash
3 × swivel
Bells
Glove
Flying waistcoat
Whistle
Rabbit-lure
Creance
Hawking knife
Leather
Leather tools: punch, grease, scalpel or leather knife, steel ruler, awl, eyelets and applicator, pliers, chopping board
Johnson's Anti-mite: pyrethrum-based
Fenbendazole (Panacur, Hoechst): de-wormer
SA 37: vitamin supplement

THE FALCONER'S KNOT.

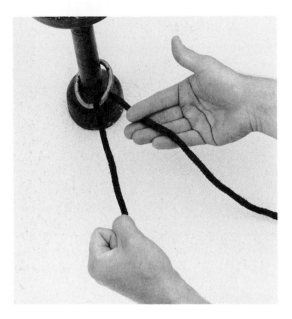

1) With the hawk sitting on the gloved left hand, and the leash secured around the little finger (do not allow the hawk to sit on a perch), pass two-thirds of the free end of the leash through the tethering ring on the perch. Hold the free end of the leash approximately 3 in from the ring with the right hand, palm uppermost. The leash should run under the end joint of the index finger and over the second third and fourth fingers.

2) Move the hand under the length of leash which runs from the swivel, grasping it in the fork between the thumb and index finger.

5) Bring the leash on the index finger to meet the point of the thumb and push the loop down, through the loop formed by the thumb, to form a figure 8.

6) Tighten the knot with the second finger and thumb.

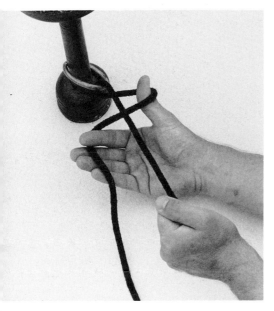

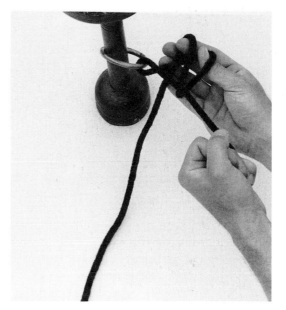

3) Hook the free end with the thumb, between the fingers and the tethering ring. Bring the thumb back, allowing the leash to slide through the fingers to the original position to form a backward figure 4.

4) Leaving the thumb in an upright position, turn the hand palm-side down and out to the right, thereby forming a loop around the index finger.

7) Pass the free end through the loop and pull tight. Slide the knot down to the tethering ring by pulling the end of the leash attached to the swivel. This completes the knot.

8) A second knot should always be tied for safety. To release, take out the free end and pull sharply.

Wound powder (aureomycin)

Silver-nitrate stick

Coping files

Dog's toenail clippers

Evostik and 'super-glue'

Bamboo canes, carbon-fibre and gloving needles

Scales and weights

Bath

Carrying crate: Vari-kennel or similar

Tail tape

Reference books – to include a good falconry manual and veterinary texts (*Veterinary Aspects of Captive Birds of Prey*, Cooper, 1978; *Recent Advances in the Study of Raptor Diseases*, Cooper & Greenwood, 1981)

Sundries as required – game licence, ferret, dog, telemetry equipment

FACILITIES

The weathering accommodation must be built in readiness to receive the hawk. Equally important, a supply of food must be located and a stock laid down in a deep-freeze. When preparing to take up falconry, it is a common oversight to forget to line up flying ground both for training and for hunting. A polite approach to landowners may yield dividends, often dependent on whether the ground is shot. It is important to get a map of the land and become familiar with the boundaries. It is also important to assess how much suitable quarry is on the ground, although this will require a tactful approach. Sometimes, the prospect of the hawk taking a rabbit is considered a bonus by the landowner, particularly in areas which are infested. Others will give permission, but specifically request that certain species of game – maybe hare or partridge – are not taken. Such requests will not be a problem with a buzzard, which is unlikely to take much more than rabbit or moorhen, but must be respected with a hawk of greater potential. Frequently, permission from one landowner will persuade his neighbour to grant you rights on his ground. It is not normal practice to pay for rough hawking rights, although considerable sums can change hands to secure a moor for grouse hawking.

It is important to seek a veterinary surgeon willing to undertake work on your hawk, should the necessity arise. There are very few raptor specialists and a falconer is lucky if he has one within reasonable distance.

Finally, it is a sound move for a beginner to join the British Falconers' Club or one of the other regional recognized clubs so that he can come into contact with other falconers at regional meetings, receive newsletters and magazines and attend field meets.

BUYING A HAWK

When purchasing a first hawk, it is always best to buy an immature straight out of the aviary, untouched, directly from the breeder. Just as one would check that a garage was reputable before buying a car from it, so one should check that the breeder has a good reputation. With the numbers of hawks now bred in captivity, it is inevitable that there will be a variation in the quality of stock and also in rearing methods. Inbreeding and imprinting are the two major problems. The former can generally be checked through reputation only, for unfortunately, as few breeders currently give a pedigree, the buyer is reliant on their word. The latter can be assessed by asking the right questions. In simple terms, imprinting occurs when an eyass is reared by hand rather than by its parents or foster parent(s). At worst, it will result in a hawk which screams constantly and which mantles over food on the glove and on the lure, dropping its wings to shield the meat, as if from a nest sibling. It can also lead to an aggressive response towards the falconer and to the vice of carrying kills away from the falconer on his approach. Whilst there is the occasional species which can be legitimately imprinted for a specific reason, the science of imprinting and imprinted hawks, and the way it affects their social and breeding behaviour, is one which merits a great deal of study before experiencing it personally. It is certainly not a field to be investigated by the beginner.

When a suitable breeder has been identified,

certain questions should be asked during the course of the initial telephone conversation. If the hawk is to be ordered in advance from the progeny of the following breeding season, it will be sufficient merely to confirm price and to ensure that it will be correctly reared. If the hawk is already available, there are further details which must be checked. Firstly, the breeder must be asked to confirm that the hawk is registered, if applicable, and that the paperwork will be in order at the time of sale. Secondly it is essential to check that the hawk is close ringed with a ring of the correct size, rather than cable tied. An untouched eyass should be feather perfect and this is worth confirming. The method of payment is also worth confirming, together with details of former diet. A parent-reared eyass of the year should never be collected before the hawk is hard penned, plus 2 weeks at least, to allow the feathers to harden off.

When setting off to collect the hawk, a box, a glove and tail tape should be taken. On arrival, some simple checks to ensure, as far as possible, that she is in good health should be carried out. The following list of checks has been compiled with the aid of Neil Forbes, MRCVS, B.Vet.Med. Ideally these checks should be carried out by an experienced falconer or better still by a veterinary surgeon who has particular expertise in this area.

CHECKLIST

The bird should be bright, alert and attentive. Before the bird is upset in any way, rate and depth of breathing should be observed to check that this appears normal. The proper movement of both wings should be checked. With an immature in an aviary this represents no problem as she should fly away from the person trying to catch her. It is advisable to let the breeder catch her. Obviously, it is preferable to see the young hawk with her parents, although if the brood has been a large one, the youngsters may have been moved to a nursery aviary to prevent overcrowding.

When the hawk is safely in the breeder's hands, she should be taken from him and the muscle covering the breast bone assessed for condition.

Each eye should be checked. They should be bright and clear, with no evidence of opacities. The nares should be clear with no sign of any discharge. The cere should be undamaged. The mouth should be opened and checked for any necrotic white areas, swollen areas or patches of abnormal reddening. There should be no unpleasant or foul smell from the mouth. Each wing should be extended in turn and the bones palpated along their length. Her feather condition should be checked, and fret marks or hunger traces, which may later result in feather breakage, should be looked for. With the hawk on her back, each leg should be extended to check that there are no abnormal swellings or deviations of the bones. The leg bones should be straight without any bowing. Any deviation of the long bones will cause weight to bear on abnormal sites on the feet. An abnormal stance will often be most easily diagnosed by studying areas of wear on the bottoms of the

A taped tail.

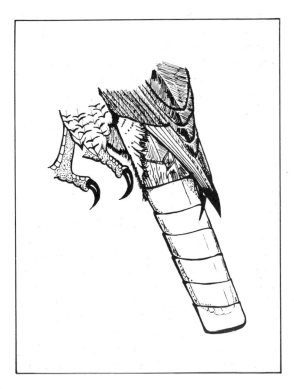

feet. Each foot should be checked for swellings, scabs or redness. Any of the latter signs are an indication of potential bumblefoot. Such a hawk should either be rejected or at least examined by an experienced veterinary surgeon prior to purchase. Grip should be tested with a gloved finger in both feet alternately.

If the hawk is in good order, her tail should be taped with masking tape and the sharp tips clipped off her talons before she is put in the box. In the UK, a declaration of captive breeding should be collected, together with the registration document if applicable – the breeder rips off and returns the bottom section, whilst the purchaser completes the back of the document fee and returns it to the DoE with the relevant fee.

If a beginner has to choose the hawk by himself, it is at least sensible for him to check that the vendor is happy to take the hawk back within a given period (e.g. 48 hours) if, following veterinary examination, she is pronounced unfit. In this situation a veterinary surgeon should be asked to write a certificate stating the reasons for the return of the hawk, which must relate to a condition which was present prior to the time of sale.

Some people buying a hawk are a little overawed by the reputation of the breeder, particularly if he is a well-known falconer, and they seem afraid of insulting him by checking the hawk over. This is not a sensible line of approach, unless one happens to know the breeder extremely well, or unless he is providing a health certificate or guarantee with the hawk. *Caveat emptor* – let the buyer beware – is particularly apt when buying livestock of any sort and an unscrupulous breeder may well claim later that any problem occurred in the box on the way home.

Having arrived home, the hawk should be removed carefully from the box and equipped, including bells. After the removal of tail tape and the steaming of any feather tips which may be bent, it is time for training to commence.

PART II
SHORTWINGS AND BROADWINGS

7 MANNING AND TRAINING

This chapter should be used in conjunction with the chapter on the individual species in question, to address variations peculiar to training of the species.

It is a complete waste of time to try to man a shortwing or broadwing thoroughly when she is at top weight. She will merely hate the sight of the austringer and long for the times when she is replaced in her weathering, for she can see absolutely no reason for tolerating human company. Once she is eating off the fist, and offered food only from the fist, she will see good reason for being with the austringer and will accept his company with qualified enthusiasm.

Having established this principle, the first task is to assess just how fat she is. If she is an eyass of the year, freshly out of the aviary, she will have been on maximum rations and should be at top weight. This should have been confirmed by feeling the breast bone at the time of purchase. The feeling of the breast bone is an important but often neglected part of the austringer's art. At first, the novice will not be able to determine his hawk's condition accurately from the flesh on her breast bone but, by feeling her keel on a daily basis throughout the training, he will learn to compare the degree of sharpness with the quality of the performance. Eventually, he will use his weighing scales merely to confirm his prognosis on her impending daily performance, rather than to determine it.

SITTING ON THE FIST

However, before there is time to take any weight off the new arrival, she must first learn to sit on the fist. This stage comes immediately after she has arrived home and been equipped, so that she can find her feet and learn of the restricting qualities of the jesses. It is of paramount importance that austringer and hawk remain undisturbed during this first lesson. Ideally, the manoeuvre should be carried out inside, in a darkened or dimly lit room. Here, having been equipped, the hawk is released from her cast position by the assistant, who should immediately beat a retreat. The jesses are held under the gloved thumb, with the leash coiled around the lower two fingers. The hawk will swing from the gloved fist, suspended by her jesses. With infinite care, the austringer must gently put a hand on her chest and lift her onto the glove, facing her forward and holding her there until her feet take up a firm stance on the fist. Upon releasing her, one will be extremely lucky if she remains there, albeit looking decidedly uneasy. It is most likely, however, that she will bate instantly and require the rescuing hand again. If she bites the right hand, the austringer has the option of either wearing a right-handed glove or picking her up from the back, rather than from the front. When she gains a foothold on the glove and stays there for an interval, it is important to remain absolutely still, for at this stage, the slightest movement may cause her to bate. With rare good fortune, she may bate but regain the glove herself. This is a most encouraging sign, but usually one which will not be witnessed for 2 or more days.

Initial efforts to persuade the hawk to stand

on the fist should not continue for more than about 20 minutes. She will be tired after her journey and, if she becomes exhausted with bating, she will lose the strength in her legs and will require time on her own to find her feet. If, during this first interval, she has stood on the fist for a matter of minutes, the austringer can count his blessings. If not, a session later in the day, or the following morning if it is late, may achieve better results. She must be tethered to her bow perch and left for a few hours to settle down. She should not be put in the weathering in daylight, for during the inevitable bating which will follow, as she discovers she is tethered, she might break her feathers. The weathering lawn represents a far safer prospect at this juncture, provided that it is quiet and secluded. She should be put in the weathering overnight, when she has stopped the incessant bating, and this should be prepared for her by adding an offcut of carpet, laid in the front half of the weathering. This will protect her primaries from fraying on the gravel. Later, when she is satisfactorily manned, the carpet can be dispensed with, although it may be necessary to leave it permanently for an *Accipiter*.

FEEDING ON THE FIST

The manning sessions, during which she is coaxed to stand on the fist for extended intervals, should be accompanied by the proffering of food, held in the gloved fist, as soon as she will stand for a minute or more. Feeding off the fist is the first sign of her acceptance of the new circumstances in which she finds herself and, as such, is the first milestone in the training process. Persuading the nervous hawk to bend her head and eat from the glove is dependent partly on the skill of the austringer and partly on how hungry the hawk is. With careful presentation of the food and just the right amount of wriggling of the gloved thumb and forefinger to attract her attention downwards to the meat, it is possible to persuade even a fattish hawk to eat on the fist. Some, however, will be much more stubborn and may go several days without food before they will overcome their nerves and eat. In the latter case, it is essential that the austringer keeps firm his resolve not to offer the hawk any food other than that offered from the glove, for, if she is allowed to eat in the weathering, all efforts to persuade her to eat from the fist will be to no avail.

During his attempts to get the hawk feeding on the fist, the austringer will notice that she is becoming steadier during these periods of handling, because her attention, whether she eats or not, is centred on the decision to take food rather than on whether or not she should sit still or bate. This is the way the whole training process should proceed – with the lesson of the previous day, once mastered, accepted as standard behaviour whilst both austringer and hawk concentrate on the next step. As soon as possible, the hawk must be persuaded to stand on the scales. The austringer will know when he is likely to achieve this – ideally it should be within the first 24 hours.

Once the first weight has been recorded, the search for the flying weight is under way. The hawk must be weighed daily at the same time before being fed. Weighing on the basis of a 24-hour cycle is important, as it ensures that the hawk has no gut content from the previous day's food and that any casting has been regurgitated. The novice is well advised to keep not only a daily record of the hawk's weight, but also notes on the amount of food fed and the performance of the hawk. In this way he will learn how much food will hold his charge steady and how much will cause her to lose weight or to put it on. When the hawk is trained and flying at quarry, these quantities will alter, as they are affected by variables, such as the amount of work she has done and the weather – she will burn off more in very cold conditions and *vice versa*. Meanwhile, they are an integral part of the weight loss equation.

It is both difficult and potentially dangerous to give an annotated guide to weight loss. It is certain, however, that to get a young hawk going, fat out of the aviary. she will need to lose a matter of several ounces (except in the case of the sparrowhawk and other diminutive *Accipiter*s). Whilst it may seem rash to point out that some hawks need to lose as much as 25 per cent of their fat weight to achieve flying weight, in case the beginner should promptly starve his unfortunate hawk to that level in a handful of days, it is a fact that most novices err on the side of extreme caution in the matter of weight loss, often keeping their hawk at too high a weight because they are nervous of dropping her lower. The skill of the matter lies in assessment.

Throughout the training process, it is the task of the austringer to observe his hawk and her progress, and to reduce the weight by measured amounts until the desired level of performance is achieved. A 'measured amount' will be greater in the early stages and less when she is flying on a creance and the optimum performance prior to flying free is being sought. By the daily feeling of the breast bone and the careful monitoring of his hawk's status, even the beginner should be able to tell if he has dropped his hawk too low, as the indications will be clearly apparent. These signs include 'slitty' eyes, 'puffed-up' feathers, a razor-sharp breast bone and a distinct reluctance to perform as well as on previous days. Bates will also be weak.

When the hawk will feed off the fist with enthusiasm the minute the meat is produced, further manning can take place and the austringer can carry his hawk around his local environs, accustoming her to the sights and sounds therein. It is advisable to tie the end of the leash onto the thong of the glove during these excursions as a precaution. Food will pave the way if there is something new and threatening to encounter and the hawk will gradually relax and take in the scenery during these daily excursions. Tirings can be used in preference to part of the daily food intake during these walks, so that the training session later in the day will not be adversely pre-empted by giving substantial rations.

STEPPING UP

As soon as the hawk is feeding confidently off the fist, which should be the day after she first fed in this manner, the austringer should progress swiftly to the next stage – stepping up for food. At this point, it is highly likely that the hawk will bate away from the austringer on his approach. Stepping up for food will alleviate this problem, as a 'pick-up piece' can thereafter be used, until she is so steady that this is no longer necessary. Stepping up also marks the first point at which the hawk actively makes an approach towards the austringer to gain the food and, as such, marks another milestone in the training process. Stepping up should be attempted either off the bow perch in the weathering or off a suitable object in the confines of a shed or garage. If it is attempted outside, the hawk will be easily distracted and success will probably not be forthcoming.

Initially, the hawk should be taken up onto the fist and given a bite to eat from the glove. After she has taken a few mouthfuls, the austringer should reverse her carefully against the chosen perch, lifting her tail clear with the right hand so that she steps back. The food can remain in the gloved hand, which is then held just in front of her, with the top of the glove at a level a little higher than her feet. She should resume her attempts to eat the meat. The austringer should ease his fist upwards each time she pulls at the meat, so that she is unable to pull off a mouthful. Irritated, her natural reaction will be to put a foot onto the glove to hold down the offending chunk of meat. With one foot on the fist, it is a simple matter to raise the fist slightly higher to persuade her to part company with the perch and complete the action of stepping up. If, for any reason, the slight lifting of the fist fails to persuade her to put a foot onto the glove, twisting the fist away from her, so that the meat is further out of reach, may persuade her to step forward to secure the food.

Opposite It is advisable to secure the leash to the glove whilst carrying a hawk.

JUMPING TO THE FIST

Once she is stepping up, she must be encouraged to jump from perch to well-garnished fist. This may be achieved on the same day, if she has learnt her previous lesson quickly. The gap is widened to a few inches, with the meat held just out of her reach. She will crane forward in its general direction and, if the length of her neck has been under-estimated, she may well succeed in snatching a bonus mouthful before the fist is moved further away. She will lean and stretch towards the meat, and even risk half falling off her perch in order to reach it, without actually jumping to the glove. She may reach out and try to snatch with one foot or, showing incredible length of leg, she may manage to connect with the glove with one foot and attempt to pull the fist closer to her; she will then follow up with the other foot and succeed once again in stepping up in a rather elaborate fashion. If she refuses actually to

Jumping to the fist.

jump, she must not be allowed too much food during her repertoire of different lines of approach, but should be left in her weathering to consider her tactics for the following day, when she will be at a lower weight.

When she has jumped properly once, the battle is usually won, for having discovered how simple it is, she should be quite willing to repeat the manoeuvre. A call to the glove should always be accompanied by a whistle. She must not be granted more than a few mouthfuls at each jump. Whole items of food, such as a day-old chick, a quail or a large chunk of beef, from which she will take a few mouthfuls, are the order of the day, as little pieces of meat placed on the fist individually will not be considered sufficient in terms of bribery.

The next stage is to increase the distance which she is jumping to leash length – approximately 3 ft. With the end of the leash secured, the distance can be increased – 6 in at a time – until she is jumping leash length. She should have no trouble in achieving these extended distances but, if she balks, her weight must again be cut. The jesses should

be brought through the middle gloved fingers, from back to front in between each jump. Up to this point, all these early attempts to inveigle her to come the length of the leash will still have been carried out somewhere inside or in the weathering. Now, she is ready to be taken to her early training ground to be put onto the creance, in preparation for the distance over which she is called to the fist to be extended. It is of paramount importance that this early training ground is as smooth as a billiard table lest it should snag the creance.

Much to the austringer's disappointment, he will find his hawk most reluctant to repeat what has already been accomplished indoors in an outdoor environment. Her eyes will be everywhere but on the proffered meat as she takes in her new surroundings with curiosity. The austringer will have no choice but to regress to attempts to feed her on the fist and can indeed consider himself fortunate if she deigns to step up for food on that day. This merely indicates that she is not really keen enough – she is happy to perform without distractions, but at the slightest excuse, her attention will wander. Her concentration can

only be commanded by a further drop in weight to sharpen the appetite.

FLYING ON THE CREANCE

The following day, provided that the scales register a satisfactory result, more progress should be made. After she has been offered a small bite from the glove to whet her appetite, she should be ready to be called short distances on the creance, into wind, for she must always be called off with the wind blowing into her chest. It would be reasonable at this juncture to hope that she will come 4 to 6 ft, although she may respond even further than this. At this stage it is far better that she comes a short distance quickly, than a longer one in her own sweet time. In the latter instance, she will learn that you will await her, food at the ready, to respond at her leisure and further evidence of this will reinforce a bad habit. It is reasonable to wait and whistle for her for maybe 30 seconds, but if she does

Flying on a creance.

not respond during this interval, either reduce the distance or cut her food for the day, according to her degree of interest and what has already been achieved during that session.

The hawk should not be called much more than half a dozen times during the daily training session, lest she becomes bored. While her weight is being reduced, she will usually receive all her food during these flights in the form of small pieces or a bite off a larger food item. Later, when the weight reduction is slowed or halted, it will be necessary to make up the rations at the end of the flying session to hold her steady.

The aim is to reach the point at which she will fly the length of the creance instantly to the fist. While extending the distance, the austringer must always keep one foot on the creance, lest she starts to come, then changes her mind mid-way and heads for the nearest tree. It is quite likely that she may rake away if the distance is pushed too far too fast, for it is important to bear in mind that, when flying a young hawk fresh out of the aviary, every flight at this point represents the furthest she has ever flown. If overfaced, she may suffer a

Harris hawk flying to the rabbit-lure.

loss of confidence and allow the breeze to catch her, drifting downwind or crosswind until she is brought up short by the creance. Alternatively, she may be such a model pupil that, realizing the game, she will be so eager to come to the fist that she will follow before she is called. The austringer, no matter how fast he runs, having deposited her on the perch or allowed her to hop back to it, will then be unable to get any distance from her. This situation requires the intervention of an assistant, to hold her until the austringer has reached the desired distance. When the hawk is responding instantly over the length of the creance, it can be considered that she has reached a point where she is close to being ready to fly free. However, as an added precaution before this momentous day arrives, she must be introduced to a lure and tested further for her reliability.

LURES

Shortwings and broadwings should be introduced to both rabbit- and swing-lures (with the exception of the sparrowhawk, which lacks the stature necessary to take a full-grown rabbit and will therefore only be introduced to the swing-lure). This familiarity with both wings and fur renders the hawk potentially capable of taking a mixture of quarry, which is more practical, as well as more pleasurable, than concentrating all efforts in pursuit of one type of prey. The swing-lure is also an essential aid for recalling a hawk which is at a great distance from the austringer, or one which is lost, for it can be seen swinging at a distance.

A lure should be introduced when the hawk is responding well to the fist, but still on the creance. Its introduction prior to flying free gives the austringer an alternative method of recall should the hawk fail to respond to the fist for any reason once she is flying free. It is generally sufficient to introduce just one type of lure at this point, so as not to confuse the hawk; the other can be introduced shortly after she is flying loose. It is normal to introduce broadwings to a rabbit-lure in the first instance and shortwings to a swing-lure, although this is not a hard and fast rule. By this stage in the training, the hawk will be flying for a certain proportion of her food only, with the balance being made up after the training session has been completed, unless a further drop in weight is considered necessary. By this time, the austringer will have worked out the various equations of weight in proportion to food given.

To introduce the lure, instead of merely feeding this balancing ration on the fist, it should be tied to the lure, reserving two small pieces for pick up. The hawk is replaced on the outdoor bow perch and the well-garnished lure is dropped out in front of her, with the food clearly visible. Upon seeing the food, she should jump down promptly to eat from the lure. If she does not respond immediately, the austringer, from his position at the end of the lure line, can give the lure a few encouraging tweaks. Normally, the first approach is somewhat cautious. The hawk will hop down onto the ground beside the lure and lean over it to pull at the meat. It is the austringer's task to gently tug the lure line, until she puts one foot on the lure, or preferably both, to hold it down. Whilst she is eating, the austringer must make in to her, keeping the lure line taut.

When a broadwing has finished the food, one of the pick-up pieces should be thrown on the ground in front of her, in such a way that she cannot reach it whilst she is holding the lure. Seeing the additional food, she should relinquish her hold on the lure and hop off to eat the extra piece. The austringer can then swiftly transfer the lure to his lure pocket and offer a further small piece of meat from the glove, for which she can hop up when she has finished and opened her feet. This is not advisable with an *Accipiter*, which should be stepped up for food off the lure in the same way as a longwing is induced to step up off her kills, directly from the prey to gloved fist.

The following day, the hawk will have made the visual association between the lure and food. One of the smaller pieces of meat for which she is regularly called to the fist can

therefore be tied onto the lure, before the end of the day's training session. The austringer can increase the distance at which the lure is dropped out and, if the response is quick, he can attempt a second flight to it, this time dragging the lure slowly along the ground. A swing-lure should be swung backwards in a circle a few times as a preliminary to dropping it out for the hawk. A rabbit-lure can be merely tossed onto the ground, taking care at this juncture that the meat is clearly showing. When the hawk is free, the austringer is aiming to reach the stage at which the hawk will take off the second she sees the lure. With the rabbit-lure, the aim is to get her chasing it, with the austringer towing it at top speed away from her, stopping when she hits it. With the swing-lure, she should fly towards it whilst it is still swinging and take it, either dropped out and tweaked along the ground, or thrown up into the air to provide a low catch. Whilst the lure should not be overused, lest she becomes lure-bound or, in the case of shortwings, refuses the fist in preference for the lure, it can be used in a fairly static fashion once or twice a day in the few days immediately prior to flying free. In this way the hawk should be thoroughly familiar with it before being entrusted to fly loose. There is only one exercise remaining before this point is reached.

TEST FLIGHTS

At this juncture, the austringer should test-fly his hawk from a tree whilst she is still on the creance, lest she should refuse to return from such a vantage point when free. If her response to the fist is as instantaneous as it has been in the training field, then one can be reasonably certain that she will acquit herself with similar credit when enjoying her early sorties completely free.

When seeking a suitable tree, the austringer should look for one with a low branch, a little higher than himself but one he can reach, so that he may reverse his hawk onto it. This branch must also be devoid of little twigs and other hazards around which the creance may get entangled. Ideally, the tree should have no other inviting branches a little above and in front of the chosen perch, lest the hawk should attempt to 'ladder up' through the branches. With the tree thus selected, the hawk should be reversed carefully onto the chosen limb and, keeping the creance taut, the austringer should retreat to a point some 20 ft or so hence. If she responds without undue hesitation, the next day should proceed smoothly. If, however, she prefers to drink in the scenery, it is painfully apparent that she has not, in fact, reached flying weight and has been performing merely out of routine, rather than because she is really keen. Her weight, in the latter case, will obviously have to be further reduced, albeit by a very small degree.

FLYING FREE

The day before flying free, as an extra precautionary measure, rations should be slightly reduced. The next day, at the regular flying time, provided that the weather is fine, she should be taken out and put on the creance, it is to be hoped for the last time that season, and called the length of the creance to the fist. Assuming that nothing has upset her, she should come instantly. Whilst she is enjoying her morsel of food on the fist, the creance should be removed, together with the swivel and the mews jesses – one at a time – and replaced with field jesses. After a transmitter has been attached she can be placed on her perch and called off as before. There is no logical reason why anything should go wrong. The hawk will be blissfully unaware that she is in fact free. When she arrives safely on the glove, the austringer should pick up the field jesses and tuck them under his gloved thumb and out through his middle fingers, to maximize his safe grip on them. Once she is flying free from the bow perch, there is little point in repeating the operation.

CALLING OUT OF TREES AND CASTING OFF

The next stage in training is calling out of trees. At the first attempt, the austringer should select a tree with a care equal to that displayed when he sought a tree out of which the hawk could safely be called on the creance. Once again, she should be placed on a suitable branch and recalled over a short distance. Once this has been mastered, she must learn to be cast into trees. The novice may take a little while to acquire the right touch when learning to cast a hawk efficiently. Once the hawk is hunting, there will frequently be occasions when she should be cast with precision to land on a particular branch which will afford her an ideal vantage point above a rabbit hole to be ferreted or a stretch of cover to be beaten beneath her. The skill of casting with such accuracy involves having the hawk well balanced on the fist, extending the arm gently backwards and launching forward and upward, through 45 degrees, opening the gloved fist to release the jesses at the end of the throwing action, thereby using them to actually propel the hawk in the right direction. It is something of a knack, with which some people are gifted at the start; others will have to practise. However, initially, a strong arm and firm touch are not essential, as the very last thing the austringer wants at this stage is his hawk at the very top of a tall tree.

In the first instance, the hawk should be allowed to hop from the glove onto a branch. This can develop into the austringer giving her a little impetus towards the branch and finally into a full-blooded cast onto a higher branch. Over the next few days, the aim should be for the hawk to become comfortable with being cast into and called out of trees, to fist and to lure. It is also an ideal time at which to introduce the other type of lure. By this time the hawk should be responding instantly and sometimes even coming before she is called. If she is not, she may not be quite sharp enough weight-wise, or the austringer may be being careless with his wind direction, casting her correctly into wind in the direction of the tree, but recalling her in the same flight path; this effectively faces her with a downwind flight, which she is unlikely to be able to master at this point. If she does

Flying free.

fly to the fist downwind, she will instinctively overshoot and will need the austringer to turn his fist to help her to make her landing into wind.

FOLLOWING ON

Straightforward flights into and out of trees and the introduction of the second lure should be mastered within 2 or 3 days of flying free. During this time, the hawk will be receiving each of her six or so small pieces of meat for individual flights. This is sufficient work for an *Accipiter*, but under this regime a broadwing is never going to get fit enough to take on quarry. The ratio of 'miles to the gallon' needs to be vastly increased and this is where the practice of 'following on' should be introduced. When the broadwing has successfully learnt to follow on, she will follow the austringer across country, responding to a whistle, from tree to tree, coming down for food only after a certain distance has been covered. At this stage, therefore, the daily training sessions expand into a walk across country. This neatly achieves three objectives – the broadwing becomes fitter as she does more work for the same amount of food, the change of scene

prevents her from becoming bored, and the act of walking across country takes her out to areas where she can see game and will hopefully start chasing. Following on, however, is unnecessary with *Accipiter*s and also encourages bad habits.

The task of teaching a broadwing to follow on is much easier if, on occasion, she is already coming before she is called. In the first instance, the aim is to get her to fly past and beyond the austringer to land in another tree. The rules of persuading a broadwing to follow on are that she may be encouraged to take off by a whistle, but she must never be shown food then denied it, for she will feel cheated and may well cease to respond promptly when being genuinely recalled to the fist.

For the initial attempt, it is important that she is in a tree beyond which, into wind, there is another tree, with branches suitable for her to land on. Early in the day's training session, before she has had too much food, she should be cast into the first tree. Whilst walking in the direction of the second tree, which should not be more than 40 to 50 ft beyond, the austringer should whistle for the hawk to follow. Bearing in mind that, up until this point, every time he has whistled, food has been offered, the broadwing should take off in his direction without hesitation. Seeing, as she flies towards him, that his fist is not raised and that there is no sign of the lure, she will look for an alternative place to land and, noticing the tree ahead, should head for that. After she has landed, the austringer should walk beyond her, further into wind and call her down to the fist for food.

Unfortunately, there are also various other possible scenarios. The broadwing, not seeing a raised fist, may not move from the original tree. In these circumstances, she may need another small reduction in weight. If this does not produce the required result, the austringer will have to offer added encouragement by briefly raising his ungarnished fist when whistling, and dropping it the instant his broadwing takes off. This should do the trick, but, as soon as she has established a pattern of following on, the raising of the glove should be discontinued and a whistle should suffice. Alternatively, the broadwing may take off promptly, but, upon noting that the fist is not raised, may land at the austringer's feet, attempt to land on his person or hit him in the back of the head. The latter is generally a trait only encountered in imprints of a particularly anti-social type. The latter variations can be counteracted by the austringer walking under the cover of a line of trees, so close to the trunks that the broadwing will not be able to reach him, but will be forced to land in the branches. Once she has done this a few times, a habit will be formed and the austringer will be able to risk showing himself openly once more when giving the follow-on whistle, which should always be distinct from the recall whistle.

Once the broadwing has learned to follow on to one tree, then to be rewarded with food, the austringer can encourage her to follow on twice before rewarding her. It is essential that these flights make progress across country, to prevent boredom from setting in. When she will follow on readily, covering several trees before being brought down to the fist, the austringer is beginning to address one of the final problems before entering her: fitness.

FITNESS

Any young hawk, bred in captivity and freshly taken from an aviary, is going to be severely lacking in both muscle and stamina. When pitted against wild game, in its natural element, these shortcomings are going to be all too apparent. Whilst there is a school of thought which supports the view that hawks only become properly fit through chasing quarry, the austringer should do as much as he can to get his hawk into condition before expecting her to achieve the first kill.

At this stage, the species in question becomes especially relevant. *Accipiter*s exude fitness without a great deal of extra effort on the part of the austringer. *Buteo*s and *Parabuteo*s will require a concerted effort to get them fit and will, particularly in the case of red-tailed

and common buzzards, take 2 months or more to achieve even an aura of semi-fitness, although they may take a few early head of game during this time.

It is a common fault of the novice to underestimate the need for fitness and, whilst some may be satisfied with the occasional simple kill, such as a rabbit with myxomatosis, hell-bent on suicide, others will be vastly disappointed when their hawk refuses to fly a pheasant, without understanding the reason why. If a hawk does not feel that she is in with a better than average chance of catching something, she will not fly it. Early optimism, when she will streak after a distant rabbit, 200 yd away and approaching its hole, will swiftly be replaced by apathy as disappointment takes its toll of enthusiasm. The novice will usually make the mistake of thinking that his hawk is still not keen enough and will reduce her weight further, weakening her and aggravating the problem.

The answer lies in instituting a proper fitness campaign and working at it, for meanwhile the hawk will still be in the field each day and can thus take advantage of any opportunities to take quarry that may come her way. Daily sessions must be extended in duration and the number and length of flights correspondingly increased. By this stage, recognition of both lures should be firmly established and they should be utilized as a means of vigorous exercise. Swing-lures can be used to call the hawk over extended distances, then thrown up for her to catch (retaining a hold on the stick), improving her footing capability. Rabbit-lures can be 'planted' along the route, tied to a creance, which is then run around a peg in the ground. With the hawk following overhead in the trees, the rabbit-lure can be made to 'break cover' by means of the austringer picking up the end of the creance and running as fast as he can, towing the lure out from under concealing vegetation. This will achieve three objectives. Firstly, the austringer will be travelling in a different direction from the lure, thus correcting any misconceptions which the hawk may be harbouring that all rabbits will be preceded by the austringer, travelling at full tilt, a couple of yards in front of them. Secondly, and depending largely on the athleticism of the austringer, the hawk will have to work hard to catch the lure. Thirdly, the hawk will learn to watch the undergrowth and to expect the unexpected. It is also useful to substitute a fresh dead rabbit at this point, so that the hawk, having made a 'kill', can be allowed to feed up on it. When the hawk can work all afternoon, following on and landing ahead of the austringer, taking either lure with vigour and burning off the extra rations necessary to work her for several hours at a stretch, she may be considered fully trained and fit for entering.

IMPRINTS

The training as outlined will be complicated if the hawk is imprinted or partially imprinted.

TYPES OF IMPRINT
CRÈCHE-REARED IMPRINT

By far the most common is the crèche-reared imprint, which is the result of a group of eyasses hand-reared together. These hawks are normally hand reared from the egg, having been hatched in an incubator and never replaced with the parents or foster parents. Such hawks are likely to scream for food, although some may not. They may also mantle over food, both on the perch when the austringer is within sight and on the fist. They may show a degree of aggression towards the austringer.

FOOD IMPRINT

The worst sort of imprint is a food imprint. This term is used to describe a hawk which has been reared by hand in isolation. Such hawks will scream to be fed and for attention when the austringer is in sight and, responding to the sound of human voices, often when he is not. During training, her familiarity with people and her consequent lack of fear can easily turn to aggression. When given food on the fist or the lure, she is likely to mantle and scream in threat. She may also be 'sticky-footed' on the fist. When on quarry or the lure, she may attempt to carry.

DUAL IMPRINT

Dual imprinting results when a hawk is reared by a foster parent, which will allow the austringer into the aviary to socialize with the eyass(es). Provided that the austringer never enters the aviary when the hawk is feeding, but only at times suitable to socialize with her, the hawk should lack the undesirable imprinted traits – and, it is to be hoped, will be confident when taken up for training, lacking all fear of the austringer. The real merit of this type of imprint has yet to be proved, for whilst it may work well, the advantage gained appears in most cases to be of questionable value; when jessed by this familiar friendly face, the hawk's confidence is often dented, leaving the austringer with the task of re-establishing it, in much the same way that he would have had to establish confidence with a hawk which had been parent-reared.

SOCIABLE IMPRINT

A fourth type of imprint is termed a 'sociable' or '100 per cent' imprint. Such imprints are reared in isolation by hand but, in contrast to food imprints, spend nearly all their time in the company of the austringer, relying on him not just for food, but also for socializing – companionship and playtime. Ideally such an imprint will never scream because she is never allowed to want for anything in the way of warmth, food or companionship. Sociable imprints will never breed with their own kind, but are usually destined for artificial insemination. In falconry terms, it is possible to fly an *Accipiter* reared in this way with a great deal of confidence as she is likely to return to the austringer as much out of friendliness as out of a desire for food. However, it is extremely difficult to make a good job of imprinting a hawk in this manner and not worth doing with a broadwing. It is very time-consuming and, if it goes wrong, the austringer will be left with a food imprint of the worst order.

IMPRINTS IN TRAINING

Many novices make the mistake of thinking

that an imprint is going to be easier to train, because it will be friendlier. Taking into account the above catalogue of vices, it can be seen that in fact the converse is true. Imprints are touchier and extremely difficult to make good. Even very experienced austringers will be hard pressed to correct the vices inherent in imprints through their conditioning and most would prefer not to try. To work an imprint successfully, the austringer has to have a keen understanding of hawk psychology to pre-empt the establishment of the vices.

IMPRINTING *ACCIPITERS*

There is some justification for imprinting *Accipiters* to a degree and, with extreme care, to achieve a steadier hawk. However, goshawks can be well made as parent-reared hawks, so an austringer wishing to imprint one for his own use should be experienced and have a clear idea of what he wishes to achieve through imprinting. Sparrowhawks are so very nervy and highly strung that a degree of imprinting is certainly desirable. In such a small hawk, a lot of the traits that are considered unpleasant in larger imprints are not, in fact, a problem with a spar. There is never any justification for food imprinting, but crèche-rearing and 100 per cent imprinting are suitable for *Accipiters*. For most people, the latter is impractical for a variety of reasons, including time. A young *Accipiter* being reared in this way will have to be kept in the house, in constant sight of people. If the effort and the mess prove to be too much, and the austringer succumbs to pressure to put the hawk out into an aviary, the damage done is irreparable. The hawk will end up as the one thing the austringer most hoped to avoid – a food imprint – as she will see or hear the austringer only when being fed and will bewail his departure back to the house.

Even taken safely to the stage when she is ready for training there are many potential dangers which can make a full imprint scream, including boredom and erratic weight control. If she is called off too quickly between flights, she may scream, for she must always be allowed to feel that she has finished all the food the austringer has on offer. Boredom will also occur if she is not flown every day. When she is on the lure or a kill, she must always be given a substantial piece of food in exchange. If these guidelines are followed religiously, the austringer may end up with the *Accipiter* of his dreams, but the odds are against it.

The crèche-reared *Accipiter* is altogether an easier proposition. However, as a number of hawks must be reared together, the austringer is reliant on the breeder to do a good job and not to hand-feed a day beyond the time that the eyasses are capable of picking up food for themselves. Like dual imprinting, the aim is to produce a hawk which is both familiar with its own kind – in this case its siblings – but also familiar with human beings, lacking fear of them. To promote this familiarity, the austringer should obtain the eyass whilst she is still a large downy – at approximately 3 to 4 weeks of age. An aviary must be provided to house the eyass, with a large and accessible nest ledge and plenty of cover. Food must be introduced through a food hatch, so that the hawk cannot see the bearer. Ideally, the aviary should be partly open, to the extent of a half to a third of the front, well screened with vertical bamboo dowelling, with the remainder of the sides solid. This open section will enable the hawk to see the austringer and his family as they move about outside, promoting a little early manning.

The austringer should spend time socializing with the eyass and making her to the hood. A lightweight hood of the right size should already be in the austringer's possession. When the hawk is accustomed to having her bare head stroked, the hood can be popped over the head for an instant, then removed. Daily practice with the hood being left on for slightly longer intervals, should ensure a hawk which will take a hood really well throughout her life.

Despite every precaution being taken, it is possible that the eyass may start to scream at the austringer out of recognition. The austringer may also fear that their daily sessions spent socializing could result in feather damage as the hawk grows more mobile. If either of these problems occur, the daily sessions must cease promptly and the open sections at the front of the aviary must be screened off. The hawk will not forget the pleasant times she has spent with the austringer, neither will she forget the hood training. Thus the austringer can rest assured that when she is hard penned and ready for training, he will be taking up a comparatively steady hawk.

HOODING

SHORTWINGS AND BROADWINGS

It is distinctly advantageous to be able to hood any hawk. However, some can be made to the hood more easily than others. The expression 'made to the hood' should be emphasized, as it is not possible to 'break' a hawk to the hood. Strong arm tactics are wholly inappropriate. In general terms, it is more important to make an *Accipiter* to the hood than a *Buteo* and usually easier too. It is not essential for a beginner to hood train a buzzard. Eagles should be made to the hood whenever possible to make transporting them and handling them easier. The main use of the hood, however, is in the field. Quite simply, a hawk can be hooded to make her sit still on the fist, without bating, until the austringer is ready to cast her off.

The making of a hawk to the hood varies according to her background and individual personality. There are three ways of making hawks to the hood, related to their stage of development and training. One has already been discussed – making the downy shortwing to the hood during total or partial imprinting. The second method, chronologically speaking, is making the parent-reared hawk to the hood right at the start of training, whereby the hood is fitted when the hawk is cast whilst her aylmeris are being put on. Hood training then continues, hawk permitting, exactly as described for making a longwing to the hood. Often, though, this approach will fail. If the austringer then wishes to persist in his desire to hood train his hawk, his only route is to attempt the third option – late-stage hooding.

Late-stage hooding

A hawk which fails to take a hood in the early stages of training will usually avoid being hooded by bating away from the right hand, which is holding the hood, as the austringer attempts to slip the hood over. If this happens consistently, the austringer should desist his efforts until later in the training when the hawk has lost her fear of the bare hand. The hood should be re-introduced at the stage when the hawk is almost ready to fly free. After weighing the hawk prior to flying, the hood should be slipped over the head and left there for no longer than 2 seconds, without the braces being drawn. When the hood is removed, the hawk should be flown as normal, with no further attempt being made to hood her that day. For the next week, the austringer should follow the same pattern, leaving the hood on for progressively longer intervals, but never so long that the hawk makes efforts to remove it. The braces can be drawn with caution after the fourth day. After a week, the hawk can be hooded on the return journey after flying and, after 10 days or so, she should be ready to wear it whilst travelling, or whilst walking out to the land over which she is to be flown at quarry. The skill of late-stage hooding lies entirely with the austringer, as the hood must be slipped over swiftly but accurately. It is unlikely that a beginner will be possessed of such skill, as it is generally only mastered after the austringer has had the opportunity to practise on at least one hawk which takes a hood easily.

Dutch hoods are inappropriate for shortwings and broadwings as they usually do not sit easily on the shape of their heads. A soft Anglo-Indian is generally the best hood to start with and, for late-stage hooding, a hood which is slightly too large is advisable for the first few attempts, as it will not make the hawk too claustrophobic. A better-fitting hood can be substituted when the hawk has become used to something being slipped over her head. The Bahreini pattern, particularly the blocked Bahreini, tends to suit *Accipiters*, whilst most broadwings are more comfortable with Anglo-Indians.

8 ENTERING AND QUARRY

ENTERING

When the day to enter a hawk dawns, the austringer must have a plan of action. If she is to be flown off the fist at a rabbit, he must have worked out a route whereby he can give her the best chance, approaching the rabbits in such a way that the hawk can surprise them and not marching in full view across the field where they are sitting, in the furthest corner, at the edge of their burrows. If she is to be entered from a tree, over a patch of undergrowth, a line of trees must be chosen which does not have dense leaf cover obscuring the ground should she ladder up through the branches.

The first major hurdle is crossed when she chases something. It is also the time when the austringer must bear in mind that if she continues to chase, but fails to catch in the first week or so, she may well become discouraged and stop chasing, believing quarry to be beyond her. It is up to the austringer to find the quarry, both in sufficient numbers and where the lie of the land will give the hawk the best possible chance.

When quarry breaks cover, the austringer should shout to get the hawk's attention and continue shouting until she gives chase. This is necessary as, surprisingly, despite their excellent eyesight, trained hawks often fail to see quarry which the austringer notices clearly. Hawks are tuned in to spotting game which is moving and some hawks can be remarkably slow to see a rabbit which has frozen in its tracks. When the hawk finally connects with her first kill, the austringer should make in swiftly and despatch it, if it is not already dead, preferably while the hawk is still in possession. She should then be allowed to feed up partially on the kill, provided that it is not something grossly unsuitable, such as a doubtful pigeon. Having broken into the warm flesh, aided by the austringer if necessary, she should be allowed a few mouthfuls before being taken up for a good reward on the fist. Under no circumstances should she be flown again that day.

Nothing succeeds like success. After the first kill, the hawk should go from strength to strength. She should not be asked to take more than one head of quarry per day for the first half-dozen kills. Only when chasing quarry will she become really fit, but in the first few months, the austringer must be prepared to put up with some refusals on her part to take on flights for which she feels she is unfit. Few shortwings or broadwings are ever flown solely at one particular quarry species, so both austringer and hawk will have to learn about the peculiarities of the different types of quarry and the best way to fly them.

TYPES OF QUARRY

RABBIT

Whilst rabbit are abundant in some areas, in others they are extremely scarce and the austringer will have to work very hard even to get a flight at them. A basic guideline to flying rabbit is that the hawk should be at least as close to the rabbit as the rabbit is to its hole or to cover, for the hawk cannot be expected to fly more than twice as fast as the rabbit can run. Some hawks are better at spotting rabbits at a distance than others and some species or individuals, particularly goshawks, will develop the skill of stealth, taking advantage of hedgerows for cover as they make up ground before the rabbit is even aware that it is the object of unwanted attention.

'Good footers' will rarely lose anything they hit, whilst others will lose head after head of quarry as it twists out of their feet. The austringer can go some way towards correcting this by using lures, particularly the swing-lure with which he can attempt, through practice, to improve his hawk's footing capability. Rabbits cover both ends of the speed spectrum – a rabbit with myxomatosis which, incidentally, will not harm the hawk, may not move at all and can therefore hardly be considered a sporting prospect, whereas a fit, clean rabbit, particularly one which is ejected from its burrow by a ferret, can show a remarkable turn of speed.

METHODS OF FLYING RABBIT

1) *Walking up rabbit* This is one of the most satisfying ways of achieving flights, mainly, because the austringer is virtually guaranteed to be able to see the whole flight. The best type of ground to walk up is rough ground, with tussocks, reeds, nettles, thistles or long grass where the rabbits can lie up. It is very rare for a hawk both to spot and take a stationary rabbit because the senses of a rabbit are so finely tuned that it will bolt when approached. Sometimes during a flight, the hawk will hit the rabbit and lose it several times before eventually securing it.

2) *Following-on flights* Wherever there are trees overhanging an area to be worked, it is sensible for a broadwing to be given the added advantage of height which these will afford. When working in this manner, particularly when going through a wood, it is essential that the hawk not just keeps up with the austringer, but works slightly ahead of him, for it is logical that the majority of rabbits will break

forward, away from the beater and, if the hawk is lagging far behind, she is unlikely to see them, far less to catch them. In theory, the higher the hawk is in a tree, the better her chances. Hawks will learn to put in the extra effort necessary to gain a higher perch by missing quarry when they have been perched too low. If a hawk misses a rabbit, she will usually mark the spot where the rabbit disappeared by taking stand on an overhead branch. When arriving on the spot, the austringer can effect a reflush, if possible.

3) *Ferreting* Ferreting is extremely useful where rabbits are scarce and, in some parts of the country, it is virtually the only way of getting a flight. Apart from the ferrets themselves, a box for transporting them into the field, a spade for digging out one which has laid up, and a tracking collar and locator are necessary. Most ferrets will thrive on a diet of day-old chicks. Ferrets should bolt rabbits over an open piece of ground, which will give the hawk a chance to catch up with them before they reach cover or another hole. For this reason, a warren should be chosen with care. If it is too large, the rabbits, if they emerge at all, will duck back into another hole without ever bolting properly. If there is too much ground cover, the hawk will not get a clear flight at them.

Ideally, a burrow should be found on a slope, so that the rabbits will run downhill, away from the hawk, who will be on the blind side of the holes, further up the slope. A tree, situated a little behind a burrow is ideal, provided that the hawk is 'ferret safe'. Murdering the ferret, particularly if it belongs to a friend, does not enhance the afternoon's sport. Hawks which are untried and untested with ferrets must be kept on the fist and held if the ferret emerges instead of a rabbit. The austringer will soon be able to gauge from her reactions whether she will be safe with the ferret. It makes sense to use a white ferret, rather than a polecat, because the hawk is less likely to associate this with food.

Austringers should not ferret in the spring, as rabbits will have young below ground

White ferrets are preferable to polecats.

which are easy meat for the ferret. If it should kill below ground, the ferret will not re-emerge for some time. The austringer/ferreter will then have to use the ferret-locator and dig down. The spade can sometimes be useful in other ways as, if planted on treeless ground immediately behind the hole, the handle can provide a useful perching point for the hawk. Rabbits nearly always have an emergency bolt-hole – a sort of back entrance, positioned some way behind the other holes. This should be located so that the hawk can be angled to incorporate this in her view. Sometimes the ferret may draw a blank whilst at other times it may be down for ages and, if either austringer or hawk allows their attention to

wander, they might miss the bolt by a fraction of a second and the hawk will lose her advantage. Good ferreting, when the action is fast and furious, can be very exciting, but slow days, when the ferret is down for a long time, with nothing going on, are extremely boring. When rabbits bolt, they generally head for another hole. A strong rabbit which has nearly reached safety may pull the hawk partly down a hole. When he retreives her, the austringer must ensure that the hawk is not pulled off the rabbit in the process.

4) *Slope-soaring flights* Shortwings are not structured for slope-soaring, but broadwings hunt naturally in this style. It is by far the most spectacular way to hunt a broadwing, but it is not particularly easy to achieve and it requires a certain amount of courage on the part of the austringer. There are three factors

which will contribute towards achieving slope-soaring flights with broadwings: the terrain, which needs to be hilly, with plenty of updraughts; the weather, which ideally should be a light breeze with warm air currents; and, finally, the hawk herself. Slope-soaring comes naturally to a few trained broadwings. Others simply will not soar, no matter how hard the austringer tries to assist them by taking them to ideal areas. Some merely require encouragement and these can be taught by being taken onto a hillside and cast off into a good breeze. The austringer then works patches of cover beneath them in the hopes of flushing a rabbit. With the advantage of height, the hawk will be able to throw in a long stoop on anything which is flushed. Beaters are useful, as a hawk which is high will command a large area. A fit hawk will be able to stay airborne in this manner for up to half-an-hour, dropping on any rabbits which are flushed, but regaining height quickly if she should miss. As a note of caution, any shortwing which goes up on the soar can probably be considered a lost hawk, allbeit temporarily.

5) *Lamping* Lamping rabbit is a technique which has been used by shooting men for many years. The same principal – using a strong beam of light to pin-point rabbits at night – can be used for hawking. It is not a safe proposition to attempt this with an *Accipiter*, but it is feasible with any reliable broadwing. Lamping is particularly useful in areas where rabbit are scarce or where it is difficult to get a flight at them. It can also help austringers with nine-to-five jobs who lack daylight hours in which to fly their hawks in the winter months.

To lamp rabbits for hawking, there are certain guidelines which must be followed for the safety of all concerned. Firstly, the landowner must be asked if he minds and also informed of the times when the lamp is to be used. If the local police are likely to spot the lamp, they should be informed in advance that it is being used legitimately. Particular care must be taken to avoid both nearby roads and fences.

Lamping equipment.

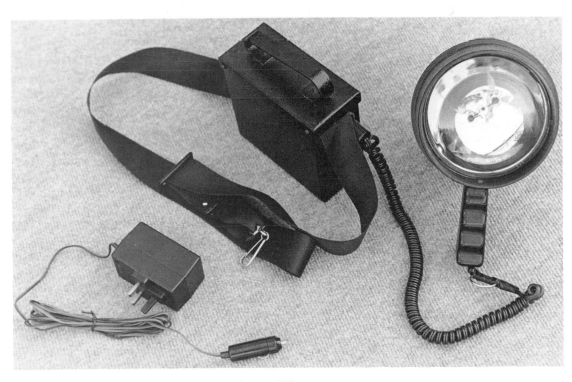

Hawking from a vehicle.

To lamp successfully, two people are necessary – the austringer and a friend to shine the lamp – for it is essential that the hawk is not slipped straight down the beam of light or she will blot it out with her wings and be unable to see where she is heading. Her bells should be taped so that she can close in silently. The hawk should be trained for lamping by practice at night on a creance; she should be called to the fist and from the fist to a rabbit-lure, which should have sequins attached to simulate the reflection of a rabbit's eyes when the lamp catches them. Telemetry is obviously essential.

When the hawk has regained the fist with the aid of the lamp, she should be accustomed to feeding up with the aid of a pocket torch, so that the lamp may be switched off before it burns out. For the first attempt, a rabbit should be found fairly close at hand, so that the hawk can see it clearly in a large pool of light. Later, when she is tuned in to looking for rabbits caught in the beam, she will see them at the fullest extent of the light's range. She should be slipped in her own time from one side, so that she will intercept without blocking the beam. The lamper must keep the rabbit in the beam when it runs. If the hawk misses, the lamp should be switched off, so that the hawk will land on the ground, then turned onto the austringer's glove, so that she

108

can see to return to the fist. Lamping can be done on foot and also from vehicles.

6) *Hawking from vehicles* Where the terrain is suitable and the austringer has a four-wheel-drive vehicle, it is possible to cover large areas of ground by flying a hawk directly out of the window. *Accipiter*s can be hooded whilst inside the car, then slipped off the fist-held out through the open window. Some broad-wings, in particular Harris hawks, can be held bareheaded inside the vehicle. It is often possible to get closer to quarry with a car than on foot. At just the right moment, the car can be turned to give the hawk the advantage before she is slipped off the fist. This should be done when the vehicle is stationary or barely moving, otherwise the hawk will get blown backwards when held out of the window. Some broadwings, upon failing to kill, will return to the fist without the austringer having to get out of the car. Hawking from vehicles is ideal for entertaining unfit friends, but it is also good for wet days, as the hawk can remain dry inside the car until the actual flight, and for large areas of ground with little cover, where the rabbits will see the austringer approaching on foot from some distance.

HARE

There are two types of hare found in the UK: the blue hare, of mountainous and moorland habitat, and the larger brown hare of the low ground. Hare have always held their charm as a potential quarry species for the majority of austringers by merit of their size. However, they represent a not inconsiderable degree of danger to hawks as they have a means of self-defence – they kick. This kick is of sufficient power to break a hawk's leg or, at worst, to cave in her rib-cage. This renders hare unsuitable quarry for all but the strongest and most experienced of hawks.

The usual method of flying hare is to walk up across the stubble fields, grassland or moorland where they can be found lying out,

Harris hawk chasing blue hare.

Harris hawk closing in on brown hare.

although it is possible for the occasional exceptional hawk to fly them from a waiting-on position.

Beaters are useful as a line can be formed to take in more ground – hare can sit very tight and will often not break unless someone virtually steps on them. When they run, hare appear to be moving slowly but, if a hawk begins to get on terms with them, they change down a gear. Blue hare will always run uphill if they can. They will also jump and, on occasion, jump right over their pursuer. Some hawks will refuse hare on sight; others will catch up with them, but, when close enough to get a good look at the size, will pull off. Some hawks will refuse after being kicked off one, for the majority of flights on hare end with the hawk being shrugged off within seconds.

The best hare hawks are golden eagles, female goshawks, female red-tails and female Harris hawks. Harrises are in with a better chance when two or more are flown together, for the first to reach the hare will know that she will quickly be receiving additional help. If the hare is caught by the rump, it will generally free itself quickly. The best way for a hawk to take a hare is in the head and any hawk which is experienced on rabbit will know this to be the best option.

PHEASANT

There is a tremendous range in the quality of flights at pheasant. This is largely related to the time of year, as pheasant at the start of the season can be pathetically easy to take, whilst, after Christmas, they represent far more of a challenge.

Pheasant will not fly unless they are hard pressed. They prefer to spend their time on the ground and the vast majority of flights therefore originate when a hawk spots a pheasant running. As the hawk closes in, the

110

pheasant will take off. If the pheasant has timed its take off well, the hawk, in anticipation of taking it on the ground, will have lost upward momentum and will usually land on the ground, looking bewildered, sometimes with a foot-full of pheasant tail feathers. Only when she is both fit and experienced will she continue immediately in hot pursuit. Although the hawk will be disadvantaged by losing her momentum, and will be trailing some distance behind, she is by no means without a chance; as good hawks will learn in time, if they continue on the trail of a pheasant, it will eventually put in and they can either crash into cover and take it on the ground or throw up to land as high as possible in a tree and mark the spot, waiting for the austringer to reflush it.

A novice will often make the mistake of staying rooted to the spot and recalling the hawk to the fist, thinking that the pheasant is lost. This is the worst thing he can do, for not only will the pheasant indeed be lost, but it will discourage the hawk from putting them in in the future. On the reflush, it is the pheasant that is at a disadvantage and it will normally be taken, hopefully in flight, although the hawk may have to put it in again before success is finally achieved. It is a good hawk indeed which will persist in this way and an exceptional immature, for most take several seasons to learn this technique.

It is wise to resist the temptation to try to drop a hawk onto a pheasant sitting tight on the ground, for although it may appear deceptively easy sitting so still, the familiar explosion of a pheasant leaving cover will nine times out of ten be the end result and the hawk will be left looking stupid on the ground. A more sensible course of action is to cast the hawk into a tree as high as possible, preferably directly over the spot where the pheasant is lying. The austringer then needs to get the hawk's attention before going for the flush. In a wooded area where the austringer knows there are a lot of pheasant, he can place the hawk high in a tree and beat towards her.

It is on flights at pheasant that the question

Harris hawk on brown hare.

of both the species and the sex of the hawk one is flying become important. The speed of a goshawk gives her a distinct advantage over other species. *Buteo*s will need to be worked extremely hard if they are to take pheasant on a regular basis. Immatures without the prerequisite degree of fitness will be quick to give up. It is an extraordinary common buzzard that can succeed on pheasant more frequently than an opportunistic snatch on the ground, whilst red-tails are certainly capable but will need to be in peak condition. Some hawks, particularly the smaller males, will develop the habit of refusing cock pheasant, which, being larger and stronger than the hens, can give a hawk quite a tussle on the ground.

The occasional broadwing will take a pheasant from a waiting-on position. This is spectacular but not easy to engineer, as any game bird is aware of a predator above them and will sit tight unless flushed with deliberation by the austringer or a dog.

MOORHEN AND COOT

Moorhen hold little appeal for the serious austringer, unless he happens to be flying a sparrowhawk. They are slow in flight and can be taken with consummate ease by a goshawk.

They are useful for entering a hawk but only one should be taken for this purpose, because, if one continues to deliberately seek them out for the purpose of swelling the bag, the hawk may well refuse more difficult quarry. In areas where an austringer is trying to achieve flights on mallard, moorhen can be a real nuisance as the hawk will always select them as the easy option.

For a female sparrowhawk or for the novice with a common buzzard, however, the moorhen is a fair flight – for the former by merit of her diminutive size and, for the latter, because it is one of the few birds which an austringer can hope to catch with a buzzard on a regular basis. Success will rarely be achieved if the moorhen reaches water deep enough to enable it to dive. Ideally, one must be encountered sitting out in a field some distance from water, so that an airborne chase can take place. Alternatively, a dog can be used to flush moorhen off water. It is also possible to achieve flights along the length of a small brook, where the water is too shallow for the moorhen to dive. Unfortunately, most moorhen are taken on the ground, but, if a spar or a buzzard manages to take one in flight, the austringer can be well satisfied with her performance.

Coot are a somewhat different proposition, being larger and tougher. They are also much harder to find away from water. Coots have quite a turn of speed when hard pressed by a hawk, so an austringer need not be ashamed to feature one or two in his game book.

DUCK

Generally, when speaking of taking duck with a hawk, one is talking about mallard, though not exclusively as the occasional other species will fall prey to a good hawk, even the redoubtable teal. There is a vast difference between 'tame' duck – those put down on mass for shoots and fed in set points on a daily basis – and true wild duck. The former will be gathered in numbers and will not be easily spooked, whilst the latter will lift off the water at the slightest provocation. The austringer can plan his campaign accordingly. If he knows the duck will sit, he is best advised to put his hawk into a tree some little distance away and let her work it out. In time, she will make her selection and work out the best line of approach. An experienced hawk will look for a duck on *terra firma*, whilst an immature in her early days is more likely to demonstrate her callow youth by attempting to snatch a duck off the surface of the water. This is not a mistake she will be quick to repeat. A mallard, and particularly a mallard drake, is not an easy prey to hold in the first place, being bulky, slippery and notoriously difficult to kill. Float these defensive attributes on water and the young hawk will find herself flapping wetly to shore, duckless.

Having learned this lesson, the hawk should limit herself to duck on dry land. Only the best of hawks will attempt to take on a duck in full flight. Usually all flights initiate with the hawk spotting a duck on the ground and most kills are achieved by dint of the hawk either managing to catch the duck before it takes off or taking one on the rise. A young hawk will quickly give up if she fails to make contact on, or close to, the ground, but later, when she is more experienced, the austringer can look forward to some spectacular rising flights as the duck takes the hawk up at a steep angle.

Wild duck are more difficult. Whilst the styles of flight are the same, the hawk is most unlikely to have the time to select her victim at leisure. Austringer and hawk will have to learn the technique of stalking their prey and a flight pond which allows both to approach under screen of vegetation will be the most likely to yield success. Flights at duck often end with the pursued and the pursuer locked together in the water. A strong drake may still manage to wriggle free by repeated attempts to dive, but generally, the hawk will maintain control and will eventually drown the duck before rowing ashore with her wings. If a hawk is locked on a duck in water, patently failing to make any progress and gradually but progressively sinking lower and lower, the austringer will feel obliged to peel off to his undergarments and go to his hawk's aid,

Broadwings can easily be encouraged to slope-soar.

vastly to the amusement of any observers. Frequently, the hawk, noting the rescuer's approach, suddenly finds new reserves of strength and rows herself and the sodden duck towards the opposite bank.

A potentially more risky scenario occurs if the hawk makes her kill on ice. For this, and for a hundred other reasons, an austringer should always carry a creance because, weighted with a suitable branch, he should eventually manage to lasso both hawk and duck and pull them across the ice towards him.

PARTRIDGE

An austringer is always proud to enter a partridge in his game book. A traditional quarry for *Accipiter*s, they can never be described as easy when taken under fair conditions. In season, partridge can be found on stubble, pastureland and on root crops.

Depending on the area of the countryside and the proximity and preferences of a local shoot, grey (English) or red-legged (French), or sometimes a mixture of the two, can be found wild. Greys are smaller than their more substantial cousins and they are quicker to take flight, whilst red-legs are more inclined to run before taking off. Partridge are generally found by walking up or with the aid of a dog.

If the austringer has suitable land, he can enhance the quality of his sport greatly by putting down a few partridge for his own purposes. Having put down his own game, the austringer will have a fair idea, early in the season, of where to find his coveys, according to the feeding points. Later in the season, coveys will pack and become wilder and it will become difficult even to get a flight at them.

113

To take a mature partridge, a hawk must be extremely fit, as well as persistent by nature, for she will generally have to chase until she puts the partridge in, whereupon she will either mark the spot or, if the cover is sufficiently thin, follow in and take it on the ground. To find a partridge in thick cover, a good dog is usually a necessity. Partridge hawking also requires the austringer to be fit, for he must keep up with the flights if he is to be of help to his hawk. An exceptional *Accipiter* can take partridge in flight. The slip will need to be a close one and the hawk will learn to climb slightly higher than the partridge and to one side so that she may cut it down in a shallow stoop. A goshawk will have little trouble dealing with a partridge on the ground, but a sparrowhawk will resort naturally to spreading her sails and train over the partridge, propping her feathers into the ground in an attempt to prevent its escape before she can despatch it or the austringer arrives to assist. Although most shortwings and broadwings appear to find the rounded-wing form of a partridge completely irresistible and will chase it with enthusiasm, it has to be admitted that most give up quite quickly and it is, indeed, a good hawk which will take them on a regular basis. More usually, it is an example of good teamwork between hawk, austringer and dog.

GREY SQUIRREL

Unfortunately squirrels can deliver a particularly nasty bite which can easily become infected and put a hawk out of action for a season. For this reason, it is not sensible to condone squirrel hawking, which is a very great pity as the flights are terrifically entertaining to watch.

THE USE OF DOGS WITH SHORTWINGS AND BROADWINGS

However good a team of austringer and hawk, it will stand a fair chance of being improved by the addition of a first-class working dog. No dog at all, however, is considerably better than a dog which is not fully under control.

Dogs are used to find game for the hawk, either by pointing it or by working cover and flushing close at hand. The former has the advantage over the latter, as the austringer will receive prior warning from the point and can allow himself the luxury of getting his hawk into the best possible position before sending the dog in to flush. It is essential that dogs which merely work cover and flush are fully under control and working close at hand. Having flushed the quarry, the dog must be trained to drop, not to give chase and tongue. Further, the dog must be able to take direction from the austringer, including turning on the whistle and dropping to command.

To train a dog to this standard will take the best part of a year, initially during the summer months and then during the season. Like hawks, dogs improve season by season, but it is essential to have trained the young dog to the point of complete obedience or the austringer will find himself in pursuit of the dog each afternoon, instead of in pursuit of game. To train a dog, a good manual and a healthy dose of commonsense are the principle requirements. Suitable manuals are aimed at gun-dog owners, so the advice therein must be adapted to suit the task in hand; obviously the austringer does not want to train his hawking dog to retrieve. The alternative is to purchase a trained dog. An austringer who specializes in training dogs professionally is the best source as he will have a thorough understanding of what is required. Gun-dog trainers should be made fully aware of the necessary criteria.

Suitable species on the pointing side include German short-haired pointers, wire-haired pointers, vizslas, Munsterlanders and Brittanys. Cocker spaniels can also be trained to point. English pointers are generally reserved for use on open ground with longwings, as their coat is not thick enough to protect them in dense ground cover. Springer spaniels are the best non-pointing propositions for working cover but, as game will be flushed without warning, they are more practical for working with *Accipiter*s than with *Buteo*s, as the former are quicker off the mark.

9 THE BROADWINGS

THE COMMON OR EUROPEAN BUZZARD (*BUTEO BUTEO*)

The common buzzard is an ideal hawk for the beginner. Traditionally, the kestrel was considered to be the hawk for a complete novice, but mercifully this view is now outdated. Kestrels, weighing only a matter of 5–8 oz on average are far too delicate to suffer the beginner's early efforts at weight control and the smallest error in judgement can result in their untimely death. In addition, kestrels can hardly be considered a species suitable for falconry as they take no quarry of interest, being limited mainly to mice and bugs. Buzzards, however, will take a restricted range of respectable quarry species. A well-heeled beginner might prefer to start with a Harris hawk. These have a much wider range of capabilities in the field than buzzards and are also easier and quicker to train. However, buzzards are by no means to be despised as a first hawk for, in comparison, the majority of Harrises have such a splendidly amiable disposition, and learn so quickly, that they can lull the novice into a false sense of security. A buzzard requires much more coaxing and subtlety to achieve good results. Thus the beginner who succeeds in entering her is perhaps better equipped to appreciate the merits of a second hawk with more potential.

In terms of temperament, buzzards vary enormously. The males generally have a better disposition than the females. Whilst this may not be apparent in the immature year, the majority of females may become more difficult to handle after their first moult. Imprinted buzzards are aggressive and will present a novice with a set of additional problems which he quite simply could do without. Parent-reared buzzards are usually steady, likeable hawks, which will put up with the inexperience of beginners without bearing them undue malice. In the field they are frequently described as lazy and lacking in persistence. It would be much closer to the truth to say that, if a buzzard's performance matches this description, the same could be said of the austringer. Any buzzard which is conditioned correctly will work to the best of its capabilities. Its capabilities, however, will be limited to a certain range of quarry species and the novice wishing to take pheasant, duck and the like will have to curb his enthusiasm while he serves his apprenticeship with a buzzard for at least one season. Buzzards can take rabbit, moorhen and a range of small fry, such as rats. Assuming proper training, fitness is the key to success and this cannot be over-stressed. In the conditioning and hunting of his buzzard, the beginner will mature with his hawk and British austringers are indeed fortunate to have such a suitable species with which to learn.

THE RED-TAILED BUZZARD (*BUTEO JAMAICENSIS*)

In the USA, the red-tail is the hawk most commonly flown by beginners. A beginner contemplating starting with a red-tail in the

Common buzzard.

it prove unsuitable in any way. He is not allowed to start with an eyass. The captive-bred red-tails available to the British austringer are a different proposition, for, being eyasses, they will not have the manners of passagers and the novice will early on become painfully aware of their not inconsiderable strength. In simple terms, the majority of eyass red-tails would frighten the average beginner. They are frequently sticky-footed in the early stages and, in the ensuing struggle as the beginner seeks to exert his inept influence over his awkward and powerful charge, the hawk is more likely to be viewed as an opponent rather than as a partner. As a second hawk, however, a red-tail is an excellent option. Similar to a common buzzard in so many respects, she will be found to be something of a supercharged version and the wider scope which she will offer in the field will be appreciated as the taking of pheasant, duck, hare and even the occasional partridge becomes a practical proposition.

Initially, a novice, with one trained buzzard behind him, may find his newly acquired red-tail to be something of a disappointment. Contrary to expectation, she will not take masterful flight after pheasant and she is likely to give duck no more than a cursory glance. Once again, fitness is the key and, whilst a hawk may be good in her immature year, she will be better the following season and will continue to improve. Thus, if he sticks with her, the austringer will have a hawk to be proud of after a few years. It is most important to fly a red-tail hard on every day made possible by the weather. She should also be flown at a range of quarry, for, if she enjoys early success on rabbit and is flown repeatedly, and with little deviation, at fur during the early months, she is later likely to refuse feathered game, believing it to be outside her range of capabilities. Varied slips will result in a hawk which is an all-rounder.

To see a red-tail at its very best is to see a red-tail which has been encouraged to slope-

UK would be well advised to reflect on the fact that, in the USA, a complete novice is required to be apprenticed to an experienced austringer for a term of 2 years and, thereby, has the inestimable benefit of referral for practical help and advice. He also has a huge wild stock of red-tails from which he can draw a passage hawk and, indeed, change it should

Opposite Red-tailed buzzard.

soar. Only in this way will she realize her full potential, for this is her natural style of flight. The red-tail should not necessarily be viewed as a stepping stone to an *Accipiter*. Many good austringers in the UK and in the USA find in a red-tail all that they require in a hawk and their early persistence whilst their hawk gains experience is well rewarded over the following seasons.

THE FERRUGINOUS BUZZARD (*BUTEO REGALIS*)

Ferruginous are slightly larger than red-tails, but have feet which proportionately are much smaller. This is unfortunate as, whilst the females can take rabbit adequately, the males are greatly disadvantaged by this shortcoming and will lose far more quarry than they will hold. For this reason the males are not ideal for falconry purposes, but the females are useful hunting birds, particularly in open, treeless countryside, similar to their natural western North American habitat.

The vast majority of ferruginous are difficult to man. To get them to sit on the fist usually proves arduous. In their natural state, they spend a great deal of their time sitting on the ground, frequently taking off and chasing game from this position. Thus, gripping onto a perching point, be it gloved fist or bow perch, is alien to them and the trained ferruginous will spend most of her time sitting beside her bow perch in the weathering, rather than on it. The easiest way to get a ferruginous to stand on the fist – and, indeed, any shortwing or broadwing which proves difficult in this respect – is to start in pitch darkness. She should be taken up before first light and walked through until dawn. After this slow start, however, events will take a dramatic upward turn as ferruginous are both quick to train and easy to enter.

They are at their best in open countryside, for they dislike sitting in trees and often cannot be persuaded to go into them at all. In the right conditions, they will quarter naturally and return directly to the glove or sit on the ground if they fail to find anything to chase.

They are surprisingly quick, both off the fist and off the ground, springing into the air, aided by their powerful legs which are a natural adaptation to this style of hunting. Their talons, blunted by time spent on the ground, need sharpening regularly. Although they take pheasant and partridge in their natural state, they do not excel at taking game birds when trained.

Primarily, therefore, the female ferruginous should be considered as a hawk for rabbiting on downland or marshland and the male should not be considered at all, except as a last resort. For those who aspire to training an eagle, a ferruginous will provide useful experience in terms of familiarizing the aspirant with the physical handling of a hawk of some size. Imprinted ferruginous are something of a dangerous menace and should be avoided at all costs.

THE HARRIS HAWK (*PARABUTEO UNICINCTUS*)

Parabuteo literally means 'similar to *Buteo*'. The Harris hawk is the only hawk thus classified. This amiable but efficient species has found a niche in British falconry and is now the number one most commonly flown hawk in the UK. The vast majority have an exceptionally easy-going temperament and are very easy to train. Harrises are not as fast as goshawks, but they can take the same range of quarry and they will waste no time stuck in trees. There are three subspecies of Harrises – *Parabuteo unicinctus unicinctus*, which is the smallest and is recognizable in adult plumage by the creamy edges to its mail; *Parabuteo unicinctus harrisi*, which, in contrast to *P. u. unicinctus*, has an adult chest of totally dark feathers; and *Parabuteo unicinctus superior*, which is the largest of the three and can be recognized by this factor.

In their natural state, Harris hawks are gregarious. They live in the deserts of the southern USA and South America in family

Opposite Ferruginous buzzard.

groups, hunting together in the manner of pack animals. The young from the previous year will stay with their parents to watch, observe and assist with feeding the following year's brood. In falconry terms, this has opened up a whole new avenue of possibilities as it is possible to fly captive, trained Harrises in a group. This does not result, as some people might imagine, in six Harrises on one rabbit; the hawk which reaches the game first will take firm possession and the others will land nearby, while a sort of Mexican stand-off ensues, broken only if the hawk in possession seems in need of assistance. In practice, it results in six pairs of eyes and consequently a great deal of sport. If one hawk gets kicked off a kill, or if the quarry should jinx sharply to evade the pursuing hawk, there will be another hawk coming up from behind to secure it. Harrises worked regularly in a team will learn to assist each other, but there is also a healthy element of competition, leading to some spectacular flying. There is a clear-cut pecking order in groups of Harrises flown regularly together. Adults will displace immatures from branches in a tree, although, interestingly, they will never attempt to take a kill from a young hawk. Sibling rivalry is also often apparent and may never subside. Occasionally one encounters a particularly aggressive individual which cannot be flown in a team. In the old-fashioned sense of a 'make hawk', an adult Harris will perform this role when flown with an immature.

Harrises will also perform very well when flown singly. Both imprinted and parent-reared Harrises are practical propositions. The former will be noisier, but the latter can rarely be guaranteed to be silent, for Harrises respond in such a familiar fashion to human beings that 70 per cent of passage hawks flown in Mexico scream until they have been intermewed. After the first moult, the voice breaks and is a good deal less piercing, and less frequently used. A Harris reared in isolation, however, as opposed to the crèche-reared Harris, will scream much more and tend to mantle. Some people strive to overcome the problem of screaming by leaving young

Immature Harris hawk.

Harrises in the breeding chamber or in a nursery aviary until after Christmas. This is a big mistake. Harrises are highly intelligent hawks which need stimulation in their formative months. Left too long, a Harris will behave like a goshawk, having none of the species' customary tameness and bright attitude towards training. Like a remedial child,

120

everything will be a struggle for her, especially game which will be strong by that time and much more likely to elude her.

Notwithstanding the advisability of taking up a Harris early, the austringer must handle her with extreme physical gentleness in the first couple of months, particularly when casting her for any reason, such as during initial equipping, for the bones of a young immature are soft and easily broken. They take several months to harden off properly and any careless handling can result in a fracture. Harrises are also highly prone to frostbite. This condition results in watery blisters, usually on the wing tips and can cause dry gangrene to set in, whereupon the hawk will lose the end of the wing. Frostbite can also deaden a petty single, turning it brown and causing it to drop off. It is essential, therefore, to take precautions against frostbite, and the temperature in the Harrises' quarters – weathering or mews – must never fall to freezing point or below. If a frost looks likely, a heat bulb, of the ceramic variety used for pigs, should be switched on behind the weathering blind or in the mews at a height of approximately 2 to 3 feet above the hawk's head. Harrises can also get blain if they get soaked in chilly weather. As with any hawk, they should never be put into the weathering or chamber wet and left overnight. If a Harris is loose in a chamber, frostbite should not be a problem as she will be able to get above frost level. Keeping a Harris in this way has distinct advantages, but should not be employed until she is fully trained or she will become difficult. Only when she has been entered, and is therefore responding as one would wish, can she be turned loose. She can be called up to the fist for food on entering the chamber and, as well as enjoying the extra freedom afforded by being kept in this way, she will be less likely to suffer from feather wear or scale displacement on her feet. Harrises are also notorious for untying leashes and this possibility is thereby avoided.

Inbreeding has been proving to be a problem with Harrises. Inbred hawks may appear normal, but will later show defects, ranging from crumbly bones to a hole in the heart. Every care should therefore be taken when selecting a breeder from whom to purchase a Harris. There can also be terrific variation in the prowess of eyasses from the same sibling group.

Unfortunately, because of bad weight control, many Harrises are downgraded by the austringer, as Harrises will work at a weight which is really far too high. A Harris hawk flown overweight will not achieve one-tenth of her potential. She will also scream far more, because, in not achieving the number of kills of which she is capable, nor concentrating on the job in hand, she will fail to grow up mentally and will whinge for food and attention like a spoilt child. Realistic weight control will produce a much better hawk at the end of the day. There is a wide range of flying weights encountered in both sexes – males fly at 1 lb 2 oz – 1 lb 10 oz and females at 1 lb 11 oz – 2 lb 8 oz.

In the early stages, Harrises respond extremely well to socializing with human beings. Time spent in their company, paying them attention, is time well spent. They neither respond well to, nor need, long manning walks, but are happier brought indoors for the evening to observe the family and relax in human company. A Harris may be trained rapidly and should not be held back. She should never be allowed to sit on the ground, but should be picked up immediately and cast into the nearest tree. Nor should she ever be rewarded with food after sitting on the ground. Harrises are intelligent enough to be able to differentiate between a 'follow-on' whistle and a 'food' whistle. Whenever the terrain is suitable, a Harris should be allowed to fly at liberty and to follow on. She will not only become much fitter in this way, but will also develop mentally more rapidly, learning to become an opportunist. Some Harrises can be surprisingly difficult to enter. They appear not to notice quarry, although they are familiar with, and quick to respond to, both lures. The answer is to use the lures unexpectedly, pulling them out of bushes and clumps of vegetation and generally getting the hawk used to expecting the unexpected.

When out with a Harris, the austringer should let her chase whatever she wishes, never holding her on a bate unless she is merely being naughty. Such is their curiosity that young Harrises will take a keen interest in all that moves, even a stone kicked by a foot or an apple falling from a tree. If she is allowed to catch these objects, her curiosity will be satisfied, she will learn that they are not edible and her reactions will become razor-sharp. If she is denied these aberrations, she will become frustrated, feeling herself to be stifled. Harrises are tremendously versatile and take an astonishing range of quarry. The males in particular, being nimbler than the females, will take a wide and ever-increasing selection of small birds. No Harris should be allowed to specialize, for, in so doing, the austringer will deprive both himself and his hawk of a great deal of sport. How much better to have an unexpected bonus flight at woodcock or a crow than to trail around on a wet day, miserable because there are no rabbit in evidence. Harrises are known to have taken well in excess of 60 species of quarry, ranging from sparrows to brown hare. Females are obviously preferable for regular flights at hare, although males can also take them, particularly if they know a female is flying with them, and will be hard on her heels to offer back-up if necessary.

The weight control with males is somewhat tricky. They must be flown tight if they are to perform well – an overweight immature male will refuse rabbit and certainly cock pheasant when, in reality, and at a proper hunting weight, he is quite capable of taking either. However, at a tight flying weight, rations must be allotted in proportion to work done and to the temperature. On cold nights, or after a particularly active day in the field, like any small hawk, a male Harris will go low if he is slightly underfed. Novices, therefore, would be better starting with a female.

It takes 4 to 5 months for a Harris to realize her potential. All styles of flight described for shortwings and broadwings are possible with Harrises, including slope-soaring, at which some individuals excel, and also lamping, to which they adapt easily. Flying Harrises out of hood is a variation which works well and one which is particularly useful when working in company, as most Harrises will object to being kept on the fist bareheaded whilst another hawk takes its turn. There is only one major drawback to Harrises in the eyes of the austringer and that is their intense and inherent dislike of dogs. In their natural state, their only competitor for food is the coyote. Even the captive-bred immature which has never seen a dog will, upon first sighting, utter a raucous shriek of dislike and disapproval. With just one immature an austringer is in with a chance of persuading the hawk that she is being silly and, using just one dog which is introduced at the outset, of getting her to accept it as a working partner in the field. Two or more Harrises are much harder to convince of the merits of canine companionship as they will set each other off, each giving vocal support and thus credence to the other's fears.

It is possible to fly a Harris right through the moult, but the moult will be protracted by so doing. The Harris which has flown right through the previous autumn and winter will be sufficiently cunning to select her slips in the summer months, always picking on young and disadvantaged quarry. In the end, this will do her no great favours for, at worst, she may become blasé and reluctant to give of her best on harder slips. An alternative for the ardent austringer who, as far as is humanly possible, is happy to restrict his hawk to vermin during the summer months whilst game is out of season, is to have a winter and a summer Harris and to moult them alternately, having started both together as immatures, but keeping one going through the summer when the other is put down to moult.

Harrises intensely dislike other species of hawk and therefore should not be flown in their company, except with experienced austringers who are prepared for a free-flying Harris to attempt to snatch another hawk off the fist. In particular Harrises hate goshawks and it is better not to mix the two, either at field meets or during informal gatherings, as both require different styles of outing and a vastly different level of concentration.

Hunting with Harris hawks is a relaxed style of hawking. There is none of the tension and worries inherent in flying *Accipiter*s. Because of this, there is a tendency to belittle Harrises, particularly from those who stick to the traditional species. This is quite unnecessary. Harrises have filled a gap in modern times for those who prefer a more laid-back and often more sociable style of hawking. Nevertheless, they require sound falconry skills and practices to achieve really good results and a fit Harris taking a pheasant in fine style merits just as much respect as a Goshawk performing the same feat.

THE GOLDEN EAGLE (*AQUILA CHRYSAETOS*)

A great many austringers in the past who aspired towards flying a golden eagle have waited many years before fulfilling this ambition and have subsequently failed to hunt the eagle with any degree of success. In part, this is often due to the fact that they live in a totally unsuitable part of the country. It takes an enormous amount of skill and dedication on the part of the austringer to hunt an eagle successfully over flat or enclosed countryside. Moreover, why carry a hawk which weighs a minimum of 5 lb when you could see far more sport with a hawk which weighs 2 lb?

Unfortunately the answer lies all too

Golden eagle.

frequently in the ego of the person in question. It is not coincidence that wild golden eagles are not found in the south of the UK. The terrain is not suitable for their natural style of hunting, which is waiting on. To achieve this, they need hilly or mountainous countryside to give them lift. Flown off the fist, unless they are extremely fit, they are awkward and cumbersome. To hunt a golden eagle successfully, therefore, one ideally needs to live in eagle country, but there is much more to be taken into consideration.

Taking into account the sheer size and strength of an eagle, the austringer will have to rethink both the equipment and the accommodation he has been using for his smaller hawks. A weathering of 12 ft in length is essential to accommodate the wingspan. All items of equipment need to be heavy duty – a stronger creance, thicker leather for jesses, a large and possibly custom-made swivel, a substantial lure, a heavy leash, large block perch, and above all else, a suitable glove. Whereas hawking gloves are usually geared to prevent the hawk from piercing them, with an eagle the crushing power of the feet also has to be taken into consideration, so the leather must be not only thick but stiff. The fingers, however, must be supple if the austringer is to be comfortable and safe in terms of being able to grip the jesses properly. A leather sleeve worn on the upper arm is a sensible precaution and an arm brace to support the weight is an addition which will be appreciated in the field.

Over and above the problems of size and strength, the austringer will also have to apply psychology to cope with the moods of an eagle. These moods will usually dominate the training and consequently the eagle will be, for the most part, unpredictable. Eagles are very territorial and it is not uncommon for an eagle in training to establish territory in her weathering. The austringer may find himself threatened when entering this territory in order to take her up or tie her down.

Imprinted golden eagles are dangerous. A minor dispute over entering territory in the weathering of a non-imprinted eagle can easily become a major incident with an imprint,

Tawny eagle.

with the austringer endangering his personal safety. Later, when flying free, an imprint which misses a kill is likely to turn her aggression on to the austringer or anyone else close at hand.

The manning and training of an eagle is a time-consuming process. A golden eagle generally needs to lose between 20 per cent and 25 per cent of her total body weight when fully fat. In the case of a large female, this can amount to as much as 4 lb. It is tempting to reduce the time necessary to facilitate such a weight loss by not feeding for days at a stretch. However, if food is withheld for prolonged intervals, the eagle will become anorexic. Far from appearing keener, she will show disdain for food when it is eventually offered, making progress impossible without feeding her right up again. A little food should therefore be fed every other day, whilst persuading the eagle to do as much as possible to earn it. Eagles will often make something of a false start at a high weight and may start responding slowly on a creance after losing only a fraction of the weight which will eventually have to be removed to achieve a response conducive to flying free. Once she is free, the austringer, noting how laboured she appears in level flight, will be tempted to take her to a slope where she can soar majestically out and gain lift. He would be better advised to call her up the slope, knowing that, every time she lands on the ground with wings hanging at her side exhausted, he is getting one step closer to getting her fit. Gliding requires little or no effort and will certainly never prepare her for chasing game. As well as flying uphill, both the distance and the number of flights must be increased. Once she is fit, then she can be encouraged to soar and wait on, for she will have sufficient stamina and speed to shut her wings and stoop hard after quarry when it is flushed. Normally, eagles are flown at ground game, preferably hare, although the occasional head of feathered game may be taken by an exceptional bird. Fox is also taken by eagles, although not without some element of risk.

To get an eagle fit to hunt off the fist is no easy task. Initially she will show a marked lack of persistence at quarry, knowing that she lacks muscle, despite being responsive to the fist and co-operative about chasing the lure. One way round this problem is to tow the lure behind a slow-moving vehicle or motorbike. The austringer can gauge the correct speed and duration of flight, which will not only give her the encouragement of catching the lure, but also make her really work for it. Daily sessions at this game, until she is hard-muscled and strong in flight, will make her far more persistent after rabbit and hare on long, clear slips.

When an eagle is waiting on at a good height she can control a large area, so beaters are helpful. It is important to reward her for prolonged periods of waiting on, therefore it is essential to fly over good ground, where one can be reasonably certain that she will at least be served. Flying an eagle which waits on over dead ground is the surest way to run into problems, for, if her attention wanders, so will she, and she is liable to go self-hunting. A fit eagle can cross between two ranges of hills in a matter of minutes, whilst the austringer can take hours to cross the same ground. For flights off the fist, open land, preferably large stubble fields or pasture land, will be necessary, where ground game can be found lying out. Beaters should form a line to walk up hare, with the austringer and eagle in the middle or keeping pace on a ridge above. When the wind is strong, it is important to walk downwind to give the eagle the advantage.

Before taking on an eagle, an austringer should consider his options very carefully. If she is to be worked properly, she will be time consuming. She will require to be worked every day possible, with little exception for bad weather, even in mid-winter when she will be at her best. Every trip to fly her will, because of her size and requirements, become something of an expedition. There are very few austringers in the UK who have made first-class hunting birds out of golden eagles.

Other species of eagle have been flown with varying degrees of success by British austringers. There are a few species being bred regularly in captivity, including the tawny eagle. Very little has been achieved with this species in terms of taking game. The celebrated Bonelli's eagle and African hawk eagle are not kept in the UK in any great number and the majority reside in aviaries for captive-breeding projects. Although they are by no means an easy proposition to train, they have realized great potential in the hands of austringers in their native countries and may, if produced in sufficient numbers in the UK through captive breeding, prove to be the answer to the prayers of those frustrated austringers who dream of eagles.

10 THE SHORTWINGS

THE SPARROWHAWK (*ACCIPITER NISUS*)

An austringer undertaking to train a sparrow-hawk should be in no doubt that he is taking on one of the most difficult hawks available. No one should attempt to fly a sparrowhawk until he has made a decent job of a goshawk, which shares many of the inherent difficulties of the sparrowhawk, but not its diminutive stature, which further complicates the job in hand. It is a sad state of affairs that, in these commercial times, sparrowhawks are a more affordable option for the novice austringer than many of their larger cousins. They are therefore considered, most unwisely, to be a good prospect and frequently fall into the hands of those wholly lacking the considerable expertise necessary. Whilst the female sparrow-hawk is correctly considered to be a highly dodgy prospect for the novice, so the musket (the male) is considered to be extremely difficult to maintain and retain, even for the most expert of austringers. Having served his apprenticeship, therefore, the austringer is advised to head firmly for a female sparrow-hawk and to avoid muskets like the plague.

Although a female sparrowhawk is somewhat more robust than a musket, she too is fragile by comparison with other species. One of the better descriptions of sparrowhawks defines them as 'hysterical little hawks'. A sparrow-hawk is troublesome to train, difficult to maintain and so demanding of the austringer that he cannot afford to let a single day pass during the season when he does not pay her attention. If she is thrown food instead of being fed up on the fist, she will prefer eating *tout seul* and is likely to adopt tactics which will result in this happening in the field, notably carrying. It is because of such tenden-cies that flying imprinted sparrowhawks has become popular. Imprinting takes the edge off an *Accipiter* in all respects but prowess in the field and with sparrowhawks is distinctly advantageous, although it in no way negates all the problems.

Having denigrated the sparrowhawk, it is time to talk of her good points. Sparrowhawks are courageous hunters and the sport to be had with them is potentially of the finest quality. Armed with a sparrowhawk, the austringer need never find himself short of a slip, for blackbirds, thrushes and the like abound in most parts of the country. Many ardent fans of the goshawk have switched their loyalty to the sparrowhawk after just one season in the company of one of these engaging and energetic small hawks.

The furniture must be well conceived and executed. The slender legs of a sparrowhawk require the support of a wide anklet. In the field she should be fitted with stiff field jesses which will not entangle in her feet or wrap around branches. Sparrowhawks are inclined to be sticky-footed. A soft and spongy glove will exaggerate this tendency to such an extent that the austringer may find it hard to slip his excitable hawk as she grips in anticipation. A glove of stiff leather is therefore an asset.

Loop perches are preferable because sparrow-hawks have comparatively long trains, the feathers of which are easily broken. Tail sheaths should also be utilized.

Because of her fragility, a sparrowhawk in training cannot endure savage weight reduction. All *Accipiter*s have a high metabolic rate and need regular meals of good quality. They are known to have a tendency to throw fits. This is frequently assigned to temperament, but more usually the fits are caused by a low blood-sugar level. A high-quality diet of beef, plus the occasional day-old chick, but preferably trapped sparrows for roughage, is ideal for a sparrowhawk. Twice-daily weighing, in the morning and before flying, is also a wise practice. The austringer can then give extra rations to bring her on weight for the afternoon if she is too low, or plan to delay his outing if she is too high when weighed in the morning.

Hood training a sparrowhawk unquestionably makes life easier in the field. Bareheaded, she will frequently see quarry before it has broken cover from the hedgerow. If she is allowed to slip too early, the quarry will not break and she will crash into the bush without a chance of securing it. If, however, she is retained on the fist once she has seen the quarry, then, until it is flushed, she is likely to be in such a high state of agitation that her bating will alert the quarry to her presence, making the task of flushing it far more difficult. She is also likely to grip the glove convulsively and miss her chance while the austringer struggles to unpick her pounces. Slipped out of hood, however, the austringer can time things to a nicety, removing the hood when the quarry is clear of the hedgerow and heading across open ground.

In the early stages, a sparrowhawk will respond much more quickly and will be sooner manned if she is not carried endlessly before she will feed up on the fist. She can then, and only then, be taken for walks to man her, armed with a piece of tiring which, from her point of view will give her time spent on the fist some enjoyable purpose. Once she is feeding on the fist, she should never be approached to be taken up without a pick-up piece. Whilst flying on the creance, sparrow-hawks are prone to smack the fist and carry on. This is generally an indication of either inadequate manning or failure to be sufficiently keen. Introducing her to the swing-lure rarely presents any problems, but it should be used infrequently or she will prefer it to the fist. As a safeguard, she should be taught to come to the lure when it is swung up into the fist, for, if she is needed in a hurry in the field but is being somewhat stubborn about being called to the fist, this is one way in which she can be retrieved quickly.

A sparrowhawk should always be entered as soon as possible, for she does not require the same rigorous regime to render her fit which a broadwing needs before being entered. It is, however, important that the austringer can recognize when his hawk is in yarak. She may appear keen when picked up from the weathering, but, once out in the field, with all its distractions, keenness can easily be forgotten if it is in any way superficial. An *Accipiter* in yarak sits slightly fluffed up, pulling her feathers in on the austringer's approach and looking very alert, with beady eyes and the feathers at the back of her head slightly raised in a small crest. She will bounce up onto the fist and grip, straining for the off and, if she is an imprint, screaming. The vast majority of *Accipiter*s will have to be carried daily for up to half-an-hour to bring them into yarak before being flown. To fly an *Accipiter* when she is too high or too low is, in the former case, to risk her loss or, in the latter, to risk temporary lowness, bordering on illness.

The traditional quarries for sparrowhawks are blackbird and thrush. The latter are the harder and both require a quarry licence. Sparrows are comparatively poor sport and a sparrowhawk should never be entered on them or she may become wedded and check at sparrows when being slipped at larger and more difficult species. Sparrows are also very easily carried and, should she ever catch one, she should not be allowed to feed up on it. Moorhen are slow in flight but their size makes them more testing for a sparrowhawk.

Flights over water should be avoided as she may be pulled under. With close slips it is also possible to take starling, partridge and lapwing, although none of these are likely to feature heavily on the game record. Wood pigeon are very rarely taken, because they need a combination of a close slip, height for a stoop and surprise. For the first few flights, the austringer should look for close slips on blackbirds, feeding up on the first taken.

The ideal terrain for flying a sparrowhawk is countryside with large fields interspersed with hedgerows. Sparrowhawking is one of the forms of hawking where beaters are most useful and can become actively involved. Flushes should be engineered so that the hawk is on the right side of the hedge. If quarry puts in, it is no easy task to persuade a sparrowhawk out of a thick hedgerow when she can see her prey through a screen of twigs. If she ignores the fist, this is a prime occasion for swinging the lure into the fist so that she may be ready for the reflush sooner, without the delay of making in.

Taking into account the problems of timing slips and sticky-footedness on the fist, and adding the necessity for a downwind slip off the fist if any success is to be achieved in a stiff breeze, it is not altogether surprising that an alternative method of slipping sparrow-hawks, or, more accurately, their cousin the shikra, was devised in the Far East. This is termed 'throwing'. This is not a misnomer, for the hawk is picked off the fist, held in the palm of the right hand and thrown like a dart at the quarry. Surprisingly, sparrowhawks rarely object to this manhandling, even on the very first occasion. A soft glove should be worn on the right hand to protect her plumage. The austringer can both time the slip and give initial impetus through the power of the throw, which is particularly useful if the quarry breaks upwind. It is not a method which should be used for every slip as it will eventually take its toll on the hawk's plumage. However, on windy days, if the hawk is being repeatedly beaten by flights into wind, it is one way of redressing the balance.

Without the luxury of beaters, the austringer will find the task of achieving slips much harder. He can walk through root crops and around the edges of suitable fields in the hope that slips may occur fortuitously, but eventually he will be forced to resort to beating for himself. With sparrowhawk on fist, he will quickly learn that all potential victims will slip unsportingly out of the far side of the hedge, whilst the sparrowhawk malingers on his fist, unsighted. The obvious solution is to find a hedgerow with a suitable perching point, from which she will be able to cover both sides of the hedge. By beating towards her it is then possible to engineer flights. Whilst this may result in kills, it also unfortunately results, in time, in a hawk which will start to show too much independence for comfort and head off to another vantage point some small distance away if action is lacking. An *Accipiter* which goes self-hunting is an *Accipiter* which is all but lost, for it is a habit which is extremely hard to break. The austringer is therefore well advised to resist the temptation to initiate deliberately flights from trees because many will occur incidentally during the course of an afternoon's sport.

Flights from trees can result in a spectacular stoop, while slips off the fist will be decided by the comparative speed of pursued and pursuer. When she is on a kill, the austringer

Throwing a sparrowhawk.

should lose no time in making in, for, thrilled with her success, she will be initially concentrating on despatching her victim for fear of losing it. If, however, the austringer stands back at a discreet distance until she occupies herself with the pleasurable business of plucking, she may, on his approach, decide that she would rather feast elsewhere, minus audience, and proceed to carry her prize in the opposite direction. Titbits of a juicy nature should always be proffered from the finger tips when making in, so that she looks forward to the approach in expectation of this reward. All *Accipiter*s are touchy and easily upset, either by their own shortcomings in the field, or by some unfortunate incident, such as a tractor looming into view at a sensitive moment. All austringers, therefore, develop tricks to persuade their charge out from the top of a tall tree where she is spurning any advances. It may be that a stone tossed into a clump of nettles will encourage her to leave her lofty perch to investigate, or that a well-garnished lure of a feathery nature, hurled upward inches from her feet, will tempt her to grab it and come to earth. No matter how recalcitrant she may be, she will be vastly worse the next day if left out overnight.

It is possible, though by no means essential, to work a dog in partnership with a sparrowhawk. A dog must work very close at hand and not be so fine-coated that it fears thorns. The late Jack Mavrogordato recommends the Clumber spaniel as the breed most likely to fit the bill, being both persevering and biddable by nature. It can also be taught to point.

THE GOSHAWK
(*ACCIPITER GENTILIS*)

The goshawk enjoys the reputation of being one of the fastest and, potentially, the most lethal of trained hawks in the field. This reputation is richly deserved, but for every trained goshawk which performs with distinction, there are two more which do not. This is nearly always the fault of the inexpert austringer who has neither the knowledge nor the ability to condition his hawk correctly. To reach their full potential, goshawks must be flown far sharper than any other species of hawk. This is the first step at which the inexperienced austringer is likely to falter. The second lies in his own early expectations of his hawk, which are generally far too high. The very best of goshawks can indeed outfly a pheasant at full stretch and bind to it in mid-air, but even the most optimistic austringer should not expect his hawk to perform such a feat during her early days in the field. Like any broadwing, she will need to be given a relatively easy chance when first being entered and this will need to be followed up with plenty of good opportunity at a variety of game, so that she may gain experience.

Sharpness should not be confused with yarak, although the one is not possible without the other. Goshawks are easily offended, unless they are the most amiable of imprints. Whilst they may be at a suitable weight on any given day, they will still require a period of carriage on the fist, prior to being flown, to bring them fully into yarak. To fly her when she is not in yarak is foolhardy, and risking her loss. True sharpness is often a state which is never reached by the trained goshawk, for she will give a good impression of being keen whilst still too high in weight. At this higher weight she may fly the easier quarry species with enthusiasm, but refuse more difficult flights, meanwhile successfully convincing the austringer that she is irrevocably wedded to this easier prey. This is not to say that the goshawk should be reduced in weight with other than extreme care and over a suitable interval, for, if she is pulled below her best flying weight, or is brought there too quickly, she is likely to suffer from a low blood-sugar level and may throw fits and die. It is because of this necessity for accurate weight control that the goshawk is not a hawk for a novice – too fat and she will be easily lost, whereas too low and she will be so sharp that she will be on the verge of expiring. Such is the nature of this, the finest of all shortwinged and broadwinged hawks.

The range of quarry which a goshawk is capable of taking is impressive. In the UK, they are flown at rabbit, wild duck of many different species, pheasant, partridge, squirrel, moorhen, hare for females, stoats, weasels, pigeon, rooks, crows and many others, even, on rare occasion, geese and red grouse. An eyass, with proper conditioning, should be persuaded to take a cross-section of quarry species without prejudice. Passage hawks are more complicated because they will have had opportunity in the wild to establish preferences and may be irrevocably disinclined to pay attention to the quarry the austringer wishes them to consider. This occurs frequently in the case of the passage male goshawk and rabbit, for the vast majority prefer feathered game which will not give them such a tussle on the ground. The austringer must therefore discover the strengths and weaknesses of his passage hawk by trial and error. Goshawks vary enormously in their ability and persistence but the skill of the austringer, and the variety of opportunity which she is given, will play a large part in determining her progress.

Like a sparrowhawk, a goshawk should not be carried for hours at a stretch in order to man her until she will feed off the fist. If forced to endure the austringer's presence before this juncture, she will grow to loathe him. Once she is flying free it is inadvisable to exercise her repeatedly from trees. Recalling from trees will happen often enough during the course of flights at quarry. It is better in the early days to slip her off the fist for, if she once becomes convinced that she is only successful on slips which initiate when she is in a tree, she will be loth to leave the tree tops to return to the fist. An imprint, however, may follow on like a broadwing, if encouraged.

Telemetry is essential for, although austringers have been successfully retrieving goshawks without it for many centuries, it will save an inordinate amount of time if the individual is one which is prone to going astray. The necessity of using telemetry is often determined by the fitness of the austringer, for a goshawk in yarak in well-stocked countryside will cover a great deal of ground very quickly. The slothful or unfit austringer, arriving on the scene too late, will

Immature goshawk.

often find that his hawk has already left, having taken on another slip. Such a pattern of behaviour is tantamount to loss of control.

Whilst austringers become fully fit chasing goshawks, goshawks become fully fit chasing quarry. There is little that the austringer can or should do to get a goshawk fit before entering her. Speed of entering is of the essence and rehearsal will only allow time for bad habits to set in. If an individual proves difficult to enter, a dead pheasant tied to a creance and thrown over the branch of a tree, where it can be jiggled up and down in mid-air, generally serves to incite her interest in the real thing. However, just because she is a goshawk, there is no excuse to overface her too early and she should not be expected to make two kills in a day until she has taken her first ten head or so. By that stage she will have learned that she is going to be fed up on kills, not ripped off them and put straight onto another slip.

If properly conditioned, there is little reason why goshawks should live up to their reputation of regularly taking stand in a tree for hours on end. Should one show a tendency to do this, the austringer, as with sparrow-hawks, will have to develop his own tricks to get her down. Often, the quality of the offering on the fist is a deciding factor. A whole quail, from which she is allowed a few good mouthfuls every time she returns to the glove, will prove far more tempting than a soggy chick leg. If she will only come out to the lure, it is a shame, but so be it. Persisting in attempts to force her to come to the fist will only waste time. Goshawks are highly prone to taking a dislike to particular strangers, who should be asked to leave the field if she takes stand.

A goshawk is fast enough to miss a rabbit, touch down, then pick herself up and overhaul it again. Sprinting comes naturally, but it is persistence which will have to be learned. Once she has discovered that she can demoralize game and put it in, even if she cannot overhaul it in flight, she will achieve many more kills, for she will either take it in cover, if she can see her way clear, or she will take it on the reflush. Males are nimbler and better able to contend with prey which jinx. Females are the heavy artillery and should not refuse cock pheasant or hare in their immature year, although they may, particularly small females, refuse them in subsequent seasons, as they lose the exuberant optimism of youth.

An austringer should always allow a goshawk with a little experience to develop her own techniques. Stalking prey, particularly on misty days, is a favourite ploy of goshawks and the austringer should leave her to it or he will spoil her chances and she will resent him for it. On other occasions, she will require prompt assistance, perhaps to reflush, or to despatch a struggling and troublesome victim. For a true partnership to develop, the aus-tringer must make an effort to understand her tactics and requirements, just as he would wish her to consider his.

To improve a goshawk over and above what has already been discussed, one can only add hood training, which is a distinct advantage, whilst not being essential, and a good dog – a German short-haired pointer or similar – which will point and work cover and must be introduced early. In the company of a first-class goshawk, the austringer is likely to find that hawking with any broadwing pales by comparison. If, however, he is deficient in either time, ability or patience, he would be better to stick to a Harris hawk, which will provide him with the sport without the stress factor.

THE BLACK SPARROWHAWK (ACCIPITER MELANOLEUCUS)

In many respects, including size, the black sparrowhawk is like a cross between a European sparrowhawk and a goshawk. A female can take all the feathered game that a goshawk can and males, whilst they are not keen on cock pheasant, will take a good cross-section of smaller birds, including doves and magpies. At home, if kept on jesses, they show a marked tendency to suffer from leg problems because they are hyperactive and they are far worse if they miss a day's flying. Wide anklets and a bumper leash should therefore be used. Their tail feathers are particularly vulnerable, so loop perches and tail sheaths, fitted at all times when the hawk is not being flown, are essential. The alternative is to keep them loose – not in a chamber with a netted roof, on which they would completely wreck their feathers but in a loose mews or suitably

Black sparrowhawk.

she is responding to the fist, she will not allow herself to be taken up each day.

Hood training, unless effected while the hawks are large downies, usually has to be late-stage, as they will rarely tolerate the approach of the bare hand whilst still being manned. Hooding is extremely useful, if not essential, for in the field some will not sit still on the fist bareheaded. Unless they can be flown out of hood, therefore, the austringer has little option but to put them up into trees and beat towards them. They are less inclined to sulk than goshawks and, if something minor upsets them, they quickly recover their good spirits. Neither do they need to be cut as fine as a goshawk in terms of weight.

In the field they are really wasted at ground game. The males are not equipped for rabbit and, if they fly them at all, they usually refuse to bind; females may take them on occasions. After feathered game, they are very quick, very persistent and will take on long slips. Often they do not climb after quarry, but persist at ground level for as long as they can keep the quarry in sight, keeping pace and awaiting the put in. Whilst they are exciting hawks to fly, only austringers who have wide experience with other *Accipiter*s are likely to be able to manage them. It takes a number of seasons to make real sense of a black sparrow-hawk and, meanwhile, the physical problem of keeping her in good condition has to be contended with.

adapted shed with a solid roof. The tail sheath should still be fitted as a precaution and, obviously, a hawk cannot be kept in this manner until she has been properly manned and has undergone early training whilst being kept on a loop perch. This is because, until

PART III
LONGWINGS

11 MANNING AND TRAINING

To train a longwing, a falconer requires certain practical skills. Hooding, making in and co-ordination with a swing-lure can be partially taught, but equally are perfected by experience. For this reason a falconer's first longwing is usually spoiled in part.

MAKING TO THE HOOD

It is essential that a longwing is hooded right at the very start of training, for if she is first manned bareheaded, the task of introducing the hood at a later stage is extremely difficult and she may never take it well. The hood should be fitted when she is first equipped, so that she may be taken up wearing it. It is inadvisable to use a smart hood at this stage as she will almost certainly spoil it by scratching. Getting her to stand on the fist hooded is rarely a problem, although some longwings puff up their feathers, clench their feet and hiss, and it requires a little time to persuade them to stand up properly. A longwing should be well made to the hood within the course of the first day. At this stage, being hooded will, to her, be preferable than being bareheaded, for when hooded, the falconer 'disappears' and she therefore feels safer. The hood should be left in place for the first hour or so whilst she is carried and becomes used to riding the glove and to the feel of the falconer's presence in her immediate vicinity. Before removing the hood for the first time, the falconer should settle himself in a dimly lit room, with no distractions.

It is a counsel of perfection when training a longwing to take her right through to the stage of flying free without her once bating from the fist. In reality, this is not easy to do and is rarely achieved, but the falconer should have this goal firmly in mind before he starts and do everything possible to pre-empt a bate. When the hood is removed for the first time, the braces should be struck smoothly and not so wide that the hood immediately falls off; it should be left in place for a few seconds before its removal, in case the longwing develops the habit of shrugging off the hood the minute the braces are loosened. When the hood is lifted off the head for the first time, by means of the hand on the top knot, it should barely come clear of the tip of the beak before it is dropped back onto the head. There is no necessity to draw the braces immediately, as this tactic of removing the hood for a few seconds initially, then for increasingly longer intervals, is going to continue throughout the next hour or so. Meanwhile, the hood only needs to be drawn periodically. Assuming that her first brief glimpse passes smoothly, the hood can be left for 20 seconds or so, then removed again, lifted just clear this time, but replaced swiftly and gently. If she bates out of the hood the second it is lifted clear, it is a great pity but she must be hooded again as quickly as possible, preferably after having been assisted to regain the fist. If she will not regain the fist, she will have to be cast in order to be hooded. She should then be alternately left hooded on a block and carried hooded for some hours, to become accustomed to the hood before the next attempt is made. It is

1) The hawk should be sitting comfortably on the gloved left hand, facing the falconer's right shoulder. The hood is held by the top knot, with the opening of the hood facing the hawk.

2) The hood is put over the hawk's head, care being taken to keep the gloved fist absolutely still.

3) Using the mouth and the right hand, the braces are drawn.

4) The beak opening should accommodate the hawk's gape.

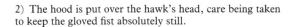

only one longwing in twenty which will behave like this – usually a prairie, saker or gyr. The vast majority will be accepting the hood readily and spending brief intervals bareheaded on the fist, without bating, by the end of the first hour. When she will tolerate the hood being taken off for 30 seconds or so, then replaced and the braces drawn, she should be blocked out on the lawn, hooded, to find her feet on a perch. When left hooded, she must be checked at regular intervals.

At this juncture it is worth mentioning common faults of novices attempting to make their first longwing to the hood. Apart from the aforementioned and ruining reluctance to make their longwing to the hood at the proper time, they also tend to be heavy handed with the hood itself. Hoods must be handled by the top knot only, never clasped with the fingers around the side panels or they will be crushed uncomfortably against the longwing's head. The braces must be struck and drawn smoothly and with even pressure on both sides. If jerked, her head will be snapped sharply to one side. The hood must be sitting square, and tipped back far enough by the fingers, before the braces are drawn. If it does not fall immediately into the right position, it can be corrected by means of the finger and thumb of the right hand easing it back by applying pressure between the top of the beak and the top knot. It can also be squared up by moving the top knot. When drawing the hood, the falconer must have his own head sufficiently far enough behind the longwing's neck so that the braces can be pulled in a smooth line. If he attempts to draw the hood when his hand and teeth are too far forward, the hood will be pulled out of position and may pinch the longwing's neck. One such error is sufficient to render a longwing hood shy.

FEEDING OFF THE FIST

Later in the same day, she can be offered food off the fist. Longwings do not require the percentage of weight loss during training that shortwings and broadwings require. They can often be persuaded to feed on the fist at the weight at which they are taken out of the aviary. Progression with a longwing can, and should be, rapid, for with the advantage of hooding, the falconer can miss so many of the awkward stages of manning intrinsic in training a shortwing or broadwing. Consequently, it is possible to get most longwings to the stage of flying free in two weeks. A longwing at this stage should never be carried more than a single pace bareheaded. Before being offered food, she should be weighed. This should always be done indoors, for she should be reversed onto the scales hooded, complete with swivel but minus leash. If she should bate and fly hooded outdoors, she would climb and keep going for as long as her strength lasted, being unable to see where to land. To reverse her onto the scales, or indeed onto a block, her tail should always be lifted over the surface of the perch with the right hand. With her feet positioned so that the back of her legs are touching the perch, she will step back. As she is hooded, to weigh her should be a simple matter. To take her up again, the gloved hand should be slotted between her tail and the back of the perch and pressure applied to the back of her legs. When food is first offered to her on the fist, the falconer should settle himself comfortably, without the risk of interruption, and remove the hood, having first placed the food in the gloved hand. If she is persuaded to eat, she should not be given too much – half a crop at most or she will not make progress the next day. If she refuses food for half-an-hour, she should be left hungry until the following day. At this stage, when she is put into the weathering for the night, she should be left hooded until dark. At night, it is important to leave her sitting on the block without a bate so her hood should be struck then removed with arm at full stretch as the falconer is exiting the weathering.

STEPPING UP

Having fed on the fist, the next day's lesson should be stepping up for food. As the falconer re-enters the weathering on the

Immature lanneret feeding on the fist.

following day, she is bound to bate, but, provided that the weathering has been carpeted to protect her plumage until she is properly manned, she will come to no harm. Having been scooped up, she should take the hood without too much difficulty if one is fortunate. She should be given a short session of manning, with the hood being taken on and off in different places to accustom her to the falconer's environs, but at no stage should she be walked bareheaded. Later in the day, after being weighed, she should be offered food off the fist once more indoors. Assuming that this is her second time of accepting food, she can then be asked to step up for it. She should be

reversed carefully, in mid-feed and therefore bare-headed, onto a suitable perch, placed at a height so that she is level with the falconer's outstretched glove. The falconer must keep a firm grip on the leash, by wrapping it around his ungloved hand. Having stepped back, she should carry on attempting to feed. It is usually a simple matter to manoeuvre her onto the fist by gently raising the gloved hand in such a way that she will put up one foot to hold the meat down. The other foot will follow if the glove is lifted slightly and she will

137

have stepped up for the first time. This exercise should be repeated half a dozen times, allowing her a few good bites each time she completes the operation. After she has consumed a suitable ration, she should be hooded to return to the weathering.

There is no merit in getting a longwing to jump to the fist at this stage in the manner of a shortwing or broadwing. Jumping is an alien action to her and one which can, if insisted upon, hold up progress needlessly at this stage. During the entire course of her training and subsequent flying at quarry, there will never be a time when it is essential that she should jump to the fist. Later, when she is fully trained, she will probably jump up for a pick-up piece anyway. The following day she should be approached with a pick-up piece. She may not yet be tame enough to approach in the weathering without a bate, but a quick bite when on the fist will remind her to look for food when approached the next time. After one more session of stepping up, during which the response should be quicker and she should be leaning forward in anticipation, she should be given the remainder of her rations tied to the swing-lure and left with her in the weathering.

INTRODUCTION TO THE SWING-LURE

The falconer's presence is not required during introduction to the swing-lure. If left to her own devices, she will see the food and go down to eat in her own time, leaving the lure to be removed later when she has finished. The alternative method, of putting her on a creance for the introduction to the lure and crouching nearby whilst she makes up her mind whether or not to go down onto it, is a waste of time, for having introduced herself to the lure unencumbered by the falconer's presence, she will recognize it the following day and will jump down onto it far more readily. As a precaution though, the lure should be pegged firmly in the weathering in such a way that she cannot carry it up to the block to feed, lest carrying becomes a habit.

CALLING OFF

During this interval, her weight should be reduced steadily. She will be becoming manned by degrees as her desire for food encourages her to overcome her nervousness and the hood protects her from anything which may potentially frighten her. The day after she has been permitted to introduce herself to the lure, she can be asked to jump down onto it in the falconer's presence. After weighing, she should be given a bite of food on the fist and tied by her leash to an outside block perch in a quiet spot. It is inadvisable to put her onto a creance just yet. The creance is more likely to get tangled than a leash at this stage and will give the falconer one more thing to worry about as he attempts to secure it whilst making in.

On a long leash, the longwing should have the lure dropped a short distance in front and to one side of her, so that she is not asked to come directly towards the falconer. As always, she should be asked to come into wind, not crosswind or downwind. Seeing the lure, well-garnished, she will recognize it as the object from which she received a good bite to eat the previous day. She should bob her head with immediate interest, but the lure will need to be given a few encouraging tweaks to attract her attention. At this point, the falconer should not stand up and tower over her, but should sit at the fullest extent of the lure line, as still as possible. The lure should be tossed towards her, not swung and dropped out, as this, at such close proximity, would frighten her. If she should refuse the lure, she is insufficiently keen, for she knows what it is and that she will get food if she goes down; she is just not prepared to risk it in the falconer's presence. She should be picked up and left until the following day when her appetite will be sharpened. When she does finally decide to jump down, it is usually not straight onto the lure, but to one side of it, whereupon she will jog diffidently over to the lure and give the meat a cautious peck. Generally, she will try to pull the lure away from the falconer, but all such attempts must

Making in and stepping up.

be resisted firmly, or she will take the lure up to her block and then be impossible to pick up. By keeping the lure line taut and tweaking it gently, it should be possible to persuade her to climb onto it and hold it down to feed.

Once a longwing is feeding from the lure in the falconer's presence, it is the falconer's task to make in and pick her up, by exchanging the food in the fist for the food on the lure. This must be accomplished without causing the longwing any alarm whatsoever, or the attempt will fail. With a tempting offering proffered in the gloved hand, which is held in front of the rest of the body, the falconer should inch his way on bended knee towards her whilst she is occupied with eating, meanwhile keeping the lure line taut by progressively winding it in. This can be accomplished by passing the line through the lowest fingers of the gloved hand to achieve tension and winding it around the stick with

the right hand. If the longwing stops eating and looks up at the falconer, he should freeze and wait until she resumes feeding. The whole business of making in, even for the first time, should not take longer than a couple of minutes. On reaching her, it is a mistake to try to take her up whilst the gloved hand is greatly extended, for the falconer will not have sufficient balance to pick her up smoothly. He should make in until he is kneeling right beside her and slide his garnished fist over the meat on the lure. If this manoeuvre is carried out with subtlety, she should continue feeding from the fist, unconcerned.

Picking her up at this point is then like stepping her up off a perch – a matter of slightly raising the gloved fist to persuade her to put up one foot to hold the meat down.

Some individuals have an annoying habit of stepping up with one foot, but leaving the other firmly locked into the lure and trying to bring this up onto the fist too. She must never be allowed to bring the lure up off the ground, or she is likely to prove hard to disentangle and may bate off with the lure. Instead, the talons must be individually unpicked with the right hand, until she is free to bring the other foot up onto the glove. Under these circumstances, the falconer will have no option but to kneel on the lure line to maintain tension.

The longwing should not be asked to come to the lure more than four times in any one daily session. Having eaten a little from the lure and the fist on each successive flight, balancing rations can, if they are required, be fed from the fist at the end of the session. The day after she comes to the lure whilst tethered by her leash, she can be put on a creance and the distance extended. If she is really quick to respond, this can even be done on the same day. The falconer will have to keep the creance taut as well as the lure line when she arrives on the lure and he is making in, lest she abandons the lure and flaps off on the creance. As soon as she is coming a distance of 15 ft or so, the lure can be swung and the whistle blown before it is dropped out. The whistle should sound as the lure hits the ground to one side of the falconer. The creance should be firmly under foot, for, if she is pushed too far too quickly, she may overshoot and must be pulled up gently by it. The lure should be swung in a backward circle a couple of times, stick held in the gloved hand and line looped through the gloved fingers, before passing to the right hand. The lure should then be dropped out at fullest extent.

If she does not come off after a few moments, this should be repeated, shortening the distance if necessary. A few gentle tweaks are nearly always needed to get her attention, until she is coming the minute the lure is dropped out. Just how far to call her on each progressive flight is a matter for the falconer's best judgement and it is not possible to lay down guidelines, as it will depend on how keenly she came off for the previous flight. Some longwings, having mastered the basics of being called to the lure, will progress so quickly that they are coming the full length of the creance within 3 or 4 days; others will take longer and will be in need of further manning and weight reduction.

When within reach of her during making in, little titbits can be given from the tip of the gloved finger to persuade her to welcome the falconer's approach. When she is coming further than 30 yd or so, the falconer can risk standing, rather than crouching or kneeling as she is called off. Many longwings will persist for quite some time in landing beside the lure, then hopping onto it. They can be encouraged to hit the lure by tweaking it as they fly towards it. Some longwings, particularly peregrines, are prone to chopping the lure so hard that they may either overshoot, then, it is to be hoped, attempt to turn back onto it, or they will carry the lure a small distance, necessitating the falconer running a few paces holding the stick to bring them down gently.

If she should ever overshoot, having either struck the lure and carried on or lost her nerve at the last moment and overshot without touching it, she will end up sitting on the ground, having been eased down by the creance. The falconer should cover most of the distance separating them cautiously, keeping the creance taut, then drop out the lure approximately 10 ft from her. Hopefully, she will run over to it and a potentially awkward situation will be overcome.

Meanwhile, her disposition should be improving and she should, by this stage, be coming up readily onto the fist for a pick-up piece prior to each day's session and be generally steady when bareheaded. She should also allow the falconer to clean her beak with his fingers before hooding her. This little courtesy will prevent the inside of the hood from becoming encrusted with food. When she is only coming short distances to the lure, there is no necessity to hood her between flights as she will still be eating her pick-up piece as she is carried back to the perch.

When she is coming more than 20 ft or so, the hood should be slipped over her head, though not necessarily drawn, as she is carried back between flights.

Rousing is important to her feeling of well-being prior to each flight and, when she is sufficiently relaxed, she should want to rouse and should be allowed time to do so both before being called off and, after feeding on the fist at the end of a training session, before being hooded.

If she is unusually slow to come off to the lure, it generally means that she needs to mute before she will fly. Sometimes a longwing will start to come before she is called. Whilst with a shortwing or broadwing, this is not a particular problem in so much as the austringer only has to raise his fist, with a longwing the falconer must get his lure out and onto the ground untangled if she is not to pass him by. For this reason, the lure should always be readied in the hands before the falconer puts any distance between himself and the longwing and whilst his back is turned. If he fails to get any distance from her, help must be sought from someone who can stand by her, while she is hooded on the perch, and remove the hood, left struck, when the falconer is ready. Such problems are short-lived, for if she is this keen, she is ready to fly free.

FLYING FREE

One of the major problems with preparing a longwing to fly free is that it is not possible to check if she will turn back to the lure, having flown past the falconer, whilst she is on a creance. Any attempt to get her to pass or stoop to the lure whilst on a creance will result in a tangle and the longwing being brought up sharp. If one is lucky, during the course of training her on the creance, she will chop the lure and turn neatly back to land on it. This gives the falconer a great deal of confidence, as she is likely to behave in similar fashion when free. If, however, she has occasionally flown over the lure without touching it and has had to be pulled up at the end of the creance, travelling to all intents and purposes

in a straight line, the converse is true; the falconer would then be best advised not to rush proceedings until she is behaving in exemplary fashion each time she is called off. More usually, she will merely come to the lure when called and land on it.

This is fine in so much as there is no reason why she should behave differently when free, but the big question for the falconer is, 'Will she turn back when I first fail to give her the lure, or will she continue in a straight line?' As soon as she is coming immediately the length of the creance, this question must be addressed.

The procedure should be to give her one flight on a creance on the chosen day, then promptly change her jesses and attach a transmitter before repeating the operation loose, which should go smoothly enough. The second flight is a different matter. To ask her to actually stoop to the lure would be a mistake, for she would be so confused that she might well lose momentum and end up sitting on the ground. It is better to walk away from her and allow her to follow. If she will do this without being called, so much the better, but she may need to be whistled or shown the lure to call her off. Under these circumstances, the lure should be hidden as soon as she is airborne. When the lure is not produced for her to land on, she will be confused and will fly past the falconer. Without asking her to turn too sharply, the falconer should blast his whistle when she is some little distance from him and, it is to be hoped, climbing. On hearing the whistle, her head will turn as she looks back towards the falconer. It is essential to throw the lure out to the same side as she turns her head or she will try to double back at a very awkward angle and may lose her nerve. She should then be allowed to take the lure on the ground in the normal fashion.

The next flight can be of longer duration. Having proved that she will turn back when called, the falconer can reasonably hope that she will circle him, awaiting the appearance of the lure. Many falconers start to get their longwings stooping straight away. This is not the best start for an eyass, who at this stage is flying the furthest she has ever flown on each successive flight. Stooping or passing to the lure requires co-ordination and control of aerodynamics which she will not possess so early in her career and consequently she may pitch. Although flying ground for a longwing should always be as open and treeless as locality will permit, she will always find something to sit on if she really wants to, including the ground. Once she forms the habit of pitching, it is very hard to break. In the early stages, it will make it extremely difficult to get her fit, as she will simply pitch to catch her breath. Later she may miss many opportunities at game, as she seeks out a perching point on which to settle and rouse before commencing her flight. Whilst pitching may occur for a variety of reasons, early stooping and confusion is a major cause. It is better first to allow her a week of flying free, merely to drift around, circling the falconer and exploring, while she gains a little muscle and learns to use the wind to her advantage.

In the first week, therefore, all the falconer has to do is to walk with her, into wind, judging the right time to call her in, when she has done a little work and her beak has just opened as she starts to pant. If pushed too hard, she will pitch. A game hawk should always be rewarded at the end of a session by being served with the lure downwind, in the same way as she will eventually be served with game. She may duck the downwind stoop at this stage, but, as her confidence and ability increase, she will take it properly. The falconer should also start to put her off the fist, rather than to call her off a perch. A longwing should never be cast off the fist when the hood is removed, in the manner of a shortwing, for she will probably want to rouse and to look around. She should therefore always be allowed to leave the fist in her own time, although, if she seems reluctant, she may be encouraged after a suitable interval to leave with a slight twist of the gloved wrist to tip her off into wind.

STOOPING TO THE LURE

As soon as she is flying free, the number of flights should be reduced to two, with a few minutes in between to allow her to catch her breath. Once this first week has been completed, the falconer can then teach her to stoop to the lure. The old adage for the training of longwings was, 'Never stoop a game hawk to the lure as it will queer her pitch'. Whilst one was advised to stoop a rook hawk hard to achieve fitness, game hawks were supposed to become fit merely by staying in the air longer each day. With passagers or haggards, this was not a particular problem – they already had muscle and the experience to enable them to gain height, stoop, pull up out of a stoop and ride the wind. With an immature eyass, fresh out of an aviary, to expect her to learn these skills merely by drifting around is asking too much and fitness will take a long time to achieve. How much better to stoop her to a lure at this point. It will not queer her pitch, for, once fit, she will learn to gain height through missing game from a lower pitch.

Below and opposite Through pass.

LURE-SWINGING

The aim of stooping a longwing is to get her fit and to teach her persistence. The falconer must place the lure in her path and then remove it or allow her to follow it through, whereupon she will lose it as it is twitched out of her way. She will then circle back to try again. The novice falconer must first put in a great many hours practising with the lure, for all the passes must be automatic by the time he starts actually practising with his hawk.

The first movement to master is the basic backward swing which links the passes together. With the stick held in the gloved hand and the line looped through the gloved fingers, the lure line should pass to the other hand and emerge from between forefinger and thumb of the right hand. With the right hand held at right angles to the body, the line should be of a length whereby the lure itself is suspended just above the ground. From here, it is swung by wrist action in slow backward circles. The falconer should be able to walk and circle to the left and to the right, maintaining the perfect circular action with the lure.

PASSES

There are four basic passes – the through, the cross, the ground and the overhead.

1) *The through pass* This is an underarm pass to the right-hand side of the body. The lure is swung forward and the gloved and right hand come together as more line is let out to accommodate the forward projectory of the lure line. The lure is then drawn back past the right-hand side of the body, with the hands separating to shorten the line. Finally, the lure is lifted out to the side and the backward swing resumed as the longwing loses the path of the lure and passes by. In the completion of this pass, the falconer's body should turn through 180 degrees as he steps forward with the left foot, then pivots, to end up facing in the opposite direction.

2) *The cross pass* Essentially the same, but this pass is to the left-hand side of the body. Most people find this easier as the backward swing after the pass can continue in the same line.

The above two passes will be reversed for left-handed people.

Above and opposite above Across pass.

3) *The ground pass* This seems simple, but care must be taken. The lure is dropped out onto the ground to one side of the falconer, but, on the longwing's approach, is tweaked sharply past the falconer in such a manner that the longwing cannot follow it, but passes it by at the point at which it was lying on the ground. Caution must be taken with this pass to ensure that the lure line is flat to the ground, for longwings will learn to anticipate this pass and will cut in in an attempt to secure the lure as the falconer is snatching it. The falconer who has been caught out in this fashion counteracts this ploy by leaving the lure still, merely pretending he is going to snatch it. If, however, the line is above ground level, the longwing may become entangled in it.

4) *The overhead pass* This is the most difficult to execute from the point of view of timing. The pass itself is performed by bringing together and raising the two hands as the circling lure is ascending. Thereby, the lure is projected skywards for a moment before being pulled down to fall into the back of the circle with the separation of the two hands. Whilst this pass is straightforward to perform in practice without the longwing, it is vastly complicated by the hawk herself, who is likely to be in the right place at the wrong time, unless the falconer is adept.

When starting a longwing on her passes, it is generally easiest to start with the cross and through passes first. Placing the lure for the ground pass too early on is a mistake, for she will believe you are offering the lure for her to take on the ground and is likely to put on the brakes. Which side she approaches and the wind direction will dictate which side the pass should be put out. The passes should be timed so that they are put as close as possible to her feet without her actually catching the lure. A good lure-swinger can get his hawk to extend her feet in anticipation of catching the lure on every pass. The sequence of passes should be put together so as to be as varied as possible and, once she is doing five or so stoops in one session, efforts should be made to include all the passes and to build up the number steadily day by day.

She must also be taught to catch the lure in

the air. This can be done by leaving the lure in the air above the head, instead of snatching it down in a pass. At no time should the falconer let go of the stick, for a fit longwing can carry a lure a long distance. Instead, she should be brought gently down to earth with the line on fullest extent. This is usually heralded by a long blast on the whistle, signifying that she can have the lure, but occasionally it is as well if she believes that she has 'caught the falconer out' by being given the lure purposefully on a pass. She then considers herself frightfully clever and will redouble her efforts again to take the lure prematurely. If she should genuinely catch the falconer out, she should always be allowed to have the lure, for if it is pulled out of her feet

Below Ground pass.

Overhead pass.

it will not only destroy her belief in the fairness of the exercise, but may also damage her feet. If she should pitch she should be recalled, but never rewarded immediately by being given the lure. Instead, she should be made to pass a few more times. If she is forever pitching, the possibility that her weight is either too low, thus weakening her, or too high, thus inducing laziness, should be investigated. This is where knowledge and skill in feeling breast bones is so important.

Lure-swinging is only a means to an end – it is not sport in itself. A longwing should never be held at this game so long that she becomes bored. Two weeks of stooping daily to the lure is usually adequate to get her fit and every effort should then be made to switch her onto quarry before she becomes lure-bound.

IMPRINTED LONGWINGS AND LATE-STAGE HOODING

Hooding is generally the first problem. Many imprints take a hood just as well as a parent-reared hawk, but some object to being deprived of the sight of the falconer and are consequently difficult to hood. Even worse are the longwings which have been rendered hood-shy by previous mismanagement. Late-stage hooding techniques are similar to those outlined under late-stage hooding (see Chapter 7) for shortwings and broadwings and include ensuring that, once the hood has been put on, the hawk is always rewarded with food after its removal. Small pieces of meat placed inside the hood and offered to the longwing will often teach her to lose her fear of putting her head inside the hood and thus it can be slipped over, but only left for a very short interval, without being drawn. Eventually, the pieces of meat will cease to be necessary. A hood which is too big will enable a longwing to overcome her fear of ill-fitting hoods and can be substituted at a later date for one which fits properly. With skill and careful consideration, a longwing which is bad to the hood can come good in time.

Imprinted longwings should never have food taken away from them during training, or tendencies to mantle, scream and carry will become exaggerated. This means effectively only calling off the imprinted longwing once a day, then allowing her a full ration. A screaming imprint can set off every other silent immature longwing on the premises. Mercifully, imprints do quieten down with good conditioning and with a few kills behind them.

HACKING

This useful practice is now restricted to those who live in suitable tracts of countryside, usually to those breeders who fly their own progeny and are prepared to run the risk of losing an eyass or two. Hacking involves placing an immature eyass in a mock eyrie before she can fly and allowing her a period of liberty in the wild whilst her feathers are completing their growth and hardening off. She can thereby learn to fly, gain a little muscle, learn about coping with the elements and even make early sorties on game before she is recaptured to take up for training. In this way, a hacked eyass is the next best thing to a passage hawk, by merit of her wider experience.

A shed with one side which opens should be positioned in a secluded spot, where the eyasses will be safe. A group of three or four eyasses is placed onto a nesting platform within the shed when their feathers are half-grown. The shed must be predator-proof and food should be given at regular times, through a hatch to prevent any risk of imprinting and tied onto a hack board so that the eyasses do not develop the habit of carrying. A hack bell is fitted, nowadays together with a transmitter with long-life batteries. Clip rings of different colours can also be fitted on the legs to facilitate identification

Over the ensuing weeks, the eyasses are permitted to branch out onto suitable perches inside and outside the hack house. Food is always made available. Soon they venture further afield and must be recaptured before they become independent. If one is seen making a kill, it is time to to recapture them. They will have to be trapped, under licence, with a manually operated bowtrap. One of the few drawbacks to hacked eyasses is that they will be familiar with pitching in trees, which may prove to be to their detriment. They also develop tastes in terms of quarry and switching their preferences can prove difficult.

12 FLYING OUT OF HOOD

ROOK HAWKING

Rook hawking is only a prospect for falconers who live in the right sort of countryside. The terrain needs to be vast and virtually devoid of cover. It is extremely tempting to attempt rook hawking purely because a suitable area lies within reach by car and can be visited periodically for hunting expeditions. This, however, invariably proves to be folly for, once having become wedded to rooks, a longwing will attempt to fly them even in the unsuitable countryside of the falconer's immediate locality, on days when he cannot travel to the rook hawking grounds and wishes merely to exercise her to the lure. Many a good hawk has been spoiled, for, although failing to catch rooks as she will in poor countryside, she will refuse to stay in good condition by stooping to the lure and will chase any way, leaving the falconer no choice but to travel daily or ground her.

A rook hawk is flown directly off the fist, out of hood. Once she is flying free, and even whilst she is on a creance, it is advantageous if the falconer can persuade someone else to unhood her and slip her. In this way, she will see the lure immediately the hood is taken off and will thereby become accustomed to responding to the flash of black wings the second the hood is removed. Casting a rook hawk at quarry tends to unsettle her and any advantage which might be gained by the initial and swift impetus is lost if she is unsighted. When stooping to the lure, she must be made to work hard. Forty stoops in one session without undue loss of breath is a fair target for her to achieve before she is entered. Rook hawking takes place in the autumn and spring, with spring rook hawking being more difficult and therefore leading to superior flights. Generally falcons are chosen to fly at rook. Tiercels can take rook, but only a small percentage make good rook hawks. Rooks can be very aggressive and will gang up on a peregrine which has made a kill and is on the ground. A falcon has a better chance of defending herself until the arrival of the falconer, although both tiercels and falcons have suffered injury from a flock of rooks under these circumstances.

Slipping at rook is quite an art and there are clear-cut rules which must be followed if the falcon is to make a kill. Firstly, the falconer needs to have a clear understanding of the way in which a rook will behave while being chased. If at all possible the rook will attempt to go downwind, for a falcon travelling downwind directly off the fist cannot gain the height necessary to do the rook any damage. Secondly, the rook will attempt to evade the falcon by taking advantage of any sort of cover which will conceivably offer it sanctuary. This can include hayricks, flocks of sheep, farm buildings and water troughs, as well as vegetation. Thirdly, even when pursued in open countryside in fair flight, rooks are past masters at the art of 'shifting' – twisting, turning and evading the stoop – and will use this tactic repeatedly, avoiding stoop after stoop until they reach the sanctuary of cover or the rookery. To combat these techniques, both falcon and falconer have to be tacticians.

The slip chosen to enter a rook hawk must be selected with particular care. Ideally, the rooks – not less than two or more than four – should be approximately 50 yd from the falcon. The falcon must be ready for the off, with hood struck. This will be the closest slip ever sought by the falconer for, once his falcon is flying rook, a longer slip will give her more time to gain a commanding position before she closes in. Short slips are a mistake, for the falcon will not have time to gain momentum before the rook turns downwind past her. If the rooks are slightly downhill, so much the better. The weather should ideally be a light breeze. Strong winds are very disadvantageous. The falcon is only likely to succeed if the flight initiates into wind, giving her time to gain height and dominate the rook. She then needs to 'shepherd' it downwind so that she can stoop.

Telemetry has made an enormous difference to rook hawking. In suitable terrain, it is possible to drive hell for leather after the flights. Rooks need to be stalked to get within suitable range. This can be done on foot or from a vehicle, but stealth is the name of the game. If the falcon flaps her wings at the wrong moment, the rooks will take to the wing. The falconer has to make an instantaneous decision as to whether the distance for the slip is too great or whether it is worth flying. An unsuspecting flock of rooks which has never seen a falcon before will sit well for a vehicle and the falcon can be slipped directly out of the window or sunroof. However, one needs a very large area of ground indeed to come across fresh rooks continually and those who see the falconer on a daily basis will become very flighty indeed and will quickly learn to recognize the car.

When slipping, there must be no rooks downwind or on the flanks of the ones the falconer wishes his falcon to chase, or she may take on a downwind flight instead. This is best ascertained by constantly travelling in search of rooks in an upwind direction. It is most helpful if the rookery is known to be upwind, for the rook is bound to try to reach

it, rather than turning downwind, and will continue upwind until sorely pressed by the falcon. Finding a suitable slip can take an inordinate amount of time.

It is essential that the rook is airborne before the falcon is slipped. Ideally, the hood should be removed as the rook takes to the air. Conditioned to chase black wings when the hood is removed, the falcon should leave the fist, after a moment to get her bearings. Initially, the fact that the rook, unlike the lure, is travelling away from her, and that the falconer is behind rather than in front of her, usually causes her to hesitate after a short distance in pursuit. She may well turn back to the falconer and await the lure. To avoid this problem, the falconer is best advised to take cover or lie flat on the ground. Such bizarre behaviour will only be necessary for the first few slips, until she starts chasing. The inexperienced falcon will follow the rook's path, but will soon realize that she must get above the rook if she is to stand a chance.

If she is only slipped at a relatively small number of rooks, she should have little difficulty in singling one out. It will be possible to fly at larger numbers when she is more experienced and has developed the ability to cut through the flock and single one out. It is also important to avoid flocks of rooks with other birds mixed in, for the falcon may check at the wrong species.

If the rook outflies the falcon into wind, and she tires or gives up before she climbs above and beyond her victim, she will be fairly beaten and will return in search of the lure. However, if she is properly fit and persistent by nature, she should, being the faster, beat the rook into wind and gain the height necessary to enable her to throw in a stoop. Seeing the falcon in such a commanding position, the rook will turn downwind and desperately seek cover. Meanwhile, the falcon will throw in a stoop which the rook will try to evade by shifting. The falcon will throw up once more and try again and a series of stoops will follow, ending either when she takes the rook or when the rook reaches sanctuary. The falconer must cover the ground quickly

Slipping a longwing.

and, if he is on foot, he will himself need to be fit. Circling or descending rooks will mark the point of a kill and the falconer, some distance behind, only needs to follow these hordes to trace his falcon on the ground. The falcon should be allowed to feed up on her first few rooks.

Some falcons do not make rook hawks. The best rook hawks are those which use their heads and develop their own tactics. The best flights are in the classic ringing style and occur later in the season when young rooks are strong on the wing, old rooks have completed the moult, and falcons are fully fit and enthused by past successes. The rook tries to outfly the falcon by circling up to gain height and the falcon follows, resulting in flights which go high into the air before one or other gives up. Slips can eventually include rooks on passage – already in flight and following a flight line. A good falcon will learn not to follow the rook directly, but to cut out to one side of it and take a different angle of ascent. Flights can cover many miles and, frequently, the rook will be taken within feet of the rookery. Any rook hawk will need to be sprayed regularly as rooks carry a great deal of livestock.

CROW HAWKING

Crows are more aggressive than rooks and can give a falcon, or particularly a tiercel, a rough time on the ground. Like squirrel hawking for shortwings, it is callous to risk one's hawk by deliberately pursuing a quarry which can do her so much damage. A crow on the ground will stab at a falcon and can cut her very badly around the eyes and beak; she may even lose an eye. Whilst the occasional falcon has been killed by mobbing rooks on the ground, crows have a far worse reputation and should therefore be avoided.

150

GULL HAWKING

Gulls will not put in until they have reached an area of water, no matter how distant. The larger gulls are easier to catch than the smaller ones, being less manoeuvrable. In flight, they will try to evade a stoop by dropping, but will twist and turn if pressed. A falcon will lose much of her advantage if she attempts to follow these twists and turns. A good falcon will climb once more, having stooped, and wait until the gull levels out or throws up, whereupon she will take it at the next attempt, when it has lost momentum. Flights in enclosed countryside are very unsafe as the falcon will soon be out of sight. Even though she may be found by telemetry, the flight will have been missed. When a falcon has choice of gull or rook, she will select the rook. In the southern UK, as gulls and rooks tend to feed in the same areas, it is hard to achieve any degree of continuity at gull. However, in Scotland it is easier to find gulls on their own and the sport is therefore more feasible.

MAGPIE HAWKING

Magpies are cunning. In full flight they are not particularly difficult, but to persuade a magpie to take flight in front of a longwing is not easy. They will let the longwing close in until she is ready to bind, then drop like a stone in front of her. If a bush is at hand, they will lodge in it so firmly that shifting them is exceptionally difficult and, even if they find themselves in the open, they will evade stoop after stoop, whilst systematically making their way closer to cover. For centuries, falconers have used a cast of longwings to combat the magpie's cunning. In theory, when avoiding the stoop of one longwing, the magpie tends to fly straight into the path of the other. In practice, the sport is now rare, for achieving a true cast is not easy. Both hawks must be trained to wait on if necessary, after slipping out of the hood, for they must frequently await the reflush over cover.

HEDGE HUNTING

Hedge hunting is one of the few ways in which a falconer who lives in enclosed countryside can fly longwings at quarry. It has really only become a possibility since the advent of telemetry as, before this equaliser, longwings were too frequently lost as they chased out of sight. Hedge hunting is the longwing equivalent of rough hawking and, as such, can employ a variety of different species. It will spoil a game or rook hawk, but beyond this proviso, tiercels not intended for greater things, lanners, luggers, prairies and suitable hybrids can be utilized. Hedge hunting essentially requires that a longwing waits on above the falconer, who beats hedgerows beneath her. She does not have to have a great pitch, but success will be partially determined by her height in relation to her position when the quarry breaks. A longwing which will wait on steadily at an optimum height of 30 ft or so, and which will stay tightly over the falconer, is the most likely to succeed.

Basically, the longwing should chase anything suitable which is flushed for her, be it pigeon, magpie, starling or blackbird. Quarry which lies on the ground can also be hunted in the same manner, such as woodcock or snipe. Beaters are helpful and can play an active role, provided that they limit their activities to times when the longwing is within sensible range and in a position whereby she will stand a chance.

A mixed bag can be achieved in the course of a season, including game birds. The falconer must, however, resign himself to the fact that his hawk will be frequently lost for long intervals and that he may fail to see many of the flights. However, for the ardent longwing enthusiast forced to dwell in short-wing country, this is the best possibility open to him, but it is not easy and the skill with which the longwing in question must be maintained must be consummate.

13 GAME HAWKING

The great mystery of game hawking for a novice is how to get a hawk to wait on. The simple answer is that most hawks learn in time through failing at a lower pitch. Those which do not learn are not cut out for the job and the falconer is better to cut his losses and try another individual. There are also naturally aerial hawks which drift up to impressive heights within days of flying free. Blessed with a hawk like this, the falconer is indeed fortunate.

It is a common misconception that a game hawk in training is taught to wait on by the falconer hiding the lure. This is not the case. If the lure is hidden, a falcon will merely circle the falconer awaiting its re-appearance. This is not waiting on, for true waiting on is when the falcon mounts to reach her pitch, then hangs high in the air, immediately above the falconer, only circling if she cannot maintain her position due to the elements. A game hawk in training has no reason to get height and will generally only go up at all if the elements lend themself to it on any particular day. This is why entering a game hawk is not easy, for initially she does not maintain her position over the falconer because she has never learnt to. She only learns by missing game then realizing that, if she had been higher, she would have been in with a better chance. Thus in the early days, the falconer only has split seconds when she is remotely in the correct position in which to call the flush.

All game hawks take time to develop and, if they have any real potential, they improve season by season. Hawks which are not good enough for grouse can often be flown successfully at partridge or pheasant, which do not need such a high pitch. Hawks which are top performers when flown at grouse should never be flown at anything else.

GROUSE HAWKING

This glorious sport deserves a book to itself, rather than a few pages. It is undoubtedly the most difficult form of hawking. However, it is this which makes it so challenging and rewarding. Peregrines, both tiercels and falcons, are the species most commonly flown at grouse.

THE HILL

Finding a moor on which to fly can, in this day and age, be both difficult and expensive. The returns from shooting grouse, with eight guns on a driven day, are obviously much higher than the return from hawking. Although it may be possible to fly on a driven hill when shooting has finished, it is too late to start a young falcon on grouse. Thus most falconers have to seek marginal ground, on which there are too few grouse for driven shoots and from which the landowner is therefore happy to see some sort of guaranteed return, albeit a comparatively modest one. The situation is further complicated by the grouse themselves. They are not, like pheasant and partridge, reared in game farms and put down on the land, for they eat fresh heather shoots and need a large expanse of heather on which to

Ready for the hill.

feed. As they therefore breed completely naturally, their numbers are never guaranteed and a moor which held a huge number of grouse one year may well have none to speak of the following season.

The hill itself is also critically important. As height is essential if a kill is to be achieved, wind and the lie of the land are most relevant. Ideally, for grouse hawking, one needs the wind blowing up the hill, so that the falcon can catch it and get lift. If the falconer takes a hill which faces in only one direction, and down which the prevailing wind blows, he is unlikely to be able to get his falcon going well. Conversely, there are hills, termed 'lift moors' which give the falcon an extraordinary amount of help by naturally providing winds which take her up to a very respectable height with the minimum of effort on her part. Such hills show off both falcon and falconer to their distinct advantage, but woe betide the falconer who regularly flies over such ground and is then invited to 'guest hawk' on a less advantageous hill, for his falcon will struggle to gain height, or not bother. If a moor is to produce good sport consistently, it must be well managed – heather burning to get rid of woody old heather on which the grouse cannot thrive, gritting to aid their digestion and vermin control are essential and have to be carried out by an experienced keeper. Any moor which has been neglected is not a good prospect.

DOGS

Grouse hawking is not possible without dogs. When tucked into the heather, grouse cannot

153

Dog on point.

be seen by the falconer, so a dog which will point is essential. The pointer must be trained in exemplary fashion and be under perfect control or it will spoil flight after flight. 'Good dogs make good hawks' is never truer than when it is applied to grouse hawking. Falconers can either beg, borrow or hire pointers annually, or they can buy their own. It is obviously not possible to train a pointer on grouse in the south of England, so a puppy purchased by a falconer who cannot train his own dog will have to be sent to a trainer. It takes several seasons for a dog to become reliable. Unreliable dogs can single-handedly wreck a season's hawking and they are no respecters of the time, effort or money which have been committed to the whole operation. As the dog may have to cover a great deal of ground before finding a point, the breed chosen must naturally be wide-ranging and quick. English pointers and setters generally fit the bill better than German short-haired pointers or wire-haired pointers in this respect. Ideally, dogs should be light-coloured, for it is commonplace to lose sight of a dark dog in heather.

A pointer must be trained on hand signals as well as a whistle. It should turn, stop and drop on command. It must also be possessed of a good nose and be extremely steady on point. Flushing on command is essential for young and inexperienced game hawks, because the falconer will not be able to find the grouse at the split second he wants them up. As a hawk will often drift out of position, a dog must also stop dead when told, even in mid-flush, until the falcon is set once more. If the falconer wants to work crosswind or down-wind, the dog, even though it will naturally want to work into wind, must comply with his wishes. Obviously a dog must also be hawk-safe, although this is generally not a problem as there seems to be a natural empathy between falcons and pointers. It is also essential that the pointer only points grouse.

Dogs should respond to whistle and hand controls.

Backing a point.

A dog which points hare is a damnable nuisance and even if the falconer reads the dog correctly and realizes before he puts his falcon on the wing, it is still a waste of time and a constant source of irritation. It is a risk to have to be totally reliant on only one dog to provide sport and, if the falconer is flying more than two falcons, he will need a brace of pointers to provide points, for one dog would be overworked. It is often necessary to back a young and inexperienced dog with an older dog, to confirm a point.

ENTERING

An immature should ideally be flown at the opening of the season. Grouse develop very fast and if she does not learn the theory of catching them early on, she is most unlikely ever to get to terms with them. To explain grouse hawking, it is easiest to describe a perfect flight first, then to deal with the problems of achieving it.

The dog is slipped to range ahead of the falconer, quartering from side to side into

wind, whilst the falconer walks behind, keeping the dog in sight but not getting too close to the dog's line. When the dog goes on point, it is allowed a little time to settle and confirm, so that the falconer can ascertain whether the point is a genuine one. When he is happy in his own mind, as far as is reasonably possible, that there are indeed grouse there, the falconer positions himself, removes the hood, allows the falcon time to rouse and mute if she so wishes, then tips her gently off into wind. She begins to climb upwind quickly and efficiently, without wasting any time and always staying close enough for the grouse to be so intimidated by her presence that they will sit still, tucked into the heather. Meanwhile, the falconer 'heads the point'. This is most important as, in order to catch the grouse, the falcon must stoop downwind. To accomplish this, the grouse must flush downwind, for, if they flush into wind, the falcon will usually be beaten. By heading the point, ending up opposite the dog's nose, upwind, with the grouse lying between the dog and himself, the falconer can call his hawk over him in an effort to ensure that the grouse will choose, when flushed, to break downwind, away from the falcon, rather than to risk passing beneath her.

The falconer awaits the time when the falcon has climbed as high as she is going to go and is waiting on, hanging high above him, so that, as he faces the dog, he can see her over one shoulder, forming a straight line with the dog's nose. When she is facing into wind – for she cannot maintain height if she is facing downwind – but just about to turn, so that her head is round watching falconer and dog and she will see the flush, the falconer calls to the dog, which instantly flushes the grouse. The grouse turns downwind and the falcon rolls over and stoops. The dog drops instantly after the flush. The falcon closes in rapidly on the grouse and binds to it in mid-air, bringing it down safely into the heather. The falconer makes in and, after allowing her to take her pleasure on the grouse for a little while, takes her up onto the fist.

So much for the theory. In practice there are a million variables. The six main factors which vary and cause difficulties are:

1) Terrain
2) Weather
3) The dog
4) The grouse
5) The falcon
6) Humans (be it falconer or spectators)

At the start of the season, whilst the grouse with young birds in the covey are likely to lie well to the point and give the falconer time, his young falcon will give him little or no time to set up a perfect flush, as she will be circling rather than hanging over him and, initially, will have little height to speak of. At this stage, the falconer should head the point before slipping his falcon. From October onwards, it is the grouse who will give the falconer little or no time. They become jumpy and will often not lie to the point. Covies will join up and great packs of grouse will break one after the other until the falconer begins to despair of ever getting another point. It is all the more irritating as the falcon, by that stage, will be going so much better, but points are so much harder to come by.

When preparing to enter a game hawk, it is important to get her into a routine of weathering and bathing (if she wishes) in the morning, before being weighed and travelling to the hill at the same time of day. In the days prior to being entered, she should always be rewarded with a dead bird rather than a lure, thrown when she is travelling downwind, onto the ground – not up into the air for her to catch, lest she carries it. If she is being flown with other falcons, they should never be left on the cadge unattended, for awful accidents can occur if one falcon should crab another when hooded. A first-class telemetry unit, which can be easily carried on the hill, is essential. A spare hood should always be carried and a field leash attached at all times when the falcon is on the fist. Initially, one is aiming for two points per falcon per day, but one should finish on one point if she makes a kill. Later, from mid-September if she is going well, three flights per day will be feasible. It is always advisable not to overface an immature and, after a kill, she should not be asked for a second flight. In her second season, she can be asked to attempt to take a brace in a day if she is reasonably successful, but, if it comes hard to her, the falconer should rest contented with a single kill on any given day.

PROBLEMS

Having described the theory of achieving flights and executing the opportunities correctly, it is perhaps easiest to give the novice a broader view of grouse hawking by describing the things which can, and frequently do, go wrong.

CANINE VICES

Common vices include:

False points On hot scent (when grouse were at a spot but have recently left) or on hare or snipe.

Losing scent When grouse run in front, or round behind the dog, they can cause it to lose the scent when the falcon is on the wing.

Pegging grouse This is when the flush is called and the grouse is so transfixed with fear of the waiting falcon that the dog is able to snatch it and kill it.

Bumping grouse When dogs flush a covey accidentally due to poor scenting conditions or not exercising sufficient care.

Following the flight A badly trained or over-excited dog follows the grouse, regardless of whether the falcon is doing likewise.

Failing to react promptly when grouse have put in downwind If the falcon puts in a grouse, the falconer will need to get the dog downwind of the point where it put in as quickly as possible to go for the reflush, at the right time and when the falcon is in the right position. Over-excited dogs tend to run in too early or from an upwind direction and flush prematurely or take so long that the falcon tires or drifts off.

Not following commands This is a constant hazard, often associated with the foibles of the dog in question. The dog, for example, may chase hare, find water and take a long bath, fiddle about in reeds or bracken, run for miles, then find a distant point on the horizon, meanwhile missing large chunks of ground and assuming temporary deafness.

Standing too far back off points Usually a problem with young, cautious dogs, this results either in the falconer not knowing how far ahead the grouse are lying and possibly wandering into them inadvertently when attempting to head off the point, or in a delay when attempting to flush.

Pulling on the lead Very few pointers will walk to heel when another dog is working. Consequently, the falconer often finds his arms being pulled out of their sockets.

Clipping the dog's lead around a belt on the waist alleviates some of the discomfort and leaves the right hand free to give hand signals.

Going on false point when tired Dogs in need of a breather may false point to allow this.

Running in When a dog does not hold a point long enough, being unable to resist flushing before the falconer calls it.

Disappearing At times of stress or excitement, the falconer's first thoughts are usually for his hawk. Dogs tend to use such opportunities to slope off in search of another point.

THE TRIALS OF BAD WEATHER
Weather conditions also play their part.

Wet days Grouse are less inclined to lie to the point when the weather is wet. After rain, they sit with their heads up, drying off on top of the heather and are easily bumped by a dog.

Windy days Grouse go very wild on windy days and the scent swirls so that a dog has difficulty in pin-pointing them. Wind must be allowed for on flushes by getting the falcon further upwind than usual, to give the grouse more 'lead'.

Still days There is no scent to enable the dog to find the grouse on still days and whatever breath of air there is may well keep changing direction so the hawking party ends up going in circles.

Hot midgy days Moors yield a variety of flies and bugs which bite, bloodsuck and irritate. These are at their worst in very hot weather when walking is particularly arduous.

Mist and low cloud levels High moors are unflyable on days when the cloud level is low, due to poor visibility.

PROBLEMS WITH THE TERRAIN
The terrain itself can also pose problems.

Wet weather clothing for hawks.

Short heather This offers too little cover for grouse, which are prone to bump in such areas.

Long heather or deer/tussock/couch grass Walking on such terrain is murderous.

Bracken The scourge of hills, bracken is beloved by grouse which put into it whenever possible, knowing that they will be extremely difficult to find.

Gorges and wide or deep areas of water The falconer will have to cross these an unreasonable number of times in the course of the season's sport.

Ditches and drainage channels Grouse seek sanctuary in these and are then most elusive.

Bad slopes On days when points are hard to come by, grouse tend to be located finally on steep slopes with the wind blowing straight down them, making it very difficult for an inexperienced falcon to get height.

Sheep ticks Hills that are grazed often carry ticks, which are transfered from sheep to heather and thence to dogs and, sometimes, to falconers.

Wild peregrines These show up at bad moments and draw one's hawk away for aerial battles. Such conflicts can result in the loss of a falcon but more frequently merely spoil a flight.

Hen harriers Such birds flush covey after covey of grouse, clearing wide strips across the moor. One often shows on the horizon when the falconer has walked unknowingly in its wake for several hours, wondering why he has not had any points.

Kestrels Like peregrines, kestrels tend to show up at bad moments and may draw off a falcon which is prone to chasing them.

Surrounding shoots Neighbouring hills may draw away a falcon on driven days when beaters are active. It is definitely worth avoiding flying on such days by requesting prior notice of shoots. Non-resident grouse which are 'shot in', will aim to return home when flushed for a falcon.

Undulating ground On such ground, the falconer can lose sight of the dog. This is a particular problem when heading the point as he may not be able to see the dog to engineer the flush.

PROBLEMS WITH HAWKS

Lack of height At the start of the season, grouse may be mown down from a height of 40 ft. Some falconers content themselves with catching a few brace in this style, then finish their season after a couple of weeks without ever experiencing proper game hawking. To catch grouse consistently later in the season, a pitch of 200 ft or thereabouts is necessary for a falcon. Tiercels need to be considerably higher. However, there are always exceptional falcons which will regularly reach 600 ft and more.

Lack of fitness This is the fault of the falconer although, in the early days, it has to be accepted that a falcon will take at least a month to become fit.

Failing to chase This happens because the hawk is too fat or she knows she is not fit enough, whereupon she will start to chase in due course. It can also occur because she was served when she was out of position, or because she has become discouraged due to lack of success.

Wasting time when achieving pitch Falcons which wander off and take too long to reach their pitch provide opportunity for the grouse to bust. This is usually a trait of an overweight hawk. It also occurs with falcons which go downwind when leaving the fist, instead of into wind to gain height.

Failing to get into position Some falcons will wait on too far away, which is a weight-related problem, or over the dog, whereupon they are not far enough forward for the flush. Flagging with the glove or running into wind away from the dog and calling to her, will often help to bring her further forward. Deliberately flushing when she is out of position should teach her to wait on in the correct position.

Failing to bind Grouse are frequently lost when a falcon knocks them in but fails to bind because, if not badly injured or severely frightened, they will make good their escape before the falcon can regain position.

Losing grouse on the ground This is always very disappointing, but occurs often.

Failing to regain height for reflush Young, inexperienced and unfit game hawks tend to potter at a mean pitch awaiting the lure when the falconer is attempting a reflush. Many grouse, if not the majority, are taken on the reflush, so it is essential that the falcon should learn to regain height and position after a grouse has been put in or knocked down.

Being awkward on the fist This can include a variety of sins, such as biting the glove, jumping about, bating, gripping and struggling when the falconer attempts to strike the braces of the hood. Although apparently indicative of being overkeen, some game hawks get over-excited when at a perfectly respectable flying weight. They are just highly strung.

Chasing other species A falcon which checks at rooks, kestrels, snipe, etc. is a nuisance. It may, in the case of rooks, be a result of bad practice, but, in the case of kestrels and snipe, it is generally a habit which hawk slips into without fault of the falconer.

Pitching A surprising number of game hawks look to pitch before starting their ascent. Often it is the fault of the falconer, as a longwing only learns to pitch through accident, incident, or mismanagement. If there is a grouse butt nearby, or a tree, it will prove irresistible to a hawk which shows a tendency to pitch. It may not spoil the flight, but it is immensely irritating and embarrassing in company.

Lowering pitch at point of flush Made falcons show a tendency to lower their pitch instantly in anticipation as the flush is called, even before the grouse have got up. Later in the season for an immature, and with a fit, made hawk at any stage, it is therefore better for the falconer to flush the grouse himself by progressively creeping in when the falcon is in the right position. By now, she will be fit enough to remain set whilst he finds the grouse.

PROBLEMS WITH THE GROUSE

The behaviour of the quarry is obviously a significant factor.

Breaking upwind Earlier in the season, this is the fault of the falconer for calling the flush incorrectly. Later in the season, grouse will sometimes risk passing under the falcon, knowing that this may be their only chance of escape.

Running If the grouse run in front of the dog, they will cause it to lose scent or find it hard to pin them down. Cunning birds, later in the season, will run behind the dog so that it loses the scent altogether.

Not lying to point This is usually due to weather, familiarity or the lateness of the season.

Busting This may be with or without due cause, but is often due to the fact that the hawk has dropped below their horizon when first put off to gain height.

Putting in in front of the stoop When a grouse is hard pressed it will drop like a stone into the heather in front of the falcon. The falcon may attempt to follow it in, whereupon it will run, then break the minute she has lost height and momentum. Alternatively, the grouse will repeat the tactic on successive reflushes.

Jinxing Grouse are quite capable of standing on their tails and turning 180 degrees or shooting upwards, just as the falcon is about to make contact.

Old cocks These usually jump first and, consequently, are frequently and unsuccessfully singled out by an inexperienced falcon, who will then be outflown. They will also lead a covey to safety by busting before a dog can be run onto them or at an opportune moment when the falcon is out of position.

Surrendering Young grouse will sometimes put in on short or burnt heather where they have no cover and give up, allowing the falcon to take them so easily that she may be spoilt by the incident, for thereafter she will be tempted to search for other easy victims, rather than putting in a more worthy effort.

Blackgame Although grey hens may be taken without undue difficulty by an experienced falcon, near the start of their season, blackgame generally, and particularly blackcock, later in the season, may appear deceptively slow but are in fact extremely quick and will, when flushed, travel a great deal further than grouse.

HUMAN ERROR

The range of problems caused by human error cannot be eliminated totally, even with practice.

Bad flushing Flushing is a real art and it takes a novice a long time to master it. Expert flushing can result in a kill even when the falcon does not really deserve it. Conversely, bad flushing will spoil chance after chance, no matter how well the falcon is performing.

Misreading dogs It takes several seasons really to get to know a dog. When this happy state has been achieved, the falconer will not put his falcon on the wing unless the point is a genuine one. Before this, it is frequently something of a gamble.

Losing sight of the dog This happens through inattention, due to difficulties in crossing terrain or sometimes through lack of fitness. It can result in wandering into a covey accidentally when the dog on point had not been spotted.

Accidentally flushing grouse This can occur for a variety of reasons, including falling over and cursing on the way round the point. Noisy spectators are prime culprits in causing a covey to flush prematurely.

Putting up another covey inadvertently Although this is not the falconer's fault, it is most irritating if the falcon is on the wing and is drawn off to chase an accidental flush for which she was out of position.

Failing to establish the correct flying weight This is a fault of novices who often incorrectly believe that the higher the hawk's weight, the more independent she will be and consequently the higher will be her pitch. Although game hawks are frequently described as being flown in 'high condition', in practice they have to be maintained with care for, if their weight is allowed to creep up too high, they will waste time reaching their pitch and may not persist, even if the covey awaits their convenience for the flush.

SPECTATORS

Spectators should be well briefed and preferably be allotted to someone well versed in grouse hawking, who can keep them entertained during the slower moments but also control them during the action. Apart from the obvious problem of noise on the hill, spectators without adequate supervision are also prone to the following behaviour:

Getting in front of the dog This usually occurs early on, for all but the most hardy are usually too tired to manage this after the first hour or so.

Standing out on the horizon A couple of spectators, or even an individual, standing out like a sore thumb on the skyline behind the point during a flight, may well cause the hawk to wait on over them instead of over the falconer. All spectators must be briefed to squat down if the falcon appears to be drawn back over them. This is a common occurrence with inexperienced falcons which are easily confused. For this reason all spectators should, for such hawks, be taken round the point.

Becoming five-minute experts There are few things more annoying than receiving advice from someone who is on the hill for the first time, or even the second.

Getting cold/tired/bored It is generally highly inadvisable to take out someone who is neither a falconry enthusiast nor practises any other field sport.

Crowding a kill Given the opportunity, spectators tend to get uncomfortably close to a falcon on a kill, so must always be pre-empted until she has been taken up on the fist.

As the season progresses, dog, falconer and hawk adjust their behaviour to compensate for the gradual change in the grouse, as they become wilder. It is no longer possible to head, or partially head, the point before the falcon is put on the wing. When the dog goes on point, the falconer will only dare to move if the point is a distant one, lest he spooks the grouse. The falcon must be put off from behind the point and the falconer can only safely move forward under her cover. As she will be fit enough by that stage to allow for the time taken to get round the point, this does not represent a significant problem, although the exercise has to be executed with precision. The falconer will also learn about breaking the rules, if the situation dictates. If, for example, the grouse are lying on a very steep slope, down which the wind is blowing, it is better to flush them into wind, uphill. The falcon, with the advantage of height, will be more likely to beat them because she will be descending while they face a steep climb. There are good days and bad days, but, whereas the latter will outnumber the former initially, while dog, hawk and falconer struggle to become a team, the good days amply reward the effort.

PARTRIDGE HAWKING

Flushing a partridge for a game hawk is, in theory, exactly the same as flushing a grouse, for the same principles of positioning and stooping downwind apply. Partridge are not as fast as grouse and can therefore be taken from a lower pitch. The best hawks will not allow this to influence them, but there is a danger that a hawk which is given a full season on partridge first may never achieve a pitch high enough for grouse, having learned that she can be consistently successful at partridge from a comparatively low height.

Partridge are found on low ground. The two species encountered in the UK are the grey or English partridge and the French partridge, or 'red-leg'. Of the two, the grey is reputed to be faster. This is probably a *trompe l'oeil* effected by their smaller size. However, French partridge have the annoying habit of running before taking off, which can spoil a precise flush and may cause a falcon to lower her pitch or, at worst, attempt to take them on the ground. Wild partridge are prevalent in some parts of the UK, but, failing this, they can be put down successfully for the purpose of hawking. Well-spaced pens in open countryside can be used to introduce partridge to the ground. Early on, these birds do not fly as well as their wild counterparts and should therefore not be flown early in the season; later, when they have been at large for a month or so, there is little or no difference.

It is possible to fly at partridge without a pointer, for covies can be spotted at a distance with the naked eye or with binoculars. The falcon must be put on the wing and, once she has mounted over the partridge, the falconer must run into position. It is usually possible to get closer in a vehicle before putting the falcon off. Partridge are remarkably good at taking advantage of anything which can shield them from the power of the falcon's stoop, taking cover behind fence posts, in any vegetation, down rabbit holes, under a vehicle and even behind sheep if they feel really hard pressed. For this reason, really open ground is essential. Wire fences are extremely dangerous. With a steady dog used to working on low ground, the flights can be engineered exactly as for grouse, with all the same rules of wind, weather and precision applying. Without a dog, the falconer will have to be familiar with his ground and quick on his feet and the hawk may have to wait on for extended intervals until he manages to flush.

PHEASANT HAWKING

Pheasant hawking is a poor second-best to either partridge or grouse hawking. Pheasant are generally found in wooded areas which are unsuitable for flying a game hawk. Even if found in the open, pheasant cause many bad habits to occur in a hawk which is flown regularly at them. They run and will thereby tempt a falcon down from her pitch; they hide so well that a pointer, taking airborne scent, may run right over the top of them on the flush; and they are often found spread about in some numbers, so that the one which takes to the air first may well not be the one for which the falconer has positioned his hawk. A single pheasant will often flush at an inopportune moment and, even if a perfect flush is achieved, there is a danger of a falcon taking it so easily that she may realize that she need not reach a good pitch to take such game. It is a great mistake to fly pheasant too early in the season, for they will be taken too easily. As a quarry species they are heavy for a falcon and even more so for a tiercel; consequently, they may be more easily knocked down than put in the bag, for they are past masters at making good their recovery and then their escape.

In open areas where there is nothing else suitable to fly at, a falconer may be tempted to turn to pheasant hawking as a last resort, but it is folly deliberately to fly a good partridge hawk and particularly a good grouse hawk at pheasant.

DUCK HAWKING

Wild duck are easily flushed by a human presence when on a small area of water. A falcon, therefore, must always be put off at some distance from the water or behind the cover of undulating ground. When she has mounted, the duck will be reluctant to flush, particularly if they have seen the falcon on a previous occasion. The falconer may have a hard time putting them up, even with a good dog, but a few well-aimed projectiles will often serve his purpose. An experienced falcon will wait until the duck have travelled a short distance away from the water and are heading over open ground because, if she makes her move too soon, they will return to the safety of the water. A mallard can take a falcon a fair distance if she does not get in a good and telling stoop right at the outset.

Most game hawks will fly duck, but are inclined to become discouraged if the duck successively return to water before they can get on terms. The falconer must use his wits if he is to save her from refusing them after initial unsuccessful sorties and is best advised to find a couple of ponds with a large enough area of open ground between them to give the falcon a fair chance. As the duck will be in the habit of frequenting both ponds, they are more likely to risk crossing the open ground than to turn on their tail back to the pond from which they were flushed. When flying at duck on streams or dykes, the falconer must be quick to follow up the flight, for the duck singled out is liable to try to put in further downstream.

A longwing which is flown at duck should ideally be specialized. Apart from the fact that a duck hawk must be trained to wait on, the sport bears only a passing resemblance to the precision of grouse and partridge hawking, for it tends to be a more 'hit and miss' affair. Duck can be taken into wind or downwind and equally can outfly a falcon in either direction. Provided that she is not too far downwind, or that the wind is not too strong, the falconer may try to flush the duck regardless of the hawk's exact position in relation to the wind, as long as she has the necessary height, but his judgement of the situation must be accurate if his hawk is to continually take on duck. Large areas of water make duck impossible to flush and will result only in disappointment and frustration for both falconer and hawk. It is pointless to attempt to make a duck hawk with only a handful of ponds at one's disposal, for the duck will become wise and sport will soon be in short supply.

14 THE LONGWINGS

THE KESTREL (*FALCO TINNUNCULUS*)

The kestrel cannot, strictly speaking, be classed as a suitable species for falconry purposes because it hardly ever catches anything. It is certainly not a hawk for a beginner because its diminutive size renders it extremely fragile and vulnerable to any mistake which a beginner might make in weight control. Its principal use lies as a first longwing. A novice who has served his apprenticeship with a buzzard, and possibly with another broadwing, can learn the techniques of hooding and lure-swinging with a kestrel, in preparation for training a larger member of the longwing family.

Most kestrels are easily trained and, whilst some, when being asked to stoop to the lure, do no more than run a shuttle service from pillar to post, with only a single pass between pitching, others will put up an impressive performance and stoop enthusiastically. Kestrels rarely show any interest in quarry and indeed are rarely asked to, although a few take a variety of small fry, such as rodents. It is most unfortunate that kestrels are viewed by certain well-meaning parents as suitable hawks for their children because, whilst they can contribute to the education of a novice with a little experience, they are invariably killed or lost by any unskilled child in whose tender care they are unlucky enough to be placed.

THE MERLIN (*FALCO COLUMBARIUS*) AND LARK HAWKING

These engaging small hawks require an expert touch. They have a rapid metabolism and need to be maintained by someone with the skill and time to weigh, feed and preferably fly them twice daily. Weighing should be accurate to $1/8$ oz. A single hour can affect her weight and, consequently, her performance. Diet, too, is important. Merlins do not thrive on the ubiquitous day-old chick, which is insufficiently high in protein. Mice, supplemented with sparrows, are the ideal diet, although beef can be used on the lure. No casting must be given in a morning feed.

The training of a merlin is usually very quick, but none the easier for that, for over and above the problem of precise weight control, the falconer must be a skilled lure-swinger and experienced enough to inhibit the merlin's inveterate desire to carry. Although it is always useful, hooding is not essential because merlins quickly become tame and they are not flown out of hood. As soon as a merlin is feeding off the fist, she should, unlike other longwings, be taught to fly short distances to the fist. This is immensely useful later on in the field, as the lure can be swung up into the fist or she can be called a short distance directly to it when hastily regrouping for a reflush. When put onto a lure, of small and suitably coloured wings, garnished with beef, she will quickly progress to many stoops in a single session, provided that the falconer can keep up with her, for merlins are both quick and agile. When making in, particular

Merlin.

immature, because they have learned to be selective when choosing a lark and, perhaps lacking the *joie de vivre* of the immature, prefer to let her do the work of bringing down a ringer, only to take possession on the ground. Later in the season, when there are no ground larks to be found, they will take on ringers if flown on their own, provided that no easier option presents itself. Lark are first flown when the old ones are in the moult and the young larks have not yet developed their full powers of flight. It is not until September that the spectacular ringing flights are encountered. To be properly tested, a merlin should be flown over open downland, where a lark, not finding easy cover at hand, will generally choose the option of ringing up high into the sky in an effort to shake off its pursuer. Many more larks can be taken by pot-hunting in enclosed areas, i.e. flying at larks which will maintain level flight, seeking cover from which the falconer can frequently dislodge them. Like early grouse hawking, there is a vast difference in the quality of flight to be had, but the good falconer should always seek to test his hawk to her limits.

When a merlin has become reasonably well muscled through flying to a lure, she should be taken out in search of her first lark. She may still be stooped if time permits each morning thereafter. Most will slip at the first lark which is put up for them. The falconer should walk across stubble or grassland into wind, with his merlin on the fist, bareheaded. Downwind flights should be avoided, for the larks will tend to streak away low to the ground and the falconer will quickly lose sight of his hawk. A dog can be used to put up lark or, better still, a pointer which will not be spoiled by the activity may be used to point them. The countryside must be open and corn which is still standing should be avoided because locating a merlin which has killed in standing corn is like looking for the proverbial needle in a haystack. For a merlin, telemetry is used by most falconers, but some fear, particularly in the case of jacks, that even the smallest of lightweight transmitters will hamper their hawk.

care must be taken. If beef is on the lure, but a mouse or sparrow is proffered in the outstretched glove, the contest of possession should be easily won by the falconer. Later, on a kill, the merlin should thereby be in the habit of welcoming his approach and a bad habit will never be formed. Prevention is always preferable to cure. Merlins love to bath before flying, sometimes more than once a day.

A licence must be acquired to take skylark – the traditional quarry for merlins and easily the best by merit of their ringing flight. The season for lark hawking is short as larks are outflying all but the very best of merlins certainly by the end and often by the middle of September. It is therefore important when acquiring a captive-bred merlin to get one from an early clutch. It is arguable that merlins fly at their best in their immature year. Many intermewed merlins 'fly cunning', especially when being flown in a cast with an

Larks are usually taken on the ground. Ringers spiral up to several hundred feet, with the merlin spiralling up in a different air space, to one side. It is a contest of strength and perseverance. The one who climbs the highest wins. If the merlin gets higher than the lark, she will throw in a series of shallow stoops on it to drive it earthwards. After avoiding several of these stoops, whilst desperately scanning the ground for cover, the lark will plummet downwards and will be taken on the ground, unless it can find sanctuary. The falconer can play a key role in the reflushing of larks. The merlin should be allowed to pitch nearby or be called to the fist if this will be more advantageous. Some merlins refuse ringers. They may be prevailed upon to change their mind when flown in a cast with a merlin of better quality. A cast of merlins will both ring up and take turns to stoop the lark. If a kill results, the falconer must ensure that the merlin not in possession is well rewarded. Some squabbling is inevitable, but there is rarely any damage done. A merlin can be flown half a dozen times a day, but should always be fed up after a particularly hard effort. During the winter months, she should not be jessed, but should be turned loose into an aviary, preferably with a potential mate for company, for they may breed during the following spring. Lark hawking is a practical form of hawking for those who have demanding work hours, provided that they live in suitable countryside, for the season occurs when the long summer evenings can be utilized to full advantage.

Immature lanner falcon.

THE LANNER FALCON (*FALCO BIARMICUS*)

In the field, lanners have proved to be somewhat inconsistent. Those which have been tried at partridge have, for the most part, been found wanting and they are no match for grouse. Neither do they make good rook hawks. Their principal use lies in their potential for hedge hunting, wherein they can take a mixed bag as suited to their capabilities, in an opportunistic fashion. Of the sexes, the lanneret is generally the better performer, being more inclined to gain height and nimbler on the turn. However, some fail to show the necessary potential, so the falconer furbishing himself with an eyass expressly for the purpose of hedge hunting may well have to try several individuals before he finds one with an aptitude for it.

The following is the quarry record taken over two seasons by Murphy, an eyass lanneret flown by Stuart Rossell:

Lanner falcon.

Lugger falcon.

8 moorhen	1 starling
5 partridge	2 thrush
2 young crows	4 coot
1 magpie	1 snipe
5 pigeon	
1 blackbird	30 total

LUGGER FALCONS (*FALCO JUGGER*)

With rare exception, luggers have not proved at all useful in the field. They show less enthusiasm for chasing quarry than lanners and they are hampered by the softness of their plumage, particularly in their immature year, when, during inclement weather, they tend to fly like wet paper bags. In terms of temperament, they generally lack the easy-going nature of the lanner, being touchier to handle,

both in the early stages and after they are manned.

THE PEREGRINE (*FALCO PEREGRINUS*)

As the native large longwing of the UK, it is hardly surprising that the peregrine is by far the best suited to the various styles of hawking available for longwings in the UK. She is quite simply the best option for rook hawking and game hawking in all its forms. Although, as in all species, there is a vast variation in the ability of individuals, the very best peregrines more than merit the high esteem in which the species is held worldwide. From the falconer's point of view, the major skill with peregrines is selecting and assessing

Peregrine falcon.

Immature peregrine falcon.

the potential of each individual. A falcon which does not put up a good showing at game may well make a good rook hawk. No peregrine should be wasted and, if an individual acquired for rook hawking shows a tendency to go up and wait on, this hawk should be passed onto someone with the time and land necessary to make a game hawk. As captive breeding progresses, strains suited to a particular style of hawking are being identified. This is immensely useful from the falconer's point of view.

The hard-feather quality of the peregrine equips her well for inclement weather. All immatures should be entered early and worked hard at quarry so that they will bulk out with muscle and develop mentally. Hacked eyasses will obviously have the initial advantage but, mid-way through the season, the unhacked hawk should be putting up just as good a showing. The grouse season opens before the annual moult is completed, but the reduction of weight necessary to bring an intermewed game hawk into condition should not harm the feather growth; it will merely retard it. Consequently, it is not unusual for a game hawk to be put down at the end of the grouse season, still with her last primary to drop and none the worse for it. After the season, peregrines should be turned loose into aviaries.

Most peregrines do not reach their full potential until they are in their fifth or sixth season. If one should miss a season's flying for any reason, the resulting effect can be most damaging. It is therefore extremely important to have continuity of purpose when starting with a peregrine, knowing with absolute certainty that it will be possible to facilitate a

Prairie falcon.

THE PRAIRIE FALCON (*FALCO MEXICANUS*)

Prairies have not made a good showing in the UK. This is a pity as they do so well in the USA. It may well be that passage hawks, which are permitted to American falconers, are vastly superior and easier to manage, but the Americans also do well with eyasses. Alternatively, it may be that, in the USA, falconers may legally serve their hawks with bagged quarry. The giving of bagged quarry is apparently an art form of its own, by means of which the Americans can teach their hawks not only to chase and kill but also to persist, gain height and wait on. It is therefore not beyond the bounds of possibility that the indisputable success of the average trained prairie falcon in the USA is initially instigated by the giving of copious quantities of live pigeon. This is not in any way intended as a slur on American falconers, many of whose hawks fly to an extremely high standard. It is simply to illustrate the point that British falconers are not legally allowed to give bagged game and thus face an additional problem to overcome in the making of an eyass.

The British falconer tackling a captive-bred eyass prairie will find her, for the most part, to be uncertain-tempered and somewhat aggressive. Throughout the early stages, these tendencies will colour initial attempts to win her confidence. For the traditional British longwing quarries of rook and game, prairies are found to be lacking in aptitude and, for hedge hunting, which might be thought suited to their habit of pursuing quarry into cover, their turning circle will transpire to be too large to facilitate efficient serving.

Thus the British falconer has always been quick to return to the tried and tested peregrine, which undoubtedly better answers his needs.

THE SAKER FALCON (*FALCO CHERRUG*)

Here is yet another species which performs

proper season's hawking not just in her immature year, but in the years that follow. Someone who merely dabbles with the species has no chance of making a first-class hawk. However, the falconer who wishes to acquire his first peregrine, with the right motivation, is indeed fortunate to be able to follow in the footsteps of falconers throughout history who, armed with the peregrine, have been able to maintain a magnificent sporting balance between this universally celebrated hawk and her traditional quarries.

Saker falcon.

cannot be taken up until October, one is then faced with the task of entering an eyass when the wind and rain are bound to prove her undoing. Although her plumage becomes much harder after the first moult, immature feathering does not equip her adequately to cut through the wind in the manner of an immature peregrine and, in wet weather, or even if she should land in wet grass, she soaks up water like a sponge. Grouse and even partridge are beyond her by the time she is fit for entering at the end of October.

In training the saker needs to be cut fine and kept that way, for she will play up at the slightest excuse, having lulled the falconer into a false sense of security. She will be found to have a most equable temperament, but this is no substitute for performance in the field. Unfortunately, therefore, one has no option but to give categoric discouragement to any British falconer likely to give the saker his consideration. He would be far better advised to ally himself firmly with a peregrine.

Despite her lack of prowess in British falconry, the captive-bred eyass saker can play a useful role in the Middle East. Although passagers are vastly preferred, it is no more difficult to make a good hawk out of an eyass saker in the Middle East, flown in a suitable environment, than it is to make one out of an eyass peregrine in the UK. It is purely a matter of knowledge and technique. The Arab training methods are geared totally around passagers, which already know how to chase, hunt and cope with wind and weather. They also still retain some of their former muscle, developed before they were trapped. In contrast, the eyass needs to learn control in the air and to develop muscle, as well as the more obvious lessons to be learned through introduction to game. These attributes can be imbued in the young hawks through stooping to the lure. Although it takes longer to prepare an eyass than a passage hawk, the difference is not vast and it may be that the eyass saker can, through the adoption of European training methods, find more favour in some quarters in the Middle East in future years.

well in many countries, but which fails to produce good results in the UK. In the case of the saker, however, the reasons are much more obvious. Sakers migrate during the months of August and September and, in the spring, in April and May. If flown at these times, they are nearly always lost and no transmitter is necessarily going to facilitate their safe recovery. Between these months lies the worst of the winter weather. Assuming that, to be within the 'safe period', a saker

Immature grey-phase gyrfalcon.

THE GYRFALCON
(*FALCO RUSTICOLUS*)

The largest and fastest of all the falcons, the gyrfalcon plays an ambiguous role in falconry worldwide. Although they are highly prized, there are many problems associated with gyrs in captivity. Many of these are health problems, stemming from holding them in climates not suited to their physiology. Any environment which features warmth, dust or humidity is alien to them and can cause respiratory problems, in particular, aspergillosis. A high percentage of captive-bred gyrs die from this in their immature year and, consequently, falconers are increasingly reluctant to put them under the stress of training whilst immature, for fear that this may exacerbate the onset of the disease. Foot problems, too, are not uncommon when these large and heavy hawks are maintained on unsuitable perching surfaces, unprotected by Astroturf. If these problems of health can be managed through good husbandry, the falconer in possession of his first gyr to prepare for the field will find her to be a vastly different hawk to any that he has previously encountered.

Once a gyr has been manned, her disposition will be found to be inquisitive and wilful. The falconer will not be able to force her to do anything she sees no point in doing. She is easily thrown off her stroke and any small upset must be quickly smoothed over if she is not to bear a grudge for at least the remainder of the day. The immature will show a butterfly quality on the creance, which completely belies her true powers of flight. Later, when fit, she will begin to show her potential but, much to the falconer's chagrin, may prove reluctant to put it to the use that he had intended. Much of the UK is too enclosed for the gyrfalcon and to try her in these regions is to risk her repeated loss. Inevitably, therefore, she will be tried against the only quarry suited to her powers which is to be found in sufficiently open areas, namely grouse, ptarmigan and blackgame. The gyr is fast enough to fly down grouse in level flight, but her wilful nature is likely to come to the fore if she is given any scope for misbehaving.

Once again, it has to be admitted that American falconers have achieved vastly better results with the gyrfalcon than have the few British falconers who have attempted to

Peregrine/prairie falcon hybrid.

introduce them to game in the UK. When flown at grouse, they have shown a reluctance to wait on, frequently backing this up with a clear demonstration that they do not need such tricks in order to be successful. However, the pleasure of grouse hawking lies in witnessing the stoop. To watch one's gyrfalcon pursuing grouse in level flight, then spending the remainder of the afternoon tracking her on telemetry really does leave a lot to be desired, even if the flight is eventually found to have ended in a kill. Unfortunately, it has once again to be pointed out that the Americans are able to make their gyrs go up with the aid of bagged pigeon. The British falconer, who can do so well in training an eyass peregrine to wait on at an impressive pitch, without bagged quarry of any sort, has so far been unable to perform the same feat with gyrfalcons.

There is a further feeling that whilst the undoubted ability of the gyrfalcon is wasted on anything less than the red grouse in the UK, even this is rather akin to taking a sledgehammer to crack a nut. This may not be altogether fair, as grouse are a worthy adversary, but it seems likely that many more captive-bred eyass gyrs will be tried at grouse in the future, before any definite conclusions are reached.

HYBRID LONGWINGS

With the ability to artificially inseminate raptors becoming more commonplace, so the spread of hybrid longwings is becoming greater. Some combinations have proved very deadly, combining as they do, due to the phenomenon of hybrid vigour, the best of both parent species. The selective breeder is able to consider what attributes are required in a longwing for a particular form of hunting and breed specifically to meet this criteria. Gyr/peregrine, prairie/peregrine and saker/peregrine have proved to be some of the more successful combinations, but there are too many variations and qualifications to list.

PART IV
A MISCELLANY

15 TRANSPORTATION

CAR

Hawks should be boxed or hooded. Carrying them on the fist is an uncomfortable experience for both parties. A hooded hawk can be carried on a box cadge – not a field cadge because a hawk in transit must have something against which to brace her tail. The beak opening of the hood must be wide enough to allow the hawk to open her beak and cast through it if necessary, although all hawks travelled in this manner should be within the driver's or a passenger's view, so that the car may be stopped and the hood removed if casting or sickness appears imminent. No hawk should be fed prior to a long journey. Provided this precaution is taken, very few hawks are car-sick.

A hawk which does not take a hood will have to be boxed, unless she is exceptionally tame. There is a risk of feather damage when transporting an unseasoned traveller in a box. Although nothing can be done for the primaries, the tail should be put in a tail sheath or taped. Care must be taken in the choice of tape for this purpose as something too sticky will be damaging to remove. Masking tape is ideal because it remains in place but can be easily unwound at the end of the journey.

No hawk should be left in a car on a hot day and, when travelling in heat, adequate ventilation must be ensured. It is safer to have a boxed hawk in the car itself rather than in the boot. Occasionally, a hawk freshly picked up from a breeder is so wild that she crashes around constantly in a box. Such hawks can

be cast and wrapped firmly in a length of material.

Hawks which are boxed regularly to be taken out into the field become seasoned travellers and taping their tails for a short distance is unnecessary. It is possible to train a broadwing to jump into a box initially by throwing in small pieces of food . Once she is accustomed to leaping in the food can be dispensed with. *Accipiter*s should either travel hooded on a cadge or in a 'modified hood'. Trained longwings should always be transported on a box cadge.

CARRIER

Red Star, who operate British Rail's livestock freight services, no longer accept birds of prey. At the time of writing, the road carrier service Amtrak will transport birds of prey door-to-door, countrywide, overnight at a very reasonable price, provided that the hawk is sent in a suitable container. The pick-up should be arranged as late in the afternoon as possible and delivery will be before 10 a.m. the following morning. Many falconers have benefited from this service, but obviously there must be trust on behalf of both the sender and the receiver of a hawk that is to be shipped in this manner.

Hawks generally travel well by train but it is a poor substitute for the peace of mind of taking or delivering the hawk personally unless the box is accompanied.

Putting a Harris hawk into a travelling box.

AIR

Hawks travel well by air but international flights are generally complicated for the sender, who will have to ensure that the paperwork is correct down to the last detail. Boxes for livestock air freight are subject to IATA regulations and care must be taken to follow these to the letter or the hawk may well be refused by the airline. The airline should be questioned about its facilities and procedures minutely before the hawk is booked, as some are very shoddy in their handling of livestock and others do not have heated pressurized holds specifically for the purpose. Like the railways, airlines charge on a volumetric basis and this can be prohibitively expensive.

SEA

Other than short ferry crossings or similar, there is probably little reason why this mode of transport would be chosen. Like human beings, some hawks will be sick.

16 LOST HAWKS

Whilst telemetry may help one to locate a hawk, it by no means guarantees her safe recovery. She may refuse to be recalled, the telemetry may fail, or she may be out of range. Additionally, there are falconers who do not use telemetry, either because they feel that their Harris hawk, or whatever, is highly unlikely to be lost, or because they have never seen fit to purchase a unit. Any fit hawk in hunting condition can potentially be lost chasing quarry. The hours spent looking for her, without the reassurance of a signal to follow, are desperately worrying.

A falconer searching for a lost hawk should enlist as much help as possible. Hawks will generally go downwind and this is the direction to search first, once the area where she was last seen and its immediate environs have been covered. Searchers should use a swing lure continually in the hope of attracting shortwings, broadwings and longwings, for the fist or a rabbit-lure will not be nearly so visible from a distance. Searching systematically, everyone should be armed with the means and the instructions for recalling her and taking her up. Mobbing birds will often help to pin-point her. It is important to be quiet and listen at intervals, as well as to blow a whistle to attract her attention. If the hawk is not recovered by nightfall, telephone calls to anyone who might help or receive information as to her whereabouts should be made, including other falconers and Licensed Rehabilitation Keepers in the vicinity, the police and animal rescue organisations, such as the RSPCA.

In areas where longwings have been flown for many years, there are normally set points where they tend to end up and these should be visited the following day. Broadwings often seek out dead trees with high vantage points. If the hawk made a kill the previous day, she is likely to be roosting somewhere, having gorged, and may not be receptive to being recalled until later in the day. If she is not recovered on day two, advertisements should be placed in local papers and the local radio station should be prevailed upon to give out bulletins reporting her loss. Someone to man the telephone is essential so that sensible reports of sightings can be followed up.

In the UK, the loss of a registered hawk should be reported to the DoE once the hope of her imminent recovery fades. If she is meanwhile picked up and reported to them, they will be able to trace her through her ring number. The keepers of unregistered lost hawks are reliant on any obvious markings, such as the close ring, or an identification tag and the manner in which they broadcast the loss of their hawk to the surrounding neighbourhood. As well as contacting other falconers, local falconry centres, LRKs, local police and animal welfare organizations, it is advisable to contact local vets, zoos, the police force's Wildlife Liaison Officer and operators of independent registration schemes.

The identichipping of hawks is now a common practice. A small chip bearing a unique number is inserted under the skin by a veterinary surgeon. Once inserted, the chip is virtually impossible to remove, but the number may be read with the aid of a special 'reader'. Several different types of chip are available and the Hawk Board is willing to advise keepers on the best options. The downfall of identichips is that unless a hawk is picked up by, or taken to, an organization such as the police or a veterinary surgery which holds a reader appropriate to the type of chip inserted, the chip is unlikely to lead to the safe recovery of the hawk. The most positive use of identichips in the future is likely to occur in cases of suspected theft.

Most trained hawks remain approachable for several days, provided that their crop is empty, and will hopefully respond to the fist or lure. *Accipiters*, however, go very wild after a relatively short period of liberty – in some cases even a few hours – and will resist all efforts to recall them, often being flushed further when approached. Any hawk whose whereabouts are discovered, but who will not allow herself to be taken up, will have to be trapped or wound up on the creance if possible.

In the UK, licences to use a manually operated bow trap for the purpose of reclaim-ing a lost hawk should be requested from the DoE. Winding up is a useful technique for hawks which will show interest in a lure but which will not allow themselves to be approached. The lure is staked firmly in an area below the hawk, in such a position that vegetation will not hinder the creance which is utilized to ensnare her. Concealed, or at a distance, the falconer, having previously secured one end of the creance beyond the lure, awaits the time when the hawk, tempted by large but well-secured quantities of food on the lure, descends to investigate. When she is busy eating, the falconer walks wide around her, progressively winding the creance around her legs as she eats. Once the creance has been passed around her legs two, or preferably three, times, the falconer can pull it taut and make in to take her up. If she attempts to fly off, hopefully the creance will hold her.

The recovery of a lost hawk brings with it an overwhelming sense of relief. Generally, the falconer knows if he is to blame for her loss in the first place, by flying her overweight or in unsuitable weather conditions.

17 CAPTIVE BREEDING AND CONSERVATION

Strictly speaking, captive breeding comes under the subject of aviculture, rather than falconry and hawking. However, as trained hawks in the UK are almost entirely drawn from captive-bred stock, it certainly merits mentioning as the future of British falconry depends on it.

Breeding hawks in captivity is not as simple as merely putting together a pair of a species in a suitable enclosure and awaiting the happy event. Hawks have to be of breeding age and they must be compatible. Certain types of imprint are unsuitable for natural reproduction. It is not uncommon for a pair of hawks to occupy an aviary for many years without any progeny being produced. Even if eggs are produced, they may be infertile or fail to hatch due to infection, incomplete incubation, damage to the shell or inclement weather conditions. Most breeders attempt to overcome some of the risks by removing eggs and placing them in an incubator, where they can assume full responsibility for their welfare. If the eggs are taken soon enough after laying, the pair may carry on laying or recycle and lay a fresh clutch. The complexities of artificially incubating eggs, and the time involved in the hatching and rearing of eyasses, are vast. It takes years of trial and error to become an expert breeder and disaster can strike at any time, wiping out a season's work. Such effort does not, consequently, come cheap and falconers must expect to pay the price if they wish to purchase eyasses of quality.

CONSERVATION

Falconers should be proud of the fact that some of their number have been intrinsic in the setting up of conservation programmes for some of the world's rarest raptors. The interests of a falconer have to extend beyond his hawk itself and include the quarry she catches and the preservation of the quarry's natural habitat. Thus falconers, like shooting men, help, by their patronage, to preserve moorland from forestry and low ground from developers. All field sportsmen are pursuing the natural pastime of hunting, without which man could not have evolved.

CONCLUSION

Falconry is brought into the public eye by flying demonstrations and falconry centres, publications and television. Provided that these represent or depict the sport in a fair light, they do no harm and may even do some good, for it is weight of public opinion which will prevail, as field sports are systematically put under pressure by those opposed to them. The vast majority of people who see demonstrations, publications, photographs or films will view them with mild interest but never think of taking up the sport. However, it is essential that those who are tempted to take up falconry are able to receive clear and sensible guidance. Courses, run to a high standard, such as those held at the British School of Falconry, are an ideal opportunity for people to receive good instruction, experience working with hawks and, most important of all, to decide before getting a hawk whether the sport is really for them. It is the responsibility of all falconers who bring their sport to the attention of others, in any way, to give a good account of themselves and to show clearly that their hawks are in first-class order, legally held and superbly maintained.

A class in progress at the British School of Falconry.

USEFUL ADDRESSES

FALCONRY COURSES

The British School of Falconry at Gleneagles
The Gleneagles Hotel
Perthshire
Scotland PH3 1NF
UK
Tel: 01764 662231 ext. 4347
Fax: 01764 664345

British School of Falconry at the Equinox
The Equinox Hotel
Historic Route 7A
PO Box 46
Manchester VT 05254
USA
Tel: 001 802 362 4780
Fax: 001 802 362 4817

LICENSING AND REGISTRATION AUTHORITIES

REGISTRATION, IMPORT/EXPORT LICENCES

Wildlife Licensing Department
Department of the Environment
Tollgate House
Houlton Street
Bristol BS2 9DJ
UK

Bird Registration Tel: 0117 987 8829
Fax: 0117 987 8393
Wildlife Licensing (sales licences, display licences) Tel: 0117 987 8700
CITES import and export licences
Tel: 0117 987 8170

SALES AND DISPLAY LICENCES, SCOTLAND

The Scottish Office
Environmental Department
Rural Affairs and Natural Heritage Division
Room 6/63

New St Andrew's House
Edinburgh
Scotland EH1 3TG
UK
Tel: 0131 244 4065   Fax: 0131 244 4785

IMPORT/EXPORT HEALTH CERTIFICATES (ADDITIONAL TO CITES LICENCE)
ENGLAND AND WALES ONLY

Ministry of Agriculture, Fisheries and Food
Import/Export Section
Hook Rise South
Tolworth
Surbiton
Surrey KT6 7NF
UK
Tel: 0181 330 8222   Fax: 0181 330 6678

AS ABOVE, FOR SCOTLAND

Department of Agriculture and Fisheries for Scotland
Pentlend House
47 Robbs Loen
Edinburgh
Scotland EH14 1SQ
UK
Tel: 0131 556 8400

CENTRES OPEN TO THE PUBLIC

The Hawk Conservancy
Weyhill
Nr Andover
Hants. SP11 8DY
UK
Tel: 0126 477 2252   Fax: 0126 477 3772
The National Birds of Prey Centre
Newent
Glos. GL18 1JJ
UK
Tel: 01531 820286   Fax: 01531 821289

EQUIPMENT SUPPLIERS

Martin Jones
The Parsonage
Llanrothall
Nr Monmouth
Gwent
Wales
UK
Tel: 01600 750 300   Fax: 01600 750 450

Ray Prior
4 Hackney Bottom
Hampstead Norreys
Thatcham
Berks. RG18 0TU
UK
Tel: 01635 200545

Northwoods Ltd.
PO Box 874
Rainer
WA 98576
USA
Tel: 001 800 446 5080/001 360 446 3212
Fax: 001 360 446 1270

BOOKS

Nicholson's Prints and Books
6935 Shorecrest Drive
Anaheim
CA 92807
USA
Tel: 001 714 281 8497
Fax: 001 714 281 0604

Robin Haigh
Abbey Bridge Farmhouse
Colonel's Lane
Chertsey
Surrey KT16 8RJ
UK
Tel/Fax: 01932 560236
(also for UK membership of North American
Falconers' Association)

TELEMETRY

L.L. Electronics
PO Box 420
Mahomet
IL 61852–0420
USA
Tel: 001 800 553 5328
Fax: 001 217 586 5733

Custom Electronics
2009 Silver Ct. W.
Urbana
IL 61801
USA
Tel/Fax: 001 217 344 3460

Falcon Telemetry
Martin Jones
The Parsonage
Llanrothall
Nr Monmouth
Gwent
Wales
UK
Tel: 01600 750 300   Fax: 01600 750 450

FALCONRY CLUBS

The British Falconer's Club
c/o John Fairclough
Home Farm, Hints
Nr Tamworth
Staffs. B78 3DW
UK
Tel/Fax: 01543 481737

The Northern England Falconry Club
c/o Steve Syree
36 Brackendale Avenue
Thackley
Bradford
W. Yorks. BD10 0SQ
UK
Tel: 01274 611446

The Welsh Hawking Club
c/o Adrian Williams
Maendy Farmhouse
Church Village
Pontypridd
Wales CF38 1SY
UK
Tel/Fax: 01443 206333

South East Falconry Group
c/o Dean White
15 Gifford's Cross Road
Corringham
Essex SS17 7PY
UK

North American Falconer's Association
c/o Alan Beske
HCR 76 Box 43
Hawk Springs
WY 82217
USA
Tel: 001 307 834 2462

GENERAL

The Hawk Board
c/o The British Field Sports Society
59 Kennington Road
London SE1 7PZ
UK
Tel: 0171 928 4742   Fax: 0171 620 1401

VETERINARY SURGEONS SPECIALIZING IN BIRDS OF PREY

Neil Forbes, MRCVS, B.Vet.Med.
Lansdown Veterinary Group
The Clockhouse Veterinary Hospital
Wallbridge Road
Stroud
Glos. GL5 3JD
UK
Tel: 01453 752555   Fax: 01453 756065

A. Greenwood, MRCVS, MA, Vet.M.B.
International Zoo Veterinary Group
Keighley Business Centre
South Street
Keighley
W. Yorks. BD21 1AG
UK
Tel: 01535 692000   Fax: 01535 690433

M. Williams. B.V.Sc. MRCVS
11 New Street
Upton on Severn
Worcs.
UK
Tel: 01684 592606   Fax: 01684 594177

N. Harcourt Brown, B.V.Sc. FRCVS
30 Crab Lane
Bilton
Harrogate
N. Yorks.
UK
Tel: 01423 508945   Fax: 01423 563899

W. McColl, MRCVS. BVM & S
Broadleys Veterinary Hospital
Dunblane Clinic
1 Station Road
Dunblane
Perthshire
Scotland FK15 9ET
UK
Tel: 01786 824400   Fax: 01786 825788

S. Spencer, B.V.Sc. MRCVS
Maison Dieu Veterinary Centre
Maison Dieu Road
Dover
Kent CT16 1RE
UK
Tel: 01304 201617   Fax: 01304 210660

GLOSSARY OF FALCONRY TERMS

Accipiter A shortwinged hawk identified by short, rounded wings, long tail and light eyes.

Austringer One who keeps and hunts short-wings and broadwings.

Aylmeris Leather anklets through which field or mews jesses can be put.

Bate To attempt to fly off the fist or perch when held or tied, in fright or at the lure or quarry.

Bells Small bells, usually of brass, nickel or monel (a type of stainless steel).

Bewits Short thin strips of leather by which the bells are fastened to the legs.

Bind To grab and hold onto quarry with the feet.

Block A perch for a longwing.

Blood feathers New feathers not yet fully grown, whose shafts contain blood at the top.

Bloom A mantle of grey sheen which protects the hawk's back feathers, keeping her water-proof.

Bob Up and down movement of the head made by longwings when especially interested in something.

Bow perch A perch used for shortwings and broadwings.

Braces Leather straps used to open or close the hood.

Brancher A young bird of prey which has left the nest, but is still learning to fly and is fed by its parents.

Break in The act of breaking through a kill's skin – usually starting at the soft underbelly.

Brown A term used to describe an immature peregrine.

Cadge A portable perch used to carry a number of longwings hooded. It is slung from the shoulders by straps and is rectangular, the cadger walking in the centre.

Cadger The person who carries the cadge, the cadge-boy.

Call off To call a hawk or falcon from a perch to the lure or to the fist.

Canceleer To make two or three sharp turns in the descent when stooping.

Carry When a hawk attempts to fly off with the quarry or lure in her foot on being approached.

Cast, a Two hawks flown together.

Cast, to To propel a hawk forward off the fist to get it airborne.

Cast, to The act of disgorging a pellet of the undigested parts of a meal – fur, feathers, bone etc.

Cast, to To hold a hawk in a cloth between the hands for imping, putting jesses on, etc.

Casting The pellet of feathers or fur disgorged by a hawk after completing the process of digestion.

Cere The bare, wax-like skin above the beak.

Check To change from one quarry to another during flight, or to hesitate because of sighting another quarry.

Condition The hawk is in high condition when she is fat, and in low condition when she is too thin. When condition is correct, she is at flying weight.

Cope To file, and so shorten, the beak and talons of a hawk.

Crab, crabbing When hawks seize each other,

either in the air or on the ground.

Creance A light line attached to the swivel of a partly trained hawk before she is allowed to fly loose.

Crines The short hair-like feathers about the cere.

Crop, a The amount of food a hawk is given at a single meal.

Crop, the The vascular sac above the breast bone which serves as the first receptacle for the food taken by a hawk before it is passed or 'put over' into the stomach.

Crop, putting over The action of a hawk when she writhes with her neck, and squeezes a portion of the contents of her crop downwards into her stomach.

Deck feathers The two centre feathers of the tail.

Diurnal Day-time hunter.

Draw the hood To pull the braces which close the hood.

Enseam To purge a hawk of superfluous fat, and so render her fit for flying.

Enter To give a hawk her first flight at prey.

Eyass A nestling, or young hawk taken from the nest.

Falcon Term actually denotes a female peregrine but is sometimes used for females of the other species of Falconidae.

Feak To wipe the beak clean on the perch with a stropping action after feeding.

Fetch To reach and turn the quarry in pursuit.

Flights or flight feathers The main feathers used in flight, the primaries.

Foot, to To strike with the feet, and clutch or bind. A 'good footer' describes a hawk that clutches well and holds.

Frounce A canker or sore in the mouth and throat, usually seen as a coloured coating on the tongue.

Fully summed When a hawk has got all her new feathers after moulting.

Gleam The substance coating a casting.

Gorge To allow the hawk to eat as much food as she can at a single meal.

Hack To allow eyasses to fly free for a few weeks until they are old enough to train.

Hack back To hack a hawk back to the wild.

Hack-bells Large heavy bells put on hawks to hinder them from preying for themselves while 'flying at hack'.

Haggard A hawk trapped in mature plumage.

Hard penned or hard down When the new feathers are fully grown and the shafts have hardened off to a quill.

Hawk A most confusing term. Strictly speaking, a hawk is an *Accipiter* as opposed to the longwinged, dark-eyed falcon. But the word is often used to cover shortwings, broadwings and longwings, and hawking is done with all of them.

Hood A close-fitting leather cap, often tooled and decorated, used to blindfold a hawk.

Hood block The wooden block on which some types of hoods are blocked to shape them.

Hood-shy A hawk that dislikes being hooded, generally through a fault of the falconer, is hood-shy.

Hybrid A cross-bred hawk, parentage of two different species.

Imp A method of repairing broken flight feathers by replacing the broken portion with part of another feather.

Imping needle A splint used to join the two parts of a feather. They are oval or triangular in cross-section.

Imprinting A complex behaviour which occurs when an eyass is not parent reared.

Intermewed A hawk which has moulted in captivity.

Jack The male merlin.

Jerkin The male gyrfalcon.

Jesses The narrow strips of leather fastened round a hawk's legs to hold her by.

Keen, to be Said when a hawk is responding with enthusiasm.

Lanneret The male lanner falcon.

Leash A long narrow strip of nylon with a button at one end, which is passed through the swivel and used to tie a hawk to its block or perch.

Longwing A term used to cover all Falconidae which have long, pointed wings and dark eyes.

Lure An imitation bird or animal used to entice the hawk in training.

Mail The breast feathers of a hawk.

Make-hawk An old, experienced hawk flown with an immature, when in training, to teach or encourage it.

Make in To approach a hawk on the lure or a kill with care, in order to take her up.

Man, to To man a hawk is to make her tame by accustoming her to man's presence.

Mantle, to To stand over a kill or food with wings lowered and spread out to hide the food.

Mantle, to The act of stretching a wing, leg and the tail, in one movement to one side of the body; generally repeated on the other side.

Mark down To pin-point the spot where quarry has put in.

Mews Building where hawks are kept at night or in bad weather. Traditionally, the place in which they were put to moult.

Musket The male sparrowhawk.

Mutes The droppings or excrement of hawks.

Nares The nostrils of a hawk.

Passage The habitual flight line of certain quarry species.

Passage hawk or passager A hawk caught on or before her migration and still in her immature plumage.

Petty singles The toes of a hawk.

Pick-up piece The piece of meat held in the gloved hand, used to cover the meat on the lure to entice the hawk from the lure or quarry onto the fist.

Pitch, the The height at which a hawk 'waits on'.

Pitch, to To land on a perching point.

Plumage The feathers of a hawk.

Plume To pluck the feathers off the quarry.

Pounces The talons of a longwing or the claws of a hawk.

Preen To clean and dress the feathers with the beak.

Primaries The longest wing feathers, ten outermost in each wing.

Put in To drive the quarry into cover; to take refuge in cover.

Put over To empty the crop into the digestive system, an action performed with a back and forth motion of the body, and particularly with the neck.

Quarry The game at which a hawk is flown.

Rake away To fly wide of the falconer, or of the intended quarry.

Rangle Small stones given to hawks to aid digestion. A hawk may pick them up and eat them of her own accord if they are put within easy reach.

Reclaim To 'man' a hawk, or to retrain a hawk that has been idle for a period.

Red-hawk A peregrine in the red or immature plumage, sometimes used to mean any first-year hawk.

Ring up To climb spirally in flight.

Ringing flight When a hawk rings up after quarry.

Rouse To raise the feathers slightly before shaking the plumage back into position.

Sakret Male saker falcon.

Sails The wings of a hawk.

Secondaries The flight feathers of the wing, between the body and the primaries.

Self-hunting When a hawk strays in search of prey.

Serve To put quarry out of cover for a hawk.

Set down to moult To put into the mews for moulting.

Shaft The central hollow strut of a feather, giving it support.

Sharp set Said of longwings when they are keen and in hunting condition.

Shortwing Term used to cover true hawks or *Accipiters*.

Slice The action employed by eagles, hawks and buzzards of evacuating mutes.

Slip To release a hawk in pursuit of quarry.

Soar When a hawk takes to the air and enjoys flying for the sake of flying, by gliding on thermals and other air currents, rather than flying at quarry.

Sore-hawk An *Accipiter* trapped during its first year.

Stoop The rapid descent of a longwing from a height, at quarry or lure, with wings nearly closed.

Strike the hood To pull the braces of a hood open.

Swivel Two rings, connected in a figure-of eight fashion with a bolt or rivet. Used to connect the jesses and the leash when a hawk is held or tied on the perch, to prevent them from getting twisted.

Take stand To pitch in a tree.

Tarsus The leg of a hawk between foot and hock.

Tiercel The male peregrine, from the French *tierce*, meaning third. The tiercel is a third less in size than the falcon (female peregrine). The term is often misused for the male of any species of hawk.

Tiring A tough piece of meat given to a hawk when in training to pull at, in order to prolong the meal and exercise the muscles of the back and neck.

Train The tail of a hawk.

Various A term used in quarry lists to cover any small fry which may have been in-advertently caught by a trained hawk.

Wait on To wait in flight high over the falconer, waiting for him to flush the quarry.

Warble To stretch both wings upwards over the back till they nearly touch and, at the same time, to spread the tail.

Weather To place the hawk on her block in the open air during the day.

Weathering ground The area where the hawks are kept on perches.

Webbing The soft strands each side of the shaft of a feather.

Wedded When a hawk prefers one type of quarry.

Yarak, to be in A term which originated in the East, usually applied only to shortwings, 'sharp set' being the correct synonym for longwings. It means fit, keen and ready to be flown.

BIBLIOGRAPHY

GENERAL

Ford, Emma, *Falconry in Mews and Field*, B.T. Batsford Ltd, London, 1982

Glasier, Philip, *Falconry and Hawking*, B.T. Batsford Ltd, London, 1978

Mavrogordato, Jack, *A Hawk for the Bush*, The C.W. Daniel Company Ltd., 1960

Michell, E.B., *The Art and Practice of Hawking*, 8th impression, The Holland Press, London, 1970

Parry-Jones, Jemima, *Falconry, Care, Captive Breeding and Conservation*, David and Charles, Newton Abbot, 1988

Webster, H. & Enderson, J., *Game Hawking at its Very Best*, Windsong Press, PO Box 1484, Denver, CO 80201, 1988

Woodford, M.H., *A Manual of Falconry*, A. & C. Black, London, 1960

VETERINARY

Coles, B.H., *Avian Medicine and Surgery*, Blackwell, Oxford, 1985

Cooper, J.E., *Veterinary Aspects of Birds of Prey*, The Standfast Press, Saul, 1978

Cooper, J.E. & Eley, J.J., *First Aid and Care of Wild Birds*, David and Charles, Newton Abbot, 1979

Cooper, J.E. & Greenwood, A.G., *Recent Advances in the Study of Raptor Diseases*, Chiron Publications Ltd, 1981

Harrison, G.J. & Harrison, L.R., *Clinical Avian Medicine and Surgery*, W.B. Saunders, Philadelphia, 1986

EDITORIAL NOTE

CONVERTING IMPERIAL MEASUREMENTS TO METRIC

Throughout this book measurements are usually given in Imperial. Those readers who are more familiar with metric might find the following useful.

To convert in to cm: $\times$ 2.54
e.g. 2 in = 5.08 cm

To convert ft to m: $\times$ 0.30
e.g. 2 ft = 0.60 m

To convert oz to g: $\times$ 28.34
e.g. 2 oz = 56.69 g

Temperature

°F	°C
32	0
50	10
59	15
68	20
77	25
86	30
95	35
104	40

INDEX